MIDI Sequencing
FOR MUSICIANS

The Keyboard magazine Synthesizer Library

From the editors of Keyboard magazine.

GPI Publications
Cupertino, California

GPI BOOKS

Director
Alan Rinzler

Editor: MIDI Sequencing For Musicians
Jim Aikin

Contributing Editor: MIDI Sequencing For Musicians
Michael Marans

Art Director
Paul Haggard

General Manager
Judie Eremo

Art Assistant
Robert Stockwell Jr.

GPI PUBLICATIONS

President/Publisher
Jim Crockett

Executive Vice President
Don Menn

Corporate Art Director
Wales Christian Ledgerwood

Production
Cheryl Matthews (Director)
Joyce Phillips (Assistant Director)
Andrew Gordon, Gail M. Hall, Joe Verri

Typesetting
Leslie K. Bartz (Director)
June Ramirez, Shirlynn Woodard

Marketing
Leah Baker, Perry Fotos

Accounting
Thomas E. Murphy (Director)
Rekha Shah
Lynne Whitlach

Cover design and illustration: Paul Haggard

Copyright © 1989 by The GPI Corporation, A Dalton Communications Company.
All rights reserved. No part of this book may be reproduced or utilized in any form or by any means, electronic or mechanical, including photocopying, recording, or by any information storage and retrieval system, without permission in writing from the publisher.

ISBN: 0-88188-911-3

Contents

Theory And Application

MIDI Sequencing, 2.

Mechanical, Analog, Digital—Sequencer History In A Nutshell, 6.

Sequencer Features, 10.

Bugs, Crashes, And Revs., 56.

MIDI Basics, 58

The Sequencer In A Music System, 64.

Beyond Sequencing, 72.

Product Reviews

Introduction, 84.

C-Lab Creator: Sequencer Software For The Atari ST, 85.

Voyetra Sequencer Plus Mark III: IBM Sequencer Software, 95.

Kawai Q-80: MIDI Sequence Recorder, 99.

Yamaha QX5: MIDI Sequence Recorder, 104.

Q-Sheet: Event Sequencer And MIDI Automation Mac Software, 108.

Coda Finale: Music Notation And Transcription Software For The Mac, 114.

Ludwig: Algorithmic Composition For The Atari ST, 127.

About The Authors, 137.

Theory And Application

MIDI Sequencing

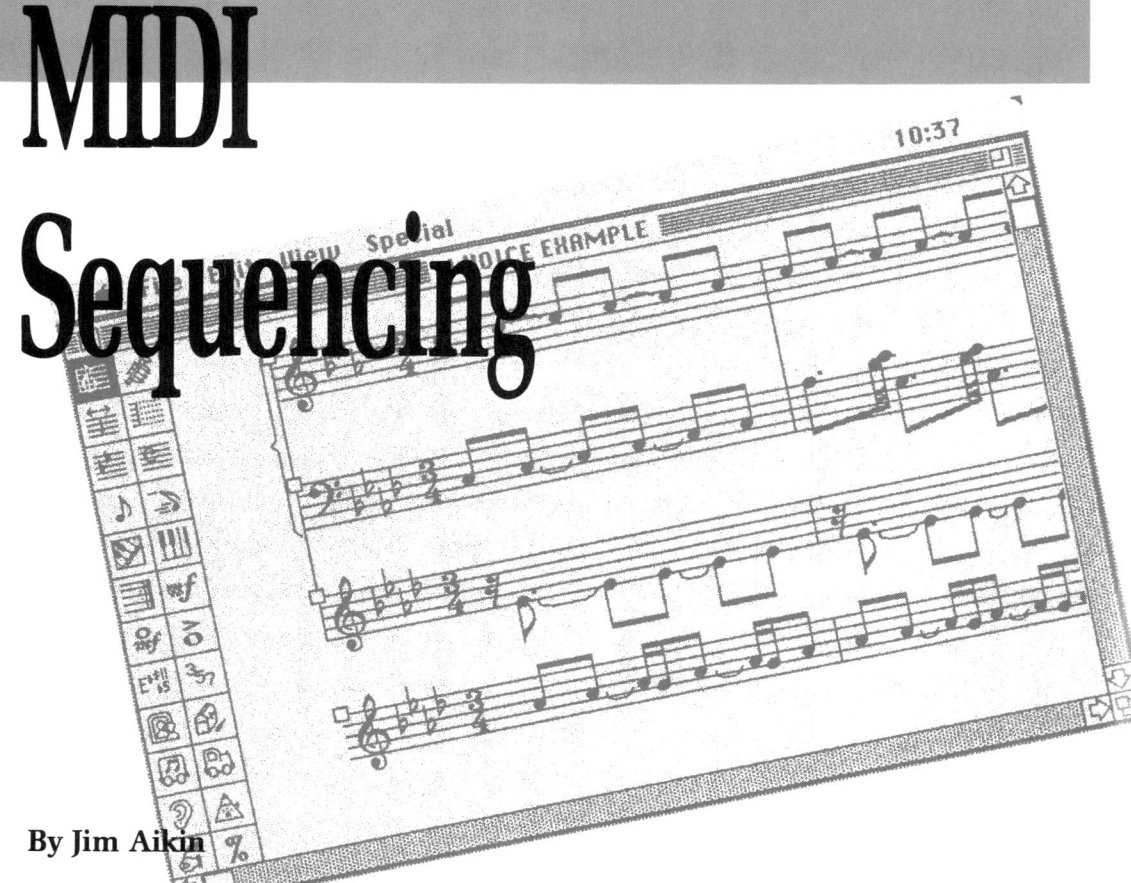

By Jim Aikin

What would you have said ten years ago if somebody had told you that within a decade, the most important new development in music technology would be a piece of equipment that didn't make any sound at all? You would have laughed, right? Music equipment that doesn't make a sound? You mean like cases and stands and cords and that little wrench you need to adjust the height of the bridge? Get serious.

But here we are. Seemingly overnight, sequencers have become an absolute necessity in many types of popular (and not-so-popular) music. By itself, a sequencer won't make a sound. Well, maybe it will beep or click through its metronome output. Not too impressive for a gadget that costs hundreds of dollars. Hook it to a MIDI synthesizer or two, though, and it becomes the brains of a composing system that Bach or Beethoven would cheerfully have cut off an arm to have access to.

If you're interested in sequencing at all, you're probably eager to learn a lot more about it than you know now. We don't have to convince you that in such a new and fast-growing field, ignorance is rampant—even, at times, among those who are most active. *MIDI Sequencing* is an attempt to shed some light in an area that badly needs it. As far as we know, this the first book-length publication ever to address sequencing in any comprehensive way.

Maybe you're entirely new to the sequencer explosion, and are simply curious to learn what all the fuss is about. Or maybe you've been working extensively with sequencers for a couple of years, and are feeling the need to upgrade your skills. Either way, *MIDI Sequencing* should have what you're looking for.

We put together an exhaustive survey and explanation of sequencer features and operations, from basic to exotic. Also in *MIDI Sequencing* you'll find an explanation of the MIDI protocol (the glue that holds everything together), a guided tour of the tools in a MIDI sequencing studio, and a peek into the future, when products that are more than simply sequencers will take an active part in helping us create entirely new kinds of music.

What's A Sequencer?

A sequencer is a word processor for music. It's a computer-based device that accepts as input the data transmitted by any MIDI keyboard or other controller. Once inside the machine, the data can be altered in various ways, played back, and stored in some permanent form, such as on a floppy disk.

A sequencer is the electronic equivalent of a self-recording player piano. Instead of paper rolls, it uses computer memory. Instead of having to buy the rolls at the store, you can punch them out yourself by playing the keyboard. (In fact, there isn't much of a market yet for pre-recorded sequencer material, partly because there are so many different sequencers on the market, and most of them use different formats for storing data. Look for this situation to change.) Because you're dealing with computer memory instead of great long sheets of paper, you can make many types of changes in the music that would be difficult or impossible to make in a physical medium. There's no need to scissor the paper apart and tape it back together, or paste solid bits over the holes that you've decided you don't want. Such things are done by giving the sequencer commands using its front panel buttons.

You can do a lot more with a sequencer, though, than sit down in the parlor and pump out "Sweet Adeline" or "Down By The Old Mill Stream." It may not be an overstatement to suggest that sequencers will prove to be the most important advance in music since the invention of notation. From pro studios in New York and Hollywood to countless living rooms and garages around the world, they're being embraced with an enthusiasm bordering on religious fervor.

Why? What's all the fuss about? Well, every art has its own set of technical challenges. Painters (representational ones, at least) have to capture three-dimensional objects on a two-dimensional surface. Writers of fiction have to create plausible human beings using nothing but ink. And until recently, musicians had to be part gymnast. It wasn't enough to have wonderful ideas; the ideas had to be executed flawlessly at concert after concert, using incredibly precise patterns of muscular movement. Only a very few musicians who bore the elite title "composer" had the luxury of going out for coffee in the middle of a melody, or fixing mistakes with a pencil eraser. When they were done, somebody else (and often 50 or 60 highly paid somebody elses) still had to do the gymnast routine with the pages of little dots.

The arrival of the sequencer has changed this picture radically. The end-product (good-sounding music) is no longer linked to the muscular process. Any musician, no matter how tentative or amorphous their ideas may initially be or how clumsy they may be about executing them, can sit down at a sequencer and produce, given a reasonable investment in the necessary equipment, finished music of amazing complexity and depth.

This is not to say that the results are *always* exceptional. Sequencers also make it possible for composers with less talent than enthusiasm to spew out large amounts of forgettable or even painfully naive music. In the last five years the quality level of bad music has risen dramatically. Outstanding music, on the other hand, is just as rare

and hard to create as it ever was. It's only harder to distinguish through casual listening than it used to be.

The linkage between muscular exertion and recorded music started to break down in the late '60s, when multitrack taping made it possible for musicians who had never even met to "play together" by laying down overdubs. A single musician with a multitrack could play all the instruments in an "ensemble." Using punch-in recording, overdubs, and tape splicing, a producer could assemble a finished "performance" that was more perfect than any of the musicians involved could actually have executed.

There are people who feel that even this degree of technical artifice is harmful to the essence of the music. But to use an analogy put forth by Glenn Gould in defense of splicing in classical piano recordings, do you insist that a movie be nothing more than a stage play performed in front of a single stationary camera? Of course not. Both film and recording are new art forms, with expressive resources quite different in some ways from those offered by drama and concert performance, whatever the degree of similarity in the raw material.

Tape overdubbing, punching in, and splicing still required muscular precision on the part of musicians, however. The groundwork for the sequencer stampede was put in place in 1983 with the introduction of MIDI (the Musical Instrument Digital Interface). With MIDI, it became relatively simple for the first time to treat a musical performance as a stream of digital data, much like the alphabetical characters in a word processor—though with several additional dimensions.

Sequencers of various kinds had existed prior to MIDI. In fact, mechanical means of playing music have existed for hundreds of years; for a thumbnail history, see page **00**. But the most advanced pre-MIDI digital sequencers only worked with instruments from a single manufacturer, while other, more generalized types were slow, clumsy, and of limited usefulness. Since the market was small, designers had little incentive to develop powerful machines.

Once keyboard synthesizers with MIDI input and output became a reality, it was possible to build a device that would record and play back any performance. And that blew the lid off.

These days, it seems, virtually everybody who makes music with electronics is using sequencers, or at least contemplating it. For musicians who aren't in a band and don't have access to a megabucks professional recording studio, a sequencer and a couple of synthesizers may be the only effective way for them to get their music down on tape in a form that they and their listeners can enjoy. Students and teachers are finding that learning about composing and arranging is vastly easier with a sequencer than with any other tool, even a tape deck, because a sequencer makes the process of trying out different musical parts largely painless. And if you can't find players you can get along with, or can't afford to keep a band together, you can fashion a rewarding career playing one-person club dates with your trusty sequencer and drum machine.

Mechanical, Analog, Digital— Sequencer History In A Nutshell

By Jim Aikin

Ever since the invention of clockwork, people have been fascinated by the idea of machines playing music. In the eighteenth century, classical composers were commissioned to write for the ornate music boxes of the day. The best music boxes had repertoires of dozens of tunes, which were stored on interchangeable metal drums or disks. Sticking metal pins into a drum or disk wasn't a real user-friendly data entry process, however, and if you wanted to be able to afford a good selection of tunes it helped if you were a king, or at least a duke or a count.

The player piano, with its paper rolls and pneumatic action, was a big step forward. Prior to the invention of the phonograph and the radio, the player piano was *the* home entertainment center. Hundreds of thousands were built, and mass-produced rolls were big business. Lyrics were printed along the edge of the roll, so that the whole family could gather around the piano and sing while one person pumped the pedals. No keyboard skill was required.

The player piano attracted some attention from serious musicians. In a 1925 interview, Igor Stravinsky expressed his enthusiasm: "There is a new polyphonic truth in the player piano," he said. "There are new possibilities.... It has a future, yes. Men will write for it." During the same period, a few concerto performances for player piano and live orchestra attracted a great deal of media attention, and technical refinements were patented that allowed the best reproducing pianos to achieve considerable dynamic nuance.

At least one artist, Conlon Nancarrow, found an original musical voice in the player piano: He composed by laboriously punching out rolls by hand. Nevertheless, the mechanical limitations of the instrument proved daunting, and when easier means were found for mass market consumption of music, the player piano went into decline.

The first step into electronic sequencing was a short one. In 1955, the RCA Synthesizer, a one-of-a-kind electronic instrument with banks of vacuum tubes, was designed to play whatever notes had been punched into a roll of paper tape. Holes in the tape tripped electro-mechanical relays, and the relays controlled a number of aspects of the sound, including pitch, envelope, and portamento. Since the RCA had no other form of input, it was strictly a sequencer-controlled device. Composer Milton Babbitt was the only person who produced any significant work on the RCA. Like Nancarrow, he was interested in compositions whose structure was determined in precise mathematical ways.

In the early '60s, electronic music experimenters were still assembling melodies (or timbral collages that served similar purposes) by the primitive method of recording oscillator tones on tape at various fixed pitches, and then chopping the tape apart and splicing the pieces back together in whatever order was desired. In the course of building his first electronic music system for the San Francisco Tape Center in 1963, Don Buchla came up with a way of eliminating the need for this type of tape splicing. He used oscillators whose pitch could be controlled by an electrical voltage, and built a device that put out a series of discrete voltage steps, one after another, automatically. His invention came to be known as the analog sequencer.

Ten years later, analog sequencers had become a standard feature on modular synthesizers, which were the most advanced electronic music devices to be found at the time. Moog, Buchla, ARP, Polyfusion, E-mu, and several other companies made them. A typical analog sequencer put out control voltages that changed the pitches of the oscillators, along with trigger or gate signals that opened up the envelope generators. Most of them were designed to use the one-volt-per-octave standard that was also employed on the monophonic keyboards of the time—a pre-digital, pre-MIDI form of standardized interfacing.

But of course there was no way to play a one-volt-per-octave keyboard into an analog sequencer so as to load its memory. The memory of an analog sequencer consisted of a row (or several rows) of hardware potentiometers. Usually these were hooked to knobs, although ARP preferred sliders, as usual. The pitch of a note in the sequence was changed by turning the knob that corresponded to that note. Each note in the sequence required a separate knob. Anybody who ever worked with an analog sequencer will remember how much fun it was to separately tune each and every note in a sequence, only to find when you finished that the oscillators themselves had drifted, forcing you to tune everything again.

The smallest analog sequencers had only eight knobs, while the largest had three or four rows of 16 knobs each. These could play three- or four-note chords, or the rows could be strung together to make single-line sequences of up to 48 or 64 notes. The sequence was played by a low-frequency clock oscillator. Each tick of the clock advanced the sequence to a new knob or vertical column of knobs, and the voltages at the output jacks changed to whatever values those knobs were set to. When the end of the row was reached, the sequencer would reset to the beginning and play the same material again.

By using a control voltage to change the speed of the clock, the musician could create irregular or syncopated rhythms. This voltage could be generated by the bottom row of pots for a regular musical repetition, or some other source could be used that might not be in sync with the repeating loop of the sequence. The most powerful analog sequencer ever built, the Touch Activated Keyboard Sequencer from Serge Modular, allowed the user to change the length of the repeating loop interactively during playback, to step forward or backward through the sequence under voltage control, or even to reset to a random step in the sequence rather than starting over from the beginning.

In spite of a few initial successes, the analog sequencer quickly developed a reputation for sounding dull and mechanical. Compounding its other, unavoidable limitations, most people simply let the clock oscillator chug along without controlling it from a voltage source. The result was an incessantly repeated pattern of eighth-notes.

The first digital sequencers were built in the mid-1970s by Dave Rossum and Scott Wedge at E-mu, by Tom Oberheim, and by Ralph Dyck (whose design was the inspiration for the Roland MC-8). Like their predecessors, these devices had control voltage and gate outputs, and were hooked up to analog synthesizers. They had more memory capacity, however—between 250 and 1,000 notes. The output could more easily be calibrated in 1/12-volt steps, so tuning problems were far less severe. And for the first time since the RCA Synthesizer, a sequence could be stored (in the form of digital data on audio tape).

The E-mu 4060, which appeared in 1976, was a microprocessor-equipped polyphonic keyboard with a built-in sequencer. The sequencer had real-time keyboard input, data tape storage, and ten memory 'bins' in which separate sequences could be recorded. No editing was possible, however, and of course the keyboard was not velocity-sensitive.

Today's universally used system of auto-correcting rhythms was pioneered by Roger Linn in 1978 for his first drum machine, the LM-1. Linn stumbled onto the idea while working with a prototype; it was initially a desperate expedient to conserve memory. The prototype, he explained to us, had 1K of RAM and eight drum sounds, and he found that the best way to save memory was to step through a single byte of memory at each clock tick. Each bit within the byte would fire one of the drum sounds if it was a 1 and not fire the sound if it was a 0. In this situation, obviously, one wanted to have the clock running as slowly as possible—at an eighth-note tempo if only eighth-notes were required. If any sixteenth-notes were to be played, twice as much memory would be used up per bar. This was *not* the system used in the production LM-1, but Linn liked the sound of the perfectly aligned rhythms, and retained that capability.

The LM-1 also introduced the idea of building complete song arrangements by chaining together short segments. This was again a way to store more music in less memory, but it was also a natural approach to drum parts, which are often repetitious. Most of today's musicians got their first taste of digital sequencing by programming patterns into one of the host of drum boxes that followed the LM-1's lead. And the hierarchical segment/song design has continued to be important in sequencing, even though memory is far cheaper than it was a few years ago.

The high point of pre-MIDI digital sequencing was unquestionably the visual score editor built into the Buchla 400 in 1983. Designed mainly to play the 400's own internal voices (though it could also put out control voltages), the score editor was a six-voice system with individual note editing, block move, delete, loop, and copy functions, patch change commands, and other goodies. A CRT that plugged directly into the instrument provided a real-time scrolling display of the sequenced music in bar-graph (horizontal piano roll) form. The clock ran at 16 pulses per quarter-note.

Better known to rock musicians was the Oberheim DSX, which interfaced with the OB-8 synthesizer and DMX drum machine to form what Oberheim called the System. The DSX spoke the same digital language as the OB-8's keyboard, but also had eight control voltage and gate outputs, which allowed the OB-8 to function as a master keyboard for analog tone modules. The DSX stored ten polyphonic sequences of ten tracks each, and could record patch changes and tempo changes. It had no individual event editing.

Several other digital sequencers were floating around in the early '80s, including popular models from Roland. They were all hardware-based, and all of them either used the one-volt-per-octave analog control voltage standard, or interfaced exclusively with instruments from one manufacturer. None stored key velocity data, as velocity-sensing keyboards were rare at the time.

One of the most powerful analog sequencers, the Touch-Activated Keyboard Sequencer, from Serge Modular.

Prior to MIDI, only two systems based on personal computers gained any degree of visibility. The alphaSyntauri and the Passport Soundchaser, while not compatible with one another, were both based on the Apple II computer, which at the time was the most popular computer around. Both generated sounds only with the aid of plug-in oscillator boards, which didn't have much to recommend them in the way of sound quality. Both systems had hardware keyboards, whose output could play the oscillators directly and could also be loaded into the multitrack sequencers that were part of the systems.

Because they were already working with a computer software system, Passport was able to offer the first-ever MIDI sequencer, the MIDI/4 for the Apple II, early in 1984.

It's been a long and winding road, and some would say we're not out of the woods yet. But it's beginning to look as if Stravinsky's enthusiastic prediction may turn out to have been right after all.

Sequencer Features

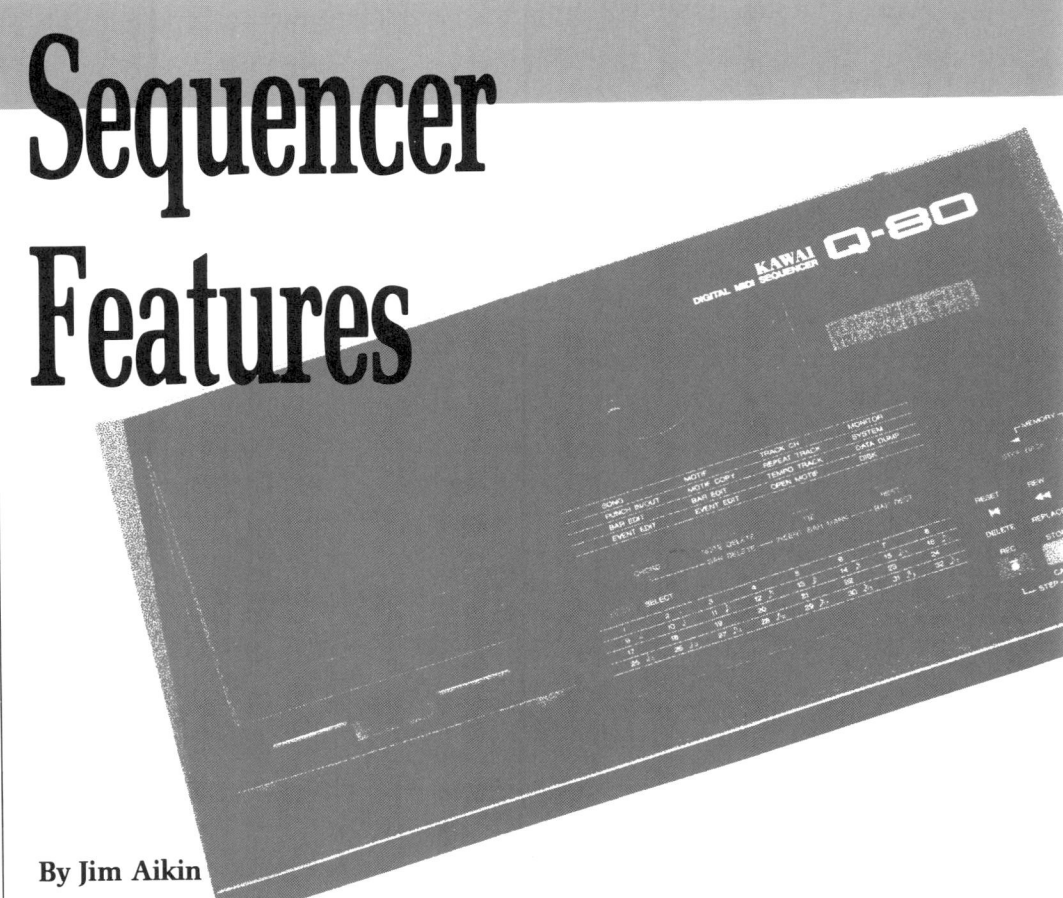

By Jim Aikin

Remember the parable of the blind men and the elephant? The programmers designing sequencer software today are a bit like blind men who have been asked not to describe an elephant but to *invent* one. Most of the beasts they've been trotting out have certain broad outlines in common. An elephant is big and gray, after all, and a MIDI sequencer has to record incoming MIDI data and send it out again on demand.

But beyond this basic level, almost everything is up for grabs. No two sequencers have the same *user interface*, which means that every time you learn a new sequencer you have to learn a new set of commands. More important, editing operations that take only a couple of quick keystrokes on one sequencer may be entirely impossible on another. Options like transposition and quantization have become nearly universal, but for every feature that becomes universal, five new ones appear, more exotic than ever before.

Several forces conspire to make the menagerie remarkably diverse. First, nobody really knows what the ultimate sequencer ought to be able to do. All of us, programmers and musicians alike, are developing new concepts at a furious pace. Second, every programmer has a different picture of what is or isn't musically important, as well as a different programming style. Third, the hardware for which sequencer software is being written may place constraints of its own on what can be accomplished. Recording and playing back music data without making any timing errors is one of the more complicated things a computer can be called on to do, and sequencers must be programmed so as to stay within the hardware limits, whether or not these are musically felicitous. And fourth, market pressures often force programmers to release their products before they can implement the functions that they might like to. One of the blind men, so to speak, may have looked over another's shoulder and seen what sort of beast the other was fashioning, but no matter how attractive the second blind man's ideas might be, the first one can't take the time to tear apart what he has already done and start over.

At bottom, the diversity of the sequencer field is a strength: A great many concepts are being tried out, and rapid evolution is the order of the day. (As in biological evolution, of course, possession of a few wonderful features is no guarantee of survival.) Musicians are free to buy whatever product comes closest to meeting their needs, without having to pay for features that they will never use. You want a four-door diesel-burning elephant with a sunroof? Step right over here.

With diversity comes confusion. Many musicians avoid this by seizing on the first sequencer that comes their way and adapting their working habits to its limitations. They might never guess that another sequencer would be better for their purposes—or they might turn elsewhere and spend more money, never realizing that the sequencer they already own has hidden commands that would allow it to meet their needs. Meanwhile, other musicians waste endless hours fighting the machine, their musical hopes buried under the immovable boulder of an inferior sequencer. Let's face it—all sequencers are not created equal. Practically every one of them has *something* unique to recommend it, but it's not unusual to see marvelously advanced concepts offered on the same menu with unforgivable design flaws. Some sequencers are clumsy to operate, some lack features that most musicians consider essential, and more than a few, due to hidden flaws lurking in the labyrinthine depths of the operating code, tend to go *crash* in the night, wiping out hours of work.

For the rest of this article, we're not going to be concerned with the confusion that arises when the sequencer doesn't work. We're going to stick (what's bad enough) with the confusion that exists when it *does* work. We're going to start with some basic definitions, and then go on to discuss in detail exactly what you might or might not find that you've gotten yourself into when you tie a rope around your new elephant and lead it home.

If you're a musician considering the purchase of your first sequencer, or thinking about upgrading to a better one, you should find in the following pages just about everything you'll need to know to ask intelligent questions of a salesperson, questions based on your own musical needs that should steer you in the direction of a sequencer that you'll be happy with. Ultimately there's no substitute for hands-on experience, but if you know what the terms mean, you'll have a much better chance of sorting through the hype.

And if you're a programmer thinking about writing a sequencer (or adding some updates to one that you've already written), maybe I'll be able to suggest a few areas that you could profitably look into. I've never designed an elephant, but in the course of writing product evaluations for *Keyboard* magazine, I've had to step around my share of elephant dung.

The Minimum Requirements

What does a sequencer need to be able to do in order to be useful for music? Well, to start with, it needs to be constantly checking its MIDI in jack for incoming messages. Each time a message arrives, it needs to store the message in its memory. It also needs to be able to send the stored messages back out through its MIDI out jack whenever the user tells it to (presumably using a front panel 'play' button). In order for the messages not to be garbled, they have to be sent out in the same order in which they were received.

A sequencer that did only this much (see Figure 1) wouldn't be good for anything. We haven't even started talking about timing yet. But already we've touched on some basic ideas that must be implemented in all sequencers. First, the sequencer needs to recognize MIDI bytes when it sees them. (It will probably translate them into some other form for storage.) Second, it's going to need an *input buffer* to hold some reasonable number of incoming bytes—perhaps 256 bytes. This is because the sequencer needs some fixed amount of time to send a byte to its memory. During this time, it can't be looking at the MIDI in jack for a new byte. (Remember, today's computers can do only one task at a time.) During periods when only a few messages are arriving, separated by times of no activity, the sequencer can clear out its input buffer and catch up. But even when the incoming data is hot and heavy, the sequencer can't afford to miss any of it.

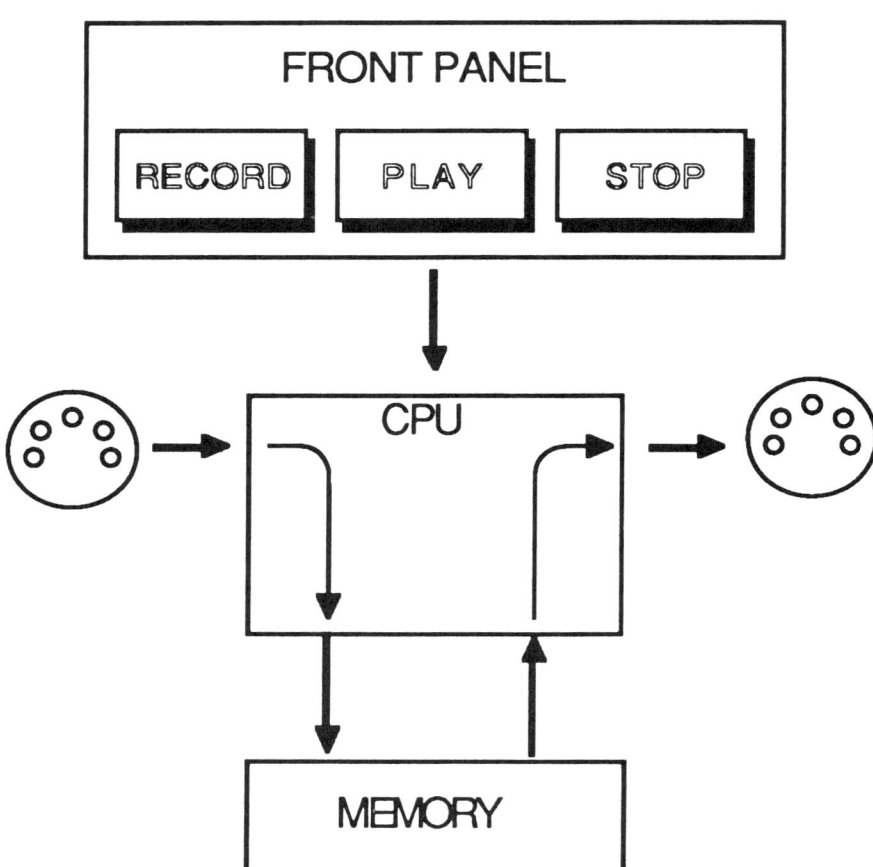

Figure 1. The simplest possible MIDI sequencer. Front panel buttons are used to tell the sequencer to begin recording the incoming MIDI data into its memory, begin playing back the contents of memory, or stop either process.

Very few sequencers today actually lose incoming data, so this is not anything you need to worry about unless you're a programmer. It's important, though, to realize that the computer must always give higher priority to some tasks than to others, deferring the lower-priority tasks until there is time to catch up on them. Many digital devices respond sluggishly to front-panel input when they're busy doing something else; this input will also be stored temporarily in an input buffer. In some devices, this command input buffer is quite small. If it overflows, portions of multi-keystroke commands may be lost before they can be carried out. If you punch a number of buttons while the sequencer is running, and nothing seems to happen in response, it's a good idea not to punch any more buttons (other than the stop button) until the machine has caught up with its housekeeping chores.

A well-designed sequencer will "lock out" any input it isn't prepared to deal with at the moment, in order to minimize potential input/output problems. For example, on a computer-based sequencer with mouse-driven graphic input, the on-screen cursor that normally moves in response to mouse movements might freeze or disappear during recording and playback. This is because the software is smart enough to know that looking at the mouse input and updating the screen will take too much of its time.

The third requirement for our primitive sequencer is a digital memory—the larger the better. And fourth, when the musician tells it to play back what's in memory, it's going to need some way of knowing when it has got to the end of the recorded material. Without such an *end-of-track* or *end-of-file marker*, it would play back the entire contents of memory each time playback was started, including the random garbage that happened to be there when the computer was switched on. Again, this concept isn't one that musicians need to deal with, as the program takes care of such housekeeping chores automatically.

In our primitive sequencer, MIDI data can be played back at only one rate—as fast as possible. This is obviously not desirable. We would like some way to slow the playback down to a reasonable rate. Even better, we would like the playback to have the same timing (rhythm) that the data had when it entered the sequencer.

But how can a sequencer—which is nothing but a computer, a glorified arithmetic machine—understand rhythmic timing? Welcome to the wonderful world of *time-stamping*. Without going into all the details of machine operation, we can simply say that every computer does have an internal clock. Of course, this doesn't look like a wrist watch, which is a good thing, because the rest of the computer couldn't tell time by it if it did. Instead, it's a few bytes of memory that are set aside as a *clock reference*, together with some circuitry that advances the clock reference at a steady rate by reading the current value, adding one to the value, and putting it back into memory. Simple arithmetic. Other portions of the machine can consult the clock reference to see what the current time is.

When a message arrives at the MIDI in jack, the computer does two things: It stores this message in its memory, and it also checks the current value of the clock and stores this value along with the packet of MIDI data. Thus the MIDI data is *time-stamped* with the current clock time, as illustrated in Figure 2.

In order to play the MIDI data back in proper rhythm, the sequencer has to reverse the process. It has to get both a clock value and a piece of MIDI data from memory, wait until the clock value in memory is the same as the current value of the running clock, and then send the MIDI data to the output jack.

A sequencer that can both time-stamp incoming MIDI data and play it back correctly with reference to the time-stamping is fully functional, though still nothing to brag about. Everything else that we will be discussing in this article is icing on this particular cake.

So far, our primitive sequencer is simply going to spit out exactly what came in. The first thing we'd like to add to it would be a bit of intelligence on the subject of MIDI. We'd like it to be able to differentiate among the various types of MIDI data. There might be certain types of data that we want it to ignore, so as to use up less memory. Or we might want it to deal with some types of data differently than others—assigning various types to different areas of memory, for example, or

Figure 2. As MIDI data enters the sequencer, each event (note-on, note-off, program change, etc.) must be stored in memory in conjunction with a number that indicates the current clock time. This linkage between the two types of data is called time-stamping. Unless the data is time-stamped, it cannot be played back in the proper rhythm. The clock time is contained in a section of memory called the clock register. The computer increments the clock register, adding 1 to it at every clock tick. Here, a note-on, caused by the depression of a key, arrives on channel 1 at bar 0001, beat 01, clock 06. The note happens to have a velocity of 87, and its note number is 60 (Middle C). At bar 0001, beat 02, clock 07, the key is released, and a note-off is recorded. (The note-off happens in this case to be a note-on with a velocity of 0.)

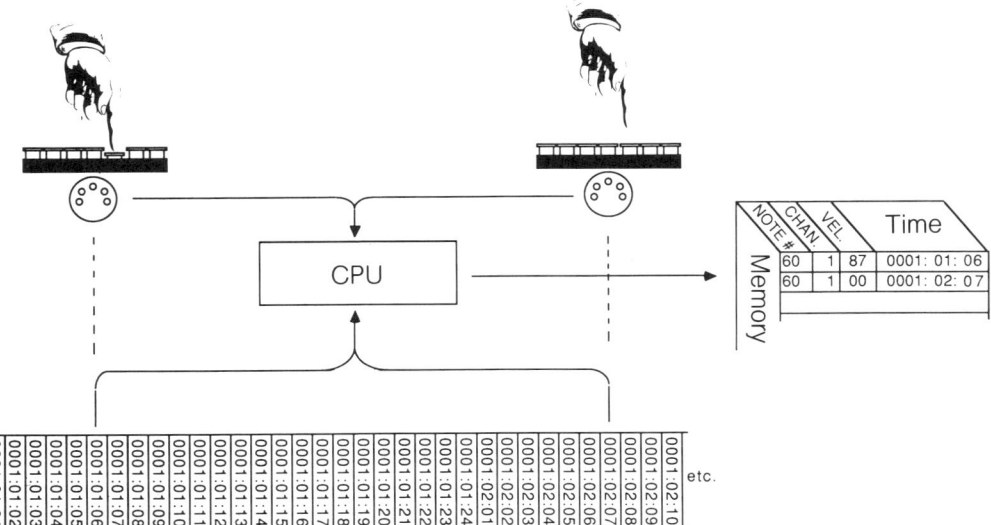

responding to them by changing its own mode of operation (as with clock and song position pointer messages) rather than recording them in memory at all.

The second thing we'd like to add would be the ability to manipulate the data once it is recorded in memory. Such manipulations are called *editing*. It's in the area of editing features that sequencers differ most radically from one another.

The third thing we'd like to add would be some form of permanent data storage, so that recorded material can be played back at a later date. Most sequencers these days use computer disks as a storage medium, but other forms of storage are found.

The fourth, fifth, and sixth things we'd like to add? Playback tempo control, yeah, and how about the ability to play back some regions of memory while skipping others? And how about ... Well, make your own wish list. And read on.

Tracks & Other Longitudinal Segments

Practically all sequencers divide their recorded material into *tracks*. The term 'track' is borrowed from multitrack tape recording. Most sequencers are designed to emulate the functions of a tape recorder, complete with rewind, fast-forward, and other familiar "tape transport" controls. Other conceptual models are possible, but the tape recorder analogy is comfortable enough to musicians to make it nearly irresistible. Sometimes you'll find a hybrid design that resembles, perhaps, a tape recorder with a built-in automated dubbing deck and splicing block.

A sequencer that emulates a tape recorder is designed so that it acts as if it contained a number of parallel tracks running from one end of the piece of music to the other, just like the tracks on a spool of tape (see Figure 3). Each track can be recorded independently with music—in this case, MIDI data rather than audio. The tracks are usually considered to be locked to one another temporally, exactly the way tape tracks are physically joined on a single width of tape. When the data in bar 5 of track 1 is being played back, the data in bar 5 of track 2 will be playing back at the same time.

But the temporal linkage between tracks is an illusion. There are no tracks in a sequencer, though there will probably be regions of memory that are partitioned off so that each track has its own assigned memory space. The sequencer may stamp each packet of MIDI data with a track designation in addition to its time-stamping, but a more efficient use of memory is for it to simply keep track of which areas of memory contain data for which tracks. Tracks may be assigned to areas of memory in some fixed fashion, or the program may allocate memory dynamically depending

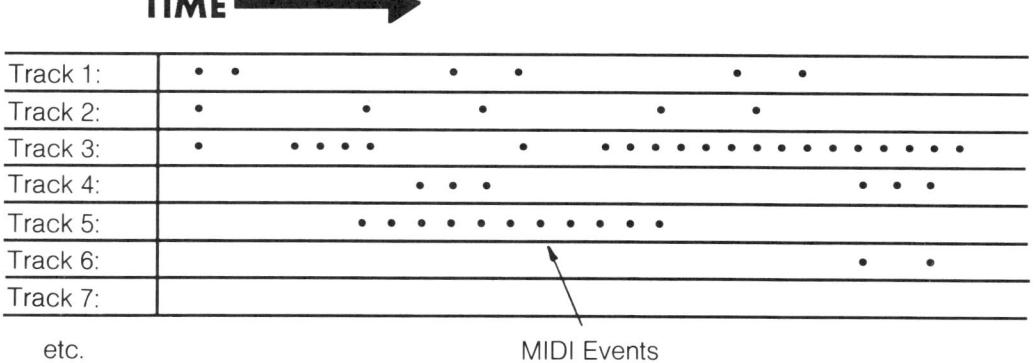

Figure 3. If a sequencer is designed to emulate a tape deck, then MIDI events will be stored in memory in such a way that they can be played back as if they were physically arranged along the tracks of a length of multitrack tape that moves at a continuous speed past a record/playback head. In fact, this arrangement is a convenient illusion; the actual physical arrangement of the stored data does not look anything like this.

on how much data you are storing in each track. If you add new data to track 1 after recording on tracks 2 and 3, the computer may use those moments when you're practicing for your next take to do a little housekeeping: It may shuffle the data for tracks 2 and 3 further down the line in order to keep all of track 1 very neatly in the same place, so it won't have to hunt for it during playback. It plays back several tracks at a time by accessing the regions of memory that it knows contain data for those

Hardware vs. Software

Hardware vs. software. While no two MIDI sequencers look alike, they are all digital devices. That is, they use the microprocessor technology found in computers. Some appear in the form a computer software that runs on general-purpose computers like the Apple Macintosh, IBM PC, and Atari ST. Others are marketed in the form of *dedicated hardware*, a box that does only one task—sequencing. Inside the box, however, are the same microprocessor circuits found in a computer, and a software program is just as necessary to a hardware sequencer as to a computer-based one.

For the purposes of our discussion of sequencer features, then, there is no need to make a distinction between computer-based and dedicated-hardware sequencers. There are three operative differences: First, a computer has a CRT (cathode-ray tube) monitor screen, and a hardware sequencer doesn't. Thus a hardware sequencer will usually be able to display at any given time only a tiny fraction of the information available on a computer sequencer's screen. Second a hardware sequencer's operating software is likely to be stored in ROM (read-only memory), while a computer sequencer will have to be loaded from disk at every session.

Therefore, a hardware sequencer can start running a minute or so quicker than its software brother if both are switched on at the same time. And third, most computers don't have built-in MIDI jacks. (The exception is the Atari ST.) A computer software sequencer must make use of a hardware *interface*, which converts the computer's output signal into MIDI.

Several MIDI interfaces are available for each of the popular computers. Some software allows the user to specify which interface is being used, but other software is only compatible (that is, it will only communicate properly) with one or two of the available interfaces. If you're shopping for sequencer software, you must be aware of which interface the software requires.

All software is originally written for some specific computer. Increasingly, though, software written for one computer is being adapted so that it will run on another. In the process of writing the adaptation, the programmer may introduce changes in the program. If you hear great things (or lousy things) about a sequencer that runs on one computer, don't assume that the same things will be true of a program with the same name that runs on another computer. Usually the programs will be similar, but they may not be identical.

By Jim Aikin

tracks. The result is that the musician hears several parallel "tracks" playing back at the same rate, even though these usually have no fixed locations in memory.

Tracks (or some other type of longitudinal subdivisions) are indispensable in editing operations. One of the primary ways of designating a region for editing is to perform the edit on one track but not on another. Most sequencers have eight tracks, or 16 or 24 or even more. Having a few empty tracks lying around can be extremely useful during an editing session. They're good for making backup copies of musical data in order to try out alternate versions of a phrase, as well as for building up a long piece out of shorter phrases that can be handled more easily because they are on separate tracks. But at least one sequencer (the MIDI DJ from National Logic) gets along very nicely with only two tracks, thanks to some special editing operations.

A sequencer that has enough display space (a computer screen, for example) will usually show a list of tracks and give some information about them, including a name typed in by the user. A typical track sheet is shown in Figure 4; we'll have a bit more to say about track sheets after we've defined the relevant terms. A good sequencer lets you write a long enough track name (16 or 24 characters) that you can display things like instrument designations and patch numbers as well as the musical function of the track in the piece. A name of eight characters or less is helpful, but not ideal.

Please don't make the mistake of confusing tracks with MIDI channels. Even seasoned professionals sometimes say "track" when they mean "channel" and vice-versa. Incoming MIDI notes and other data can be on any of the 16 MIDI channels. In most sequencers, this data can be recorded on any available track, no matter what the data's channel designation might be. A single track might easily contain data for many channels. You might run into an obsolete sequencer somewhere that forces a numerical correspondence between tracks and channels. In this case, there is no need for the device to record the channel designation of the incoming data. This scheme saves memory, but doesn't have much else to recommend it.

Virtually all sequencers today have *polyphonic* tracks. That is, chords and multiple lines of counterpoint can all be stored on a single track. Even a 4-track sequencer can play 16 or more simultaneous musical lines. At least one early sequencer program that we know of (Moog Music's Song Producer for the Commodore 64) had monophonic tracks. This type of design seems to have fallen pretty much by the wayside.

Building Songs. The simplest way, at least conceptually, to create a complete piece of music in a sequencer is to pretend that it's a tape deck, whose tape rolls from one end to the other in a linear fashion. But there are reasons why the tape deck model is not perfect for all applications. What if your tune uses a two-bar bass line that repeats 48 times? Wouldn't it be a more efficient use of memory to record the bass pattern only once, and then to tell the sequencer to repeat it as often as needed? You bet it would.

Not only does looping save memory, it can make the process of editing a lot easier in some cases. What if you decide, after listening to your bass riff, that one note in it ought to be changed? If the sequencer is playing a repeating *loop*, you can make the edit once, in a single two-bar pattern, and it will magically appear in all 48 repetitions. On the other hand, if you decide you want to change that one note in the 35th repetition of the loop but leave it unchanged in every other repetition, you're going to have to paste together a much more complicated playback structure with a looping sequencer than you would in a tape-deck-style sequencer.

Drum machines normally offer some form of segment/song architecture, in which a "song" consists not of a complete list of what drum sounds are to play on which beats, but of a much shorter list of segments or patterns that are to be played in a given order, perhaps with a certain number of repeats for each pattern or group of patterns. The song list may also contain things like tempo changes and changes in dynamics. The patterns, often (though not necessarily) two or four bars long, contain the actual musical material. The list merely contains instructions pointing to specific numbered patterns.

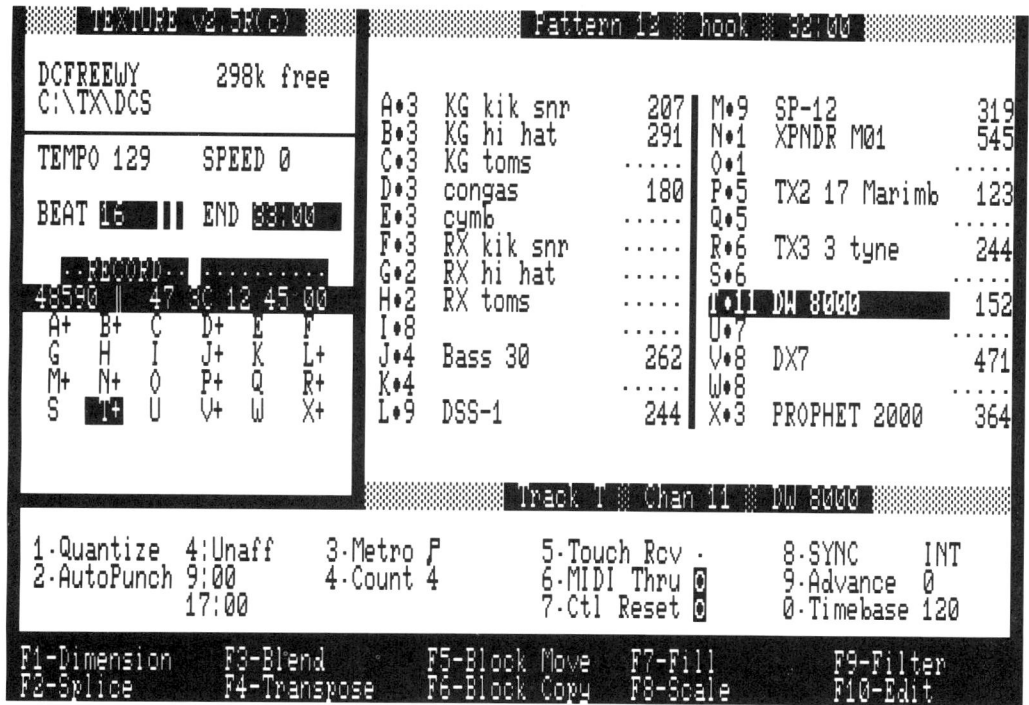

Figure 4. The main screen of Roger Powell's Texture software for the IBM PC. The largest area (upper right) is the track sheet display. All 24 tracks (lettered A through X) are shown, together with their output channel, name, and the number of bytes of memory used by that track.

This is a slick way to design a drum machine, because it corresponds to the way drum parts are usually built up by drummers. But when we transfer the concept to a sequencer, we have to address several issues. For one thing, the sequencer is playing several parts at once, not just the drums. As a result, a single list of song segments ("play pattern 03 twice, then pattern 51 four times," etc.) puts some limits on how the musical material can be organized.

Nevertheless, some very good sequencers are designed this way. Roger Powell's Texture software (from Magnetic Music) for the IBM PC is an example. Their memory may be organized into a number of independent "sequences," each with a number of parallel tracks. To build a song, you string sequences together. (In Texture, this is called *linking*.) In addition, such a sequencer might offer a "song track," a single track that runs the entire length of the song instead of being tied to a single sequence. This can be useful for non-repeating musical parts, such as improvised melodies.

On some sequencers and drum machines that allow a single pattern or sequence to be repeated (looped), a footswitch input may be provided that will command the machine to exit from the loop. This can be quite useful if the sequencer is being used to accompany a live performance in which an improvised section might change length from night to night.

Another approach is taken by the Steinberg Pro-24 software for the Atari ST. It uses only one multitrack sequence, which plays back linearly according to the tape deck analogy. Each track, however, is built up out of short patterns, which can be strung together in any order.

The most generalized approach is the one taken in Dr. T's Keyboard Controlled Sequencer, a program that was written for the Commodore 64 and has been further developed on the Atari ST. This software has a number of completely independent sequences, which are not subdivided into tracks (though they can contain multiple channels of music). Sequences can be started and stopped independently, and can loop independently. In addition, any sequence can contain "sequence start events," which activate other sequences. On other sequencers, the independent looping concept is implemented in somewhat different ways. Keeping track of what's going on in such a non-linear environment can be mind-twisting—but for some types of music, working with independent simultaneous sequences can be a fruitful approach. It invites us to take a close look at our concepts of musical structure.

When a sequencer is equipped to play longitudinal segments independently on command, there is no particular reason why the command has to come from the sequencer itself. A couple of sequencers allow a track or sequence to be started when a MIDI note is received. This might be a single note assigned to that sequence, allowing the musician to activate several sequences from a single octave of the keyboard. Or we might assign each sequence a range of notes, using individual notes within the range to transpose playback up or down. We might want playback to continue on its own, or we might want it to be gated, continuing only as long as the key is held down. There are a lot of possibilities in this area, but most sequencers are not yet equipped to take advantage of them.

Timing Is Everything

All sequencers time-stamp incoming data with the current (internal) clock time while storing the data in memory, in order to keep track of the rhythms of the music. Not all sequencers have the same *clock resolution*, however. Some of them have internal clocks that run much faster than others.

Why is this important? Because as far as the sequencer is concerned, nothing happens musically except on a clock-tick. It's not capable of knowing that it's supposed to send out a message "about 2/3 of the way from 0001:03:17 to 0001:03:18, but hold back a little so it will swing more."

Imagine an absurdly simple sequencer clock that ticked once per second. No matter what rhythms we used when playing into the sequencer, it would time-stamp everything that arrived during second 17 with a 17, everything that arrived in the following second with an 18, and so on. When playback time rolled around, it would check to see which MIDI events were time-stamped with a 17 and send these all out in a quick burst. Then it would do nothing for the rest of the second. A second later, it would send out a burst containing everything time-stamped with an 18.

No matter how high the clock resolution, the sequencer will introduce some timing errors like those just described. But by dividing the time into smaller increments, we can keep the errors smaller. Figure 5 shows how a higher clock resolution reduces timing errors.

So how much clock resolution does a sequencer need? This is usually figured in clock *pulses per quarter-note*, which is abbreviated *ppq* (or sometimes *ppqn*). By

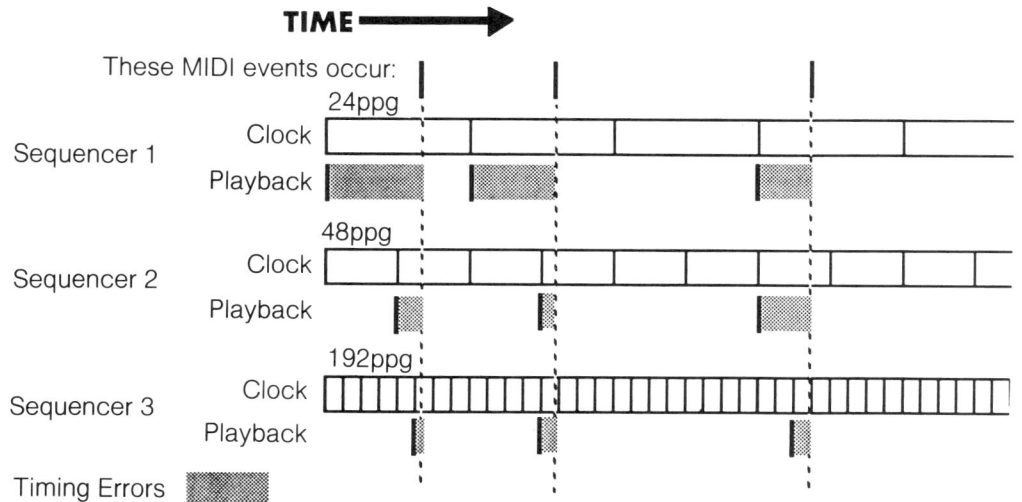

Figure 5. The higher the clock resolution, the more intervals time is divided into, and thus the smaller each interval will be. Since sequencer data can only be represented in memory as having arrived at the times corresponding to these intervals, a higher clock resolution will cause events to be represented more accurately with reference to when they were played. On playback, each event will be sent out at the beginning of the "correct" time interval, because there is no way for the sequencer to represent a smaller time interval.

the way, please don't confuse ppq with *bpm* (beats per minute), an entirely different number that also relates to timing. A sequencer's ppq will usually be the same, no matter what the tempo in bpm might be.

If all of our music is in sixteenth-note rhythms, in theory we might need only a sequencer with a 4 ppq clock, since there are four equally spaced sixteenths in a quarter-note. But what if our music contains some thirty-second-notes? We'd better increase the clock rate to 8 ppq, just to be safe. And what if we want to play some evenly spaced triplets? Obviously, eight is not divisible by three, so there's no way to assign one of the triplets to each clock pulse at 8 ppq and have them come out even at the end of the beat. (See Figure 6.) We need to multiply our clock resolution by three, to 24 ppq, in order to handle triplets.

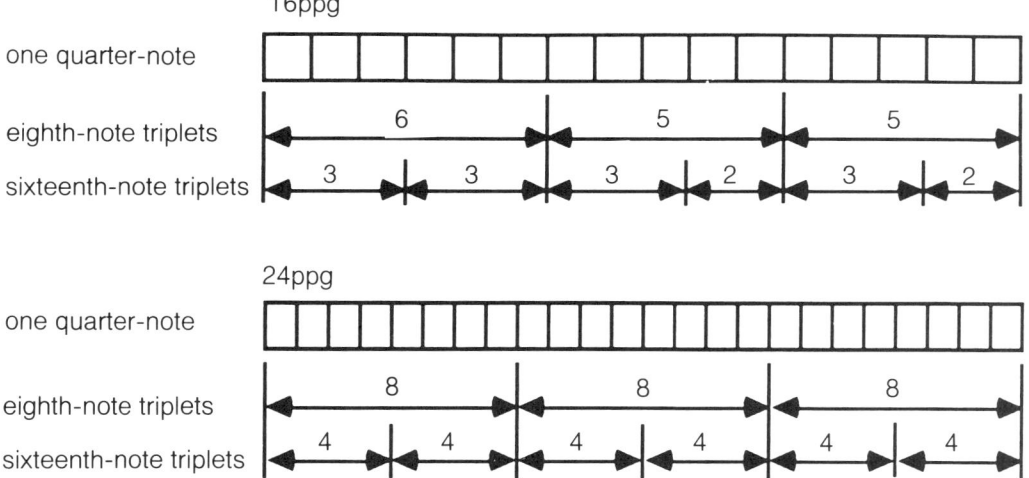

Figure 6. In order for triplets to be given an even spacing by software, the clock rate in ppq (pulses per quarter-note) must be evenly divisible by 3. In a 16 ppq sequencer, trying to divide a quarter-note into 3 or 6 equal groupings results in a lopsided rhythm, because some of the subdivisions must be larger then others. In a 24 ppq sequencer the division into triplets can be even.

The standard timebase for many MIDI sequencers and drum machines is 24 ppq. This is enough timing resolution to handle many standard musical tasks. It's also the rate at which MIDI clock signals are transmitted. If we sync our sequencer to an external MIDI clock, it will automatically be running at 24 ppq, unless the programmer does some pretty fancy timing interpolation.

But is 24 ppq really enough? Many programmers and musicians argue that it isn't. For one thing, we might want to play some evenly spaced quintuplets, which is only possible with a timebase, such as 60 or 120 ppq, that's divisible by five. More important than this (since most of us don't use quintuplets very often) is the question of time perception.

To see why this is important, let's do a bit of math. A 24 ppq clock running at a tempo of 80 bpm (a normal slow tempo) is pulsing 32 times every second. So the pulses are more than 31 milliseconds apart. Unfortunately for our 24 ppq sequencer, the human nervous system is quite capable of distinguishing time intervals far smaller than 31 ms. If everything that happens musically is happening on these 31 ms clock pulses, we will be able to perceive that the sequencer's playback is just a bit more rigid and mechanical than the supple, expressive rhythm that it was trying to record. In order for the sequencer to be able to fool our ears into thinking they're hearing a human musician, we need a higher clock rate.

How high? This is a matter of debate. There's some convincing evidence that, given the right context (that is, surrounding rhythmic material that is chugging along at a fixed rate), the human ear can distinguish a 1 ms lag. So ideally, we'd like our 24 ppq clock to run 30 times faster—around 720 ppq.

While extremely high clock rates are found on a few sequencers, most programmers feel that the drawbacks outweigh the advantages. For one thing, a faster clock rate requires a higher computer processing speed. It also requires more memory (because every packet of timing data to be stored has more bytes in it). Besides, at high speeds we run head-on into the time limitations of MIDI itself. A standard three-byte MIDI message takes 1 ms to transmit or receive. What if we crank the metronome of our 720 ppq clock up to 150 bpm? Not an unreasonable tempo, but now the clock is screaming along at 1,800 pulses per second—and half of those pulses are wasted, because it takes nearly two pulses for a single MIDI event to arrive!

In practice, sequencer designers compromise between clock resolution and practical considerations of memory and machine performance. Resolutions of 24, 48, and 96 ppq are quite common, and some sequencers offer 120 ppq or more. The Fairlight runs at a whopping 384 ppq. A few sequencers allow you to set your own clock resoluion. And if you need higher resolution for a particular piece, you can always crank the tempo of the sequencer up to double-speed. The machine will think it's playing quarter-notes while you're playing eighth-notes, which will automatically double the clock resolution.

Another reason why extremely high clock resolutions aren't needed in MIDI systems is that there are many potential sources of timing problems other than the sequencer's clock resolution. When the sequencer is sending lots of data down the MIDI cable, the data output can get backed up, because it takes 1 ms to send a single message. To send a single 12-note chord takes 12 ms, so one of the notes in the chord is going to start 12 ms *after* one of the other notes. This can be a perceptible delay if the synthesizer patch being played is one that has a sharp attack.

And what we've just said assumes that each synthesizer in the system responds instantly to incoming MIDI messages. This is not true at all. Some older instruments may take between 10 and 20 ms to turn on a single note. As long as we're on the subject, though, it's *not* true that daisy-chaining MIDI devices (sending the data from each device to the next using MIDI thru jacks) causes time delays. Daisy-chaining more than four or five devices in a row could conceivably cause data to become garbled, but that's another story.

Another hidden assumption is that the sequencer has nothing to do except spit out MIDI messages whenever the clock says to. In fact, it may have internal housekeeping chores to take care of between transmissions. Normally these are invisible to the user, because they don't take much time. But when the sequencer is being asked to spit out large amounts of data at fast tempos, it can get bogged down and start to lag quite badly. This is why some sequencers are designed so that, even though they have a large number of tracks, only a limited number of tracks can be playing back at any given time. The programmer prevents time lags by not letting his machine try to do more than it can do in a timely manner. Some sequencers provide a number of MIDI output jacks, so that data intended for one instrument won't hang up the transmission of data being routed to another.

Pitch-bends and modulation require the transmission of many more bytes of data in a short period of time than notes: A single quick pitch-bend may contain hundreds of MIDI messages. This is a potent source of timing problems, so programmers often create some method of data filtering that will get the pitch-bends, after-touch, and so on out of the data stream.

Standard tempo settings for sequencers range from 20 or 30 bpm up to 250 or so. When you change tempo, you're not actually changing the speed (some millions of cycles per second) with which the computer's internal clock is running. What you're doing is telling the machine how many machine clock cycles you want to go by before it updates its clock reference register. At fast tempos, it updates this register more often.

Many sequencers these days give the user a display of clock times in measure/ beat/tick format. For example, the clock value might read 0017:03:29, which means that we're in bar 17, beat 3, tick 29 (a little over halfway to beat 4, if this is a 48 ppq sequencer). But there is some variety in this area. Some sequencers display only measures and ticks, others only beats and ticks. A few oddball sequencers display the current time only as a total number of clocks, or in SMPTE hour/minute/second/ frame format.

Also, some sequencers start counting with 0, and some with 1. Beats normally start with 1 rather than 0, because this is the musical convention: The first beat of a bar is beat 1, not beat 0. But you might find that this beat is displayed as 01:00 in one sequencer and 01:01 in another. Accordingly, the last tick before the next beat (in a 48 ppq system) could be either 01:47 or 01:48. Doing the math to figure out what rhythm value falls on what clock tick can definitely get a little crazy at times.

Input

There are at least four ways to get notes and other MIDI data into a sequencer. These can be referred to as real-time recording, step entry, loop recording, and score entry. Each type of input procedure has advantages and drawbacks, and a well-equipped sequencer includes both of the first two types in some form. Loop recording is the type customarily found on drum machines; it is also found on a few sequencers in some form. Score recording is less common.

Real-Time Recording. Real-time recording, which is what we have been discussing up to now, is closely analogous in practice to recording sound on a tape deck. The sequencer's internal clock advances at a steady pace, just the way the reels of tape advance, and MIDI data enters the sequencer somewhat the way audio data (sound) enters the tape deck. When a MIDI event arrives, the sequencer time-stamps it and stores the event bytes and timing bytes in an area of memory. The event is associated with a particular time in much the same way that recorded sound is always associated with some particular location on the tape. Unlike tape, of course, sequencer memory is inherently a plastic medium, and the time relationships, along with many other aspects of the data, can be changed afterward by editing.

There is no requirement in our definition that the internal clock be advancing at the same tempo that will be used when the piece of music is played back. When recording parts that are tricky to play, musicians will often slow the sequencer's clock down. This allows them to execute the part more reliably at the slower tempo. After the part is recorded properly, the clock can be sped up for playback. Since what is being recorded is MIDI data rather than audio, changing the playback rate will have no effect on the pitch of the sound. This is another important difference between sequencing and tape recording.

To make slowed-down recording easier, a few sequencers include 'tempo registers.' By storing the actual tempo of the piece in one memory register and a slow tempo in a second register, the musician can switch back and forth between the desired recording tempo and the playback tempo with a single command. In the absence of such registers, changing tempos must be done by scrolling through all of the intermediate tempo values with increment/decrement keys or entering the numbers for a new tempo using a data entry command.

During the recording process the sequencer must do two things at once. It must record new data, and also play back previously recorded data. Since a microprocessor can do only one thing at a time, it has to alternate very rapidly between storing incoming data and retrieving other data from memory to play back (see Figure 7). A device that didn't allow us to hear the other parts of an arrangement while inputting a new part would be nearly useless musically.

Again, we can think of the sequencer as being like a multitrack tape deck: One track is in record mode, while the other tracks are in playback mode. We could call the process playback/recording or overdubbing if we wanted to, but in practice, the term 'recording' refers to this entire process. Unlike a tape deck, most sequencers will record on only one track at a time.

When real-time recording takes place, the data is usually stored in an area of memory called the record buffer. When the recording is finished, the user may be prompted with a menu listing the things that can be done with the record buffer. The options may include erasing the buffer, copying the buffer into some specific track while erasing whatever was previously in that track, and merging the buffer with the contents of an existing track. The record buffer stores data temporarily; when a new recording is started, the previous contents of the buffer will be erased.

On some sequencers, a track must be designated for recording before recording can begin. In this case, only two choices will be offered: keep the recorded material (i.e., store it in the designated track), or erase it so as to be able to try again. On some sequencers with a limited number of tracks, such as the Yamaha QX5, all recording must be done to track 1, but track 1 can later be copied to any other track and its contents erased. Thus track 1 is functioning both as a track and as the record buffer.

Procedures For Real-Time Recording. Some sequencers require several keystrokes to ready the machine to receive data. Others are ready to record at all times, and can be set up so as to start playback/recording automatically from a stopped condition when they receive a MIDI event. More commonly, the user is required to give a 'record' command.

When the record command is given, the sequencer does not necessarily begin recording immediately. It may begin by playing a *count-in*, so that the musician can

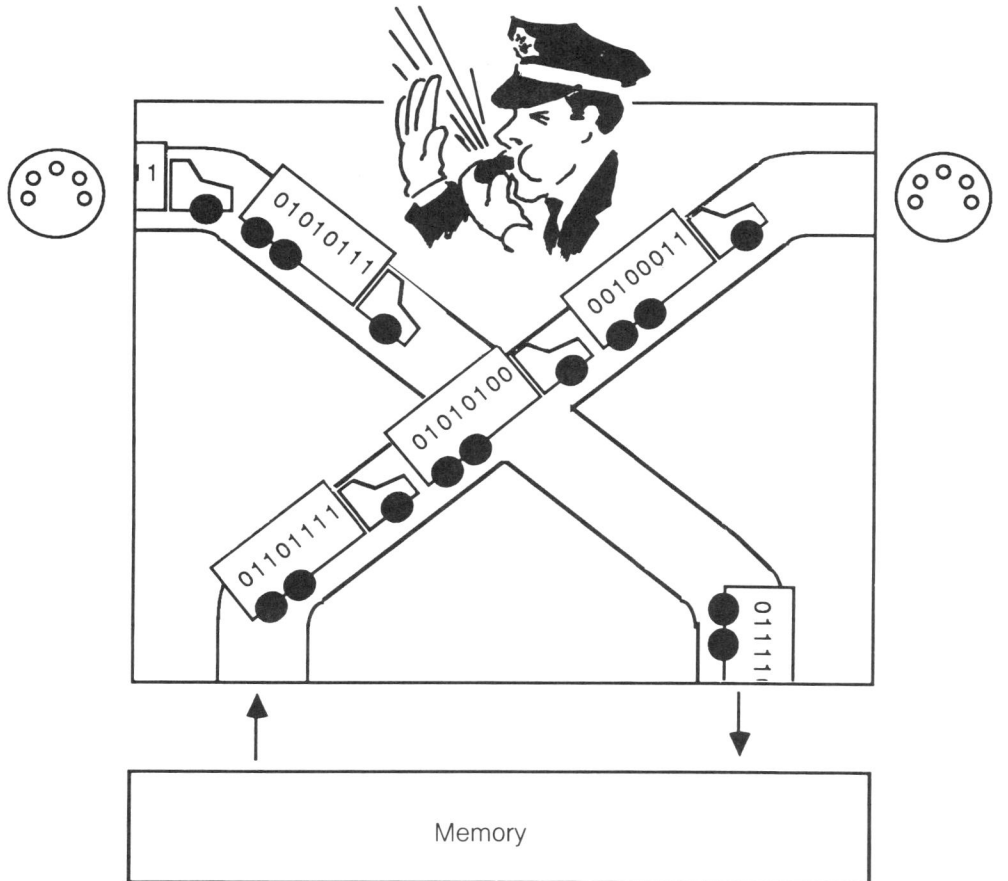

Figure 7. During the recording process, the sequencer must be doing two tasks at once. It must store incoming data in memory, while simultaneously playing back portions of the data already stored. Since the processor can do only one thing at a time, the programmer must work out some efficient form of traffic management so that neither stream of data will get backed up.

hear the tempo of the music. This count-in will be heard on the sequencer's internal metronome, if it has one. If it doesn't, the manufacturer will usually provide some alternative, such as an option to begin sending MIDI clocks (to an external drum machine) during the count-in.

The length of the count-in is generally selectable by the user in beats and/or bars, and can be switched off if desired. Some sequencers, such as the Sonus SST software for the Atari ST, offer a variable length count-in, in which the metronome will continue to click until the musician plays a MIDI note, at which time recording will start. Normally, the count-in is heard only prior to recording, not prior to playback. On a few sequencers, unfortunately, the count-in must be switched on or off for all operations with a single command. This is not very convenient, as it forces you to either switch back and forth constantly or listen to a count-in before every playback.

A sequencer's metronome can usually be switched to various beat values (such as eighth-notes or quarter-notes). Some metronomes automatically provide a louder or higher-pitched click at the beginning of each bar. This is helpful, unless you happen to be trying to record a piece that changes time signatures on a sequencer that doesn't.

If the sequencer is ignoring incoming events that occur during the count-in, it can easily lose the first note if the player plays it slightly early. This can be quite annoying. As a result, many sequencers do actually record during the count-in, but any events that arrive are time-stamped with the first clock *after* the count-in. In effect, these events are adjusted so that they fall on the first beat of the first bar (assuming that recording is beginning on the first beat of a bar).

It is also necessary, as we've just hinted, to tell the sequencer where in the piece of music we want the recording to begin. If we couldn't do this, we would have to start every take from the beginning of the piece, which would get quite tiresome when recording pieces of any length. Some sequencers only allow recording to begin at a bar line, but many will allow the starting point to be specified with bar/beat/clock accuracy. Most sequencers allow the take to continue as long as you'd like, but a few insist that an end-of-recording point also be specified before recording begins. When this point is reached, the machine will stop recording automatically, or begin to loop.

When the take is finished, we may want to save it, or we may want to try again immediately. In the latter case, we need to reset the internal clock somehow to the point at which we want recording to begin. Many sequencers contain an *auto-rewind* feature that will do this automatically, resetting the clock to any specified bar/beat/clock location each time we stop the playback.

A few sequencers are equipped with a special feature that allows the musician to do a number of takes of the same material automatically. The machine performs all the necessary housekeeping tasks: When the end of the designated recording region is reached, it automatically copies the record buffer to the next available empty track, mutes that track (so you won't have to listen to the previous take while playing the new one), auto-rewinds to the point where recording is to begin, and goes back into record mode. After doing as many takes as desired (up to the limit of the number of tracks available for storing the takes), you can unmute them one at a time, choose the best one, and erase those that are not needed.

Another approach to multi-pass recording, found on both Texture and the Atari version of KCS, allows the user to listen to previous takes, which loop automatically while a new one is being recorded. Multitrack improvisations can be built up without the annoyance of having to stop and start the sequencer.

Normally, all of the material being recorded during a single take will be arriving on one MIDI channel (the channel that the master keyboard is transmitting on). In some circumstances, however, such as when an entire sequence is being transferred from one sequencer to another via MIDI, material may be arriving on many channels. This can cause problems if the receiving sequencer insists on storing on a single track all incoming data that arrives during a single take, and if it has no method for unmerging tracks by channel. (For more on unmerging, see the section on editing.) To deal with this situation, a sequencer might have a special command that causes the record buffer to be stored onto several consecutive tracks, with each track receiving the data that arrived on one channel.

Loop Recording. A few high-end drum machines (notably the Linn 9000 and Sequential Studio 440) incorporate both MIDI sequencing and standard drum machine functions. But all drum machines are sequencers in the sense that they allow data recordings to be made that will play their own internal sounds. The sequencers built into drum machines have an unusual architecture. Because of the repetitive nature of most drum patterns, it is more efficient in terms of memory usage to build a piece of music out of a number of short *segments* (also called *patterns*) which can later be chained together by a song list to create a complete piece of music.

For this reason, drum machine recording generally takes place in a region as short as one or two bars. Under the circumstances, it would be silly for the region (that is, the segment) to play through once and then stop. Instead, it cycles through over and over while the user adds drum hits on the desired beats (see Figure 8). Unlike most sequencers, drum machines usually quantize the incoming data before storing it, so that all of the drum hits fall on some beat or other. (See the section on input and output processing for more on input quantization.)

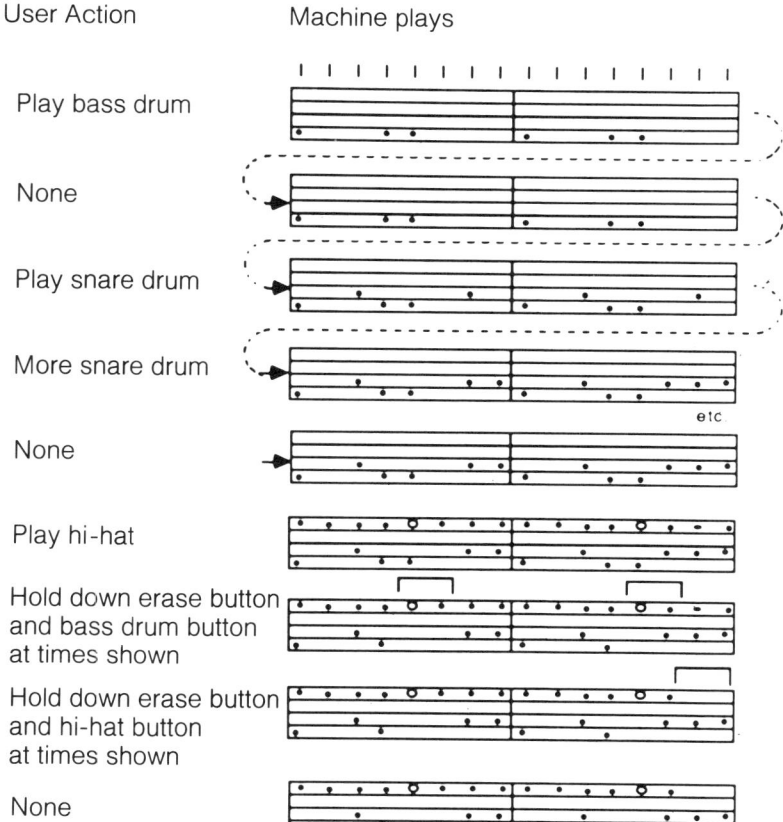

Figure 8. Drum machines use a special form of recording that is also found on a few MIDI sequencers. A short loop (often two bars long) plays over and over while the user adds and subtracts notes. A special form of erasure allows notes to be removed from the loop without affecting other notes on the same beats.

But what happens if you play a drum sound on the wrong beat? It sure would be a pain if you had to stop the loop record/playback in order to perform an erase operation to get rid of the offending note. To deal with this situation, drum machines offer a special type of erasure that we might call *scoop-out* erasure. A special 'erase' key is held down, and any notes that are played while this key is held are interpreted as erase commands rather than as record commands. Loop recording and scoop-out erasure are found on only a few non-drum machine sequencers.

Loop recording differs from track-oriented recording in that it is not normally possible to monitor (play back) any other pattern while recording a new pattern. All of the notes in the pattern that is currently being recorded will obviously be heard on every iteration of the loop.

Step Entry Recording. Step entry (which is also called step recording, single-step recording, and step-time recording) differs from real-time recording in that the sequencer's internal clock does not advance at a steady pace. Instead, it advances when commanded to do so by the user. This command may be relatively transparent to the user. That is, it may be incorporated into some other action, so that fewer keystrokes are required. But it is generally present in some form, except when pure data is being entered directly from the computer keyboard.

Step entry is somewhat a laborious process at best. It can be the method of choice when recording parts with complicated rhythms and articulations and long passages in regular rhythm (such as sixteenth-note ostinati). It is also useful in conjunction with punch-in recording for replacing wrong notes with new notes that must fit precisely into an existing passage.

Two types of step recording must be distinguished. One is pure data entry, in which all of the sequence data is generated (in some manner) directly from the computer keyboard. A hybrid type is somewhat more common (see Figure 9). In this type, a MIDI keyboard or other controller is used for generating some of the data while other portions are generated at the computer keyboard. The hybrid type is easier for most musicians to deal with, because the musical element of pitch can be played directly, rather than being translated mentally into some other form, such as letters and numbers.

In real-time recording, all of the aspects of a MIDI note (starting time, channel, pitch, velocity, and duration) are recorded as they occur. But in step recording, some or all of these may have to be specified in some other manner—usually from a menu of options offered to the user.

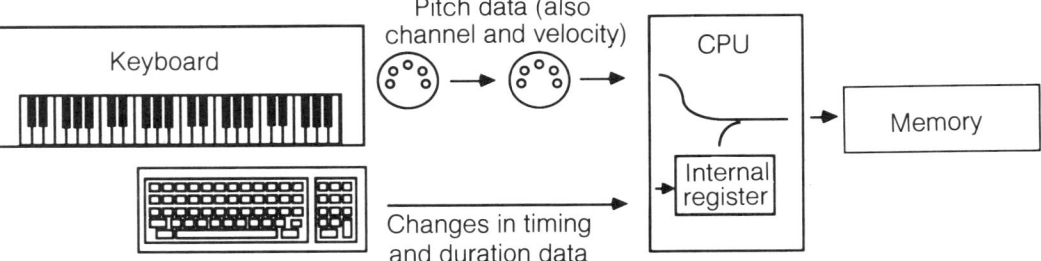

Figure 9. In hybrid forms of step entry, the sequencer receives portions of the data for a single event from two sources. In one possible arrangement, pitch, channel, and velocity are input from a MIDI keyboard while timing and duration are loaded from an internal data register. Changes in the values of this register can be specified from the computer's QWERTY keyboard.

On a typical step recording screen (see Figure 10), the user might have three menus: rhythm value, duration, and velocity. One item will be selected in each menu—for example, quarter-note rhythm, eighth-note duration, and a velocity of 64. When a MIDI note is received at the input, its pitch and channel are recorded. It is time-stamped with the current clock position, and given a duration corresponding to an eighth-note at the current clock resolution. (With a 24 clocks per quarter-note sequencer, for example, it would get a duration value of 12.) Finally, the internal clock is advanced automatically to the next point specified by the rhythm value—in this case, to the next quarter-note. Some sequencers allow the actual key velocity to be recorded during step recording instead of a velocity chosen from a menu.

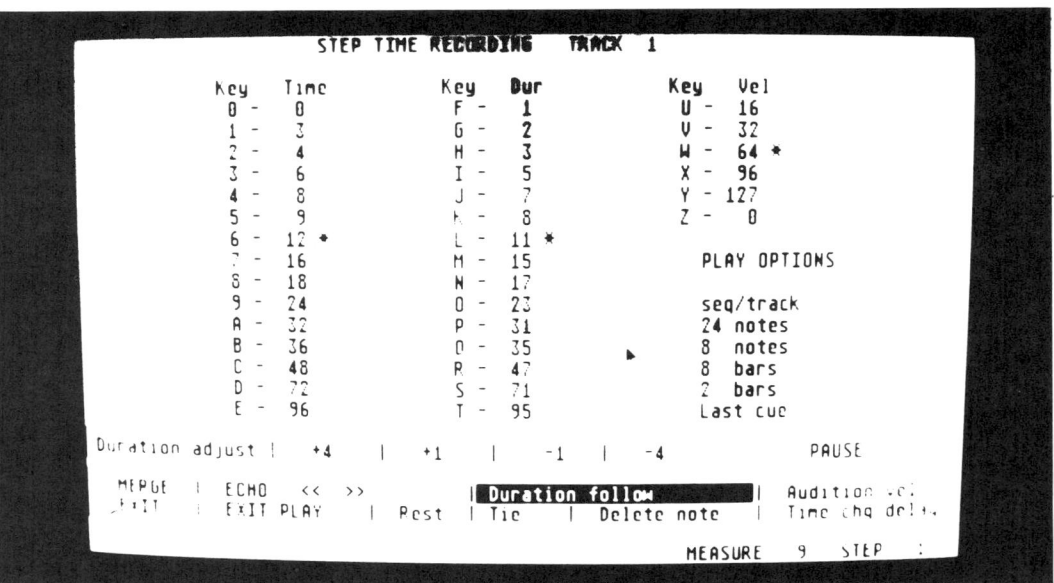

Figure 10. The hybrid step entry menu for Dr. T's KCS Rhythm (the amount by which the clock will be advanced) is selected in the column at left, the duration of the note in the middle column, and the velocity in the right column. Note number and channel are entered directly from a MIDI keyboard.

At first glance, it might appear difficult to record chords with this system, because the internal clock advances after every note. This situation is usually dealt with by having the clock advance *when all MIDI keys have been lifted.* Several keys can be pressed down at once in a more or less haphazard fashion, and they will still be recorded together as a chord. The clock will advance when the sequencer's logic tells it that there are now no keys pressed down.

This type of hybrid recording allows passages in which a single rhythm value is repeated over and over to be entered as quickly as the musician can press and release keys on the MIDI master keyboard, because the menus keep their current values until the user changes them. The user only needs to use the menus when changing from one rhythm, duration, or velocity to another.

The simplest rhythm and duration menus may offer only duplet and triplet values directly related to the current time signature. This system severely limits the musical possibilities, as it does not allow for dotted and tied notes, to say nothing of staccato articulations, quintuplets, and compound rhythms. More flexible systems include a user-specifiable item at the top or bottom of each menu, or at the very least provide a command for tying the note now being entered to either the last note or the next one.

Sequencers can store note duration data in two different ways. The note-on and note-off can be recorded as separate MIDI events, each of which is individually time-stamped. Or the note-on can be recorded, and the machine can calculate a duration value, to be stored as part of the note event, basing the calculation on when it receives the corresponding note-off. The second method is more memory-efficient, and also makes certain editing operations easier. But it leaves no way of recording note-off velocity. Most sequencers will not record note-off velocity, though it is defined in the MIDI Specification, but this is not usually a problem because most MIDI keyboards don't transmit it.

Another type of hybrid step entry gives the user no way of specifying duration as a separate parameter. Instead, the user advances the clock manually while holding the key down, and releases it when the desired end-point is reached. Note-on and note-off are then time-stamped separately. In this case, the sequencer may be equipped with commands (accessible from the computer keys) for advancing the clock by different amounts—a single clock, a sixteenth-note, and a quarter-note, for example. Hybrid Arts' Miditrack ST software for the Atari ST uses this system. It allows for more flexibility in terms of staccato/legato articulation of step-entered passages, but requires that the user do a bit more work to obtain good musical results.

The most rudimentary step entry systems may offer no method of backing up to a previous note to change it. Also, there may be no way of playing back your work to check what it sounds like, other than by exiting the step entry environment and returning to playback mode.

Another form of hybrid step entry found on at least one sequencer (the Steinberg Pro-24 software for the Atari ST) allows you to record new pitches and/or velocities into an existing track while retaining the current durations. By making several copies of a track in this sequencer and then entering new pitches into the copies, you can easily step-enter block chords. All the notes in a given chord will have the same articulation. It also allows wrong notes in a track to be fixed quite easily. Within a few years, we'll probably be seeing more input systems that allow certain types of data (such as velocity or duration) to be isolated at the input stage, stored separately, and combined with already recorded data in creative ways.

Pure data entry—i.e., typing in values from a computer keyboard—is a more cumbersome process than either real-time entry or hybrid step entry. It can be convenient when there is no MIDI keyboard handy, and is also the method of choice for non-note data in some situations. Typing in program change commands, for example, assures that they will occur at exactly the point in the music where they are required. Entering a program change in real time leaves more margin for error, and this can be difficult to correct, depending on how the editing functions affect non-note events. Pure data entry is quite similar to event editing, and generally uses the same features, so there is no need to discuss it further here.

Score Entry Recording. Score entry is used in graphically oriented sequencers, such as Deluxe Music Construction Set from Electronic Arts (see Figure 11). In score entry, the computer screen shows one or more music staves, and the user manipulates a visual cursor (often with the aid of a mouse) to select musical symbols (such as eighth-notes) and position them on the staff. Since there is no precise method of indicating the many possible non-legato durations in traditional notation, no way of indicating exact MIDI note velocity, and no way of indicating non-note events, score entry is only of limited use in a full-function MIDI sequencing environment.

Score entry is generally too slow for musicians who have any keyboard facility, but it can be quite useful for amateurs whose main interest is in playing printed sheet music with the sequencer, and for composers who work more with graphic processes than with reference to the feel and sound of a physical instrument.

A score display can also be helpful in editing, and some sequencers can be interfaced with score printing programs for the production of sheet music. The transcription of MIDI input into rhythmic notation that is both readable and true to the player's intentions is not a simple task for software, however.

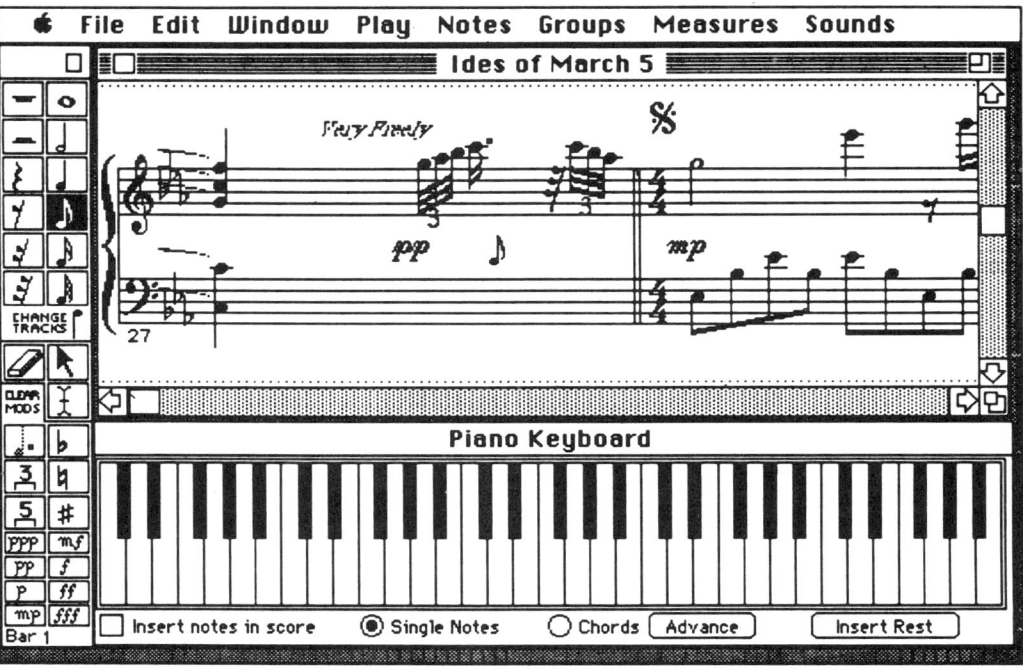

Figure 11. The score entry screen on Deluxe Music Construction Set, a Macintosh program from Electronic Arts. Notes can be played on a MIDI keyboard, or can be placed on the score manually by clicking with the mouse.

Punch-In Recording. Punch-in recording might properly be considered a form of editing rather than recording, since it involves changing some of the material in an already recorded track. But it is usually thought of as recording, so we will discuss it here. It often happens during a recording session that most of a track is perfect, but one passage contains mistakes, or is simply wrong for the music. For whatever reason, the present data must be erased and replaced with new data. Punch-in recording is the most direct process by which this can be done.

Punch-in recording is done most often in real time. Some sequencers allow you to do punch-ins in step-record mode, but since this is less common, we will discuss punching in as if it were exclusively a real-time process.

Punching in is a process that originated in tape recording. Tape playback is started several beats or bars before the offending passage. This is called the pre-roll. When the passage is reached, the engineer puts the track containing the offending passage into record mode, and the musician plays a 'fix' that is recorded onto the track. Up until the moment when the track is put into record mode, it is playing back. This allows the musician to listen to what has previously been recorded, so as to get oriented and to match the feel of the performance. When the end of the offending passage is reached, the engineer punches out and stops the tape.

Note that in normal tape recording, the erase head erases whatever has previously been on a track whenever that track is placed in record mode. When the track is not in record mode, however, the erase head is inactive. Thus, any material that may already have been recorded on a given track before the beginning of the punch, or after the end of the punch, will be unaffected by the punch. When the tape is next played back, we will hear the old material on that track up to the punch-in point, the newly recorded material, and then, after the punch-out point, the previously recorded material again.

This is how we would like sequencer punch-ins to work (see Figure 12). We would like to be able to specify a 'punch track,' which is the track containing the material to be replaced. We would like to start sequencer playback several beats or bars before the punch-in point, and we would like to be listening to the punch track, along with any other non-muted tracks, as we approach the punch-in point. Once the punch point is reached, however, and we begin the process of recording new material, we would like the punch track to be automatically muted. (Listening to the wrong notes while trying to play the right ones can be rather disorienting!) Next, we would like to be able to punch out at any time and leave the material beyond the punch-out point on the punch track unaffected. Since we're operating a computer, we would like the convenience of being able to specify the punch-in and punch-out points ahead of

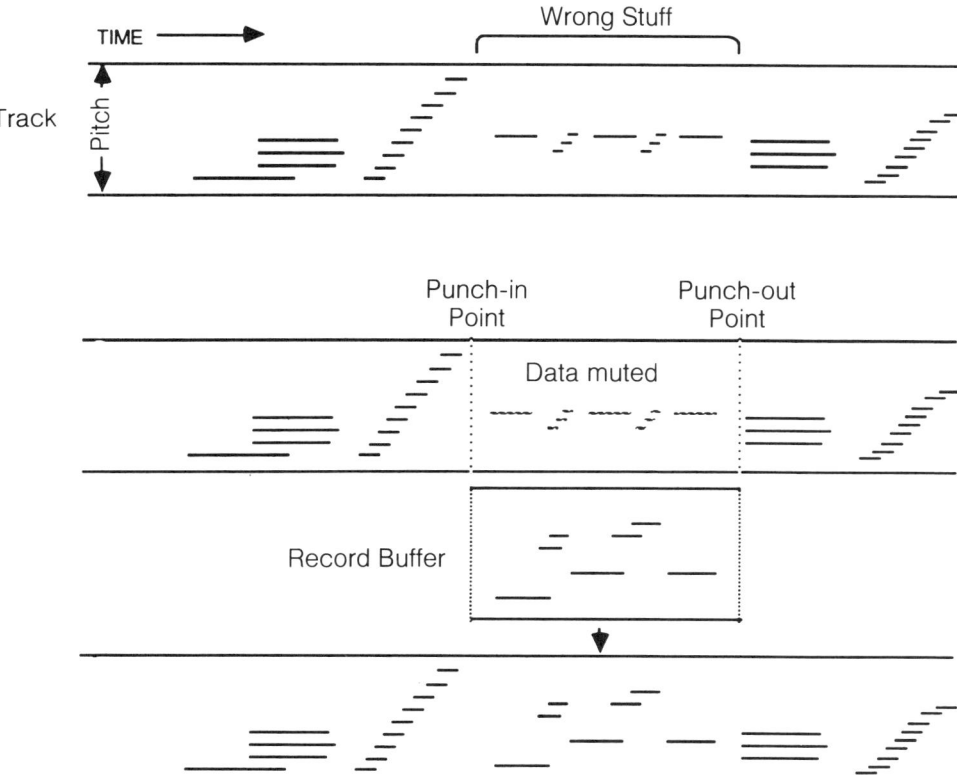

Figure 12. In punch-in recording, wrong notes in the middle of a track can be replaced with new material. The existing material on the track will be muted between the punch-in point, when recording begins, and the punch-out point, when it ends. The new material recorded during the punch-in will initially be in the record buffer, it will be inserted in the track, overwriting previous material, if the user gives the appropriate command.

time, so that we can use our hands for playing music rather than hitting the punch-in command. Finally, we would like to be able to choose among several options for what to do with the contents of the record buffer, including (a) erase the buffer and try again without altering the material on the selected track, (b) replace the offending material in the selected track with the contents of the buffer, and (c) copy the buffer to an empty track, so as to be able to listen to the two versions of the material alternately.

Some sequencers will do exactly this type of recording. Unfortunately, many of them won't. You may encounter many different constraints on the punch-in process, depending on what sequencer you are working with. These constraints range from the mildly irritating to the intensely infuriating.

Some sequencers won't do punch-in recording in any direct way. On these, the same end can be accomplished by the rather elaborate process illustrated in Figure 13. The idea is to create a hole in the track, into which to drop the newly recorded material. We have to make an extra copy of the track (just in case we don't like the new recording and want the old one back), mute the copy, and erase the offending region within the track, which may require copying some regions to still other tracks. Then we make a new recording and merge the new material with what remains of our working copy of the initial track.

Problems can appear during the punch-in process. Here is a major one: If the sequencer is time-stamping and storing note-ons and note-offs separately, it may have no way of knowing which note-ons correspond to which note-offs. So what

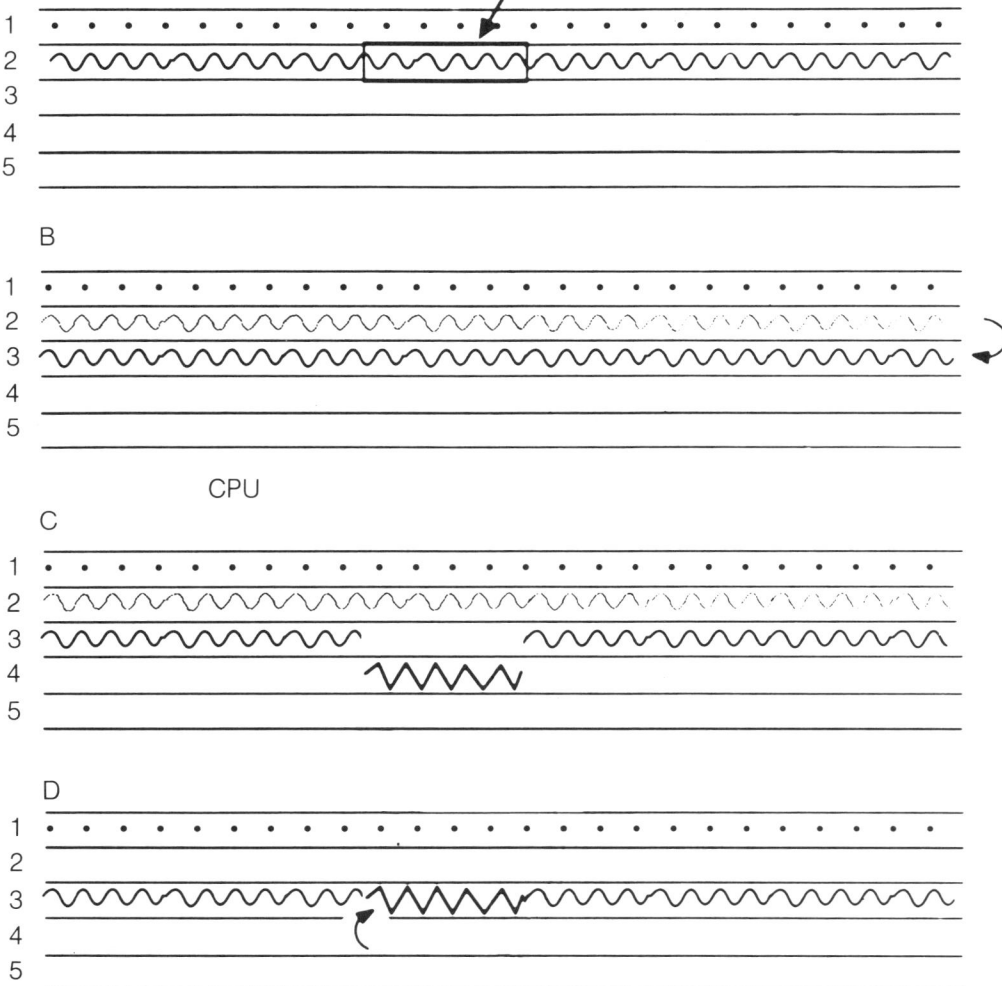

Figure 13. In a sequencer that does not offer punch-in recording, a section of a track can be replaced by a more roundabout method. (a) Track 1 is fine, but track 2 has a passage that might be improved. However, we're not sure we can improve it, so we don't want to erase it. (b) Track 2 is copied to track 3, and track 2 is muted. We can now do anything we like to the data on track 3 without affecting the original on track 2. (c) A section of track 3 is erased, after which a new take of the passage is recorded onto track 4. We have to erase the material from track 3 if we want to monitor track 3 up to the point where the new recording starts, because this sequencer is not capable of muting a track during punch-in recording. (d) If the new recording is satisfactory, track 4 is merged with track 3, and track 2 is erased.

happens when we erase all of the MIDI data between the punch points? If a note begins on the punch track before the punch-in point, but ends after the punch-in point, when we punch in we will erase its note-off without erasing the corresponding note-on. This will cause the note to ring on forever.

The easiest way for the programmer to deal with this problem is to instruct the sequencer to scan through the track looking for note-ons prior to the punch-in point that don't have note-offs, or, conversely, to look for note-offs within the punch region for which there are no note-ons within the punch region. It can then insert corresponding note-offs at the punch-in point, after which erasing the data in the punch region won't hurt anything.

That takes care of the ringing note effect, but it doesn't necessarily solve all of our musical problems. What we've just done is change the length of a note, which is likely to be audible and may not be desirable. Even if you aren't a programmer, you need to be aware of the logic with which the punches on your sequencer are executed, because if you punch in during the middle of a sustained note (intentionally or accidentally) you may hear the musical result as the note is shortened. If your sequencer stores durations rather than note-offs, you won't have this problem.

Some sequencers allow pre-roll, punch-in, and punch-out times to be programmed before playback/recording starts. They may even have a number of different punch registers for storing and recalling this type of data—quite handy when you're juggling blocks of material in various ways. Other sequencers allow you to punch in by entering record mode manually on the currently designated track during playback. In this situation, the sequencer may not understand how to play notes on the punch track and then mute this track at the proper moment; you may have to choose between muting the track before playback begins, or not muting it at all. This is not true punch-in recording.

In some sequencers, you may find that everything following the punch-in point on the selected track has been irretrievably erased. In other words, there is punch-in but no punch-out, and no opportunity to change your mind and save the previous material once you have punched in. This form of punch-in is found on the built-in sequencer in the Ensoniq ESQ-1 and SQ-80 synthesizers, but few musicians find it really satisfactory.

Input & Output Processing

There are three times when we can make changes in MIDI data with a sequencer: as the data is arriving, while the data is in memory, and while the data is being sent out again. The second option, which is at the core of many vital sequencer functions, will be covered in the next section. Right now we're going to look at the first and third options.

Input processing can be used for several things. We can strip out data that we have no use for. This saves the computer a lot of time: It can concentrate on things that are musically important. We can also make changes in the data as it arrives. This can be risky, because the data in its original form will be lost, but when we're sure that we're going to want the changes, it is again a time-saver. And finally, we can perform special tasks with certain of the incoming data rather than recording it.

Input filtering is found in some form on most sequencers. To begin with, there are certain MIDI messages, such as the active sensing byte, that the sequencer absolutely does not need to worry about. These are screened out by automatic filtering that is not user-selectable.

At a higher level, the user will usually be offered a list of options as to which types of data to record. The MIDI data stream is often filled with various items, especially after-touch data, which is sent out in great profusion by any keyboard that has after-touch sensing. Since even the largest sequencers have a limited amount of memory, we would like to be able to avoid recording after-touch. Better still, we would like to be able to choose whether or not to record it.

A typical menu of input filter options includes after-touch, pitch-bend, modulation wheel, other controllers, and perhaps program change commands and system-exclusive messages. A more powerful sequencer will give separate switching for polyphonic after-touch and channel after-touch, and will let us choose individually to record or not record any of the 128 controller messages defined by the MIDI Spec. Recording of key release velocity can be switched on or off on some machines; not many MIDI instruments can use the data, even if our master keyboard sends it, and recording it uses up extra memory (up to twice the memory per note).

An under-designed sequencer, on the other hand, may offer only a single on/off switch for recording "controllers," including after-touch, pitch-bend, all 128 controllers, and program changes in this category. It also might strip out release velocity automatically.

Another input processing function goes by several different names, including *record-thru*, *thru on input*, and *MIDI echo*. The idea here is that we may have our MIDI hardware set up so that a master keyboard or other controller is plugged into the sequencer's input, while the 'slave' synthesizers or tone modules (which have no keyboards of their own) are plugged into the sequencer's output, as shown in Figure 14. This arrangement will work fine when the sequencer is playing back—but we won't be able to hear the tone modules at all while recording, unless the sequencer is passing the incoming data through to the output.

But what if the same sequencer is hooked to a single keyboard synthesizer? In this case, we want to switch off the in/thru function. If we don't, every time we play a note on the keyboard, the synthesizer will play two identical notes, one because it sees its own keyboard being played, and the other because it is receiving a MIDI message (from the sequencer) to play that note. This can give your synthesizer a thicker sound, but it does use up twice as many synthesizer voices, which is not usually helpful. And if the synthesizer happens to also be set up in a non-standard way so that it echoes its input at the MIDI out jack (rather than the thru jack), MIDI messages for a single note can fly back and forth in a feedback loop that will lock up both devices completely! So we would like our sequencer to let us switch the thru-on-input on or off.

A few sequencers allow you to perform various kinds of processing on the incoming data before sending it to the output—rechannelizing, for example, or transposing. This concept is the tip of an iceberg. As sequencers become more sophisticated multipurpose tools for music, we'll be seeing lots more real-time data processing options, including time delays, harmonization, and arpeggiation.

We can also make changes in the incoming data as it is being stored in memory. *Rechannelizing* on input can be especially useful when an older DX7 is our master keyboard, as it always transmits on channel 1. If the sequencer has only a limited number of tracks, it may be crucial that we store several channels of data on a single track, and rechannelizing is a quick way of being sure that notes that we want played

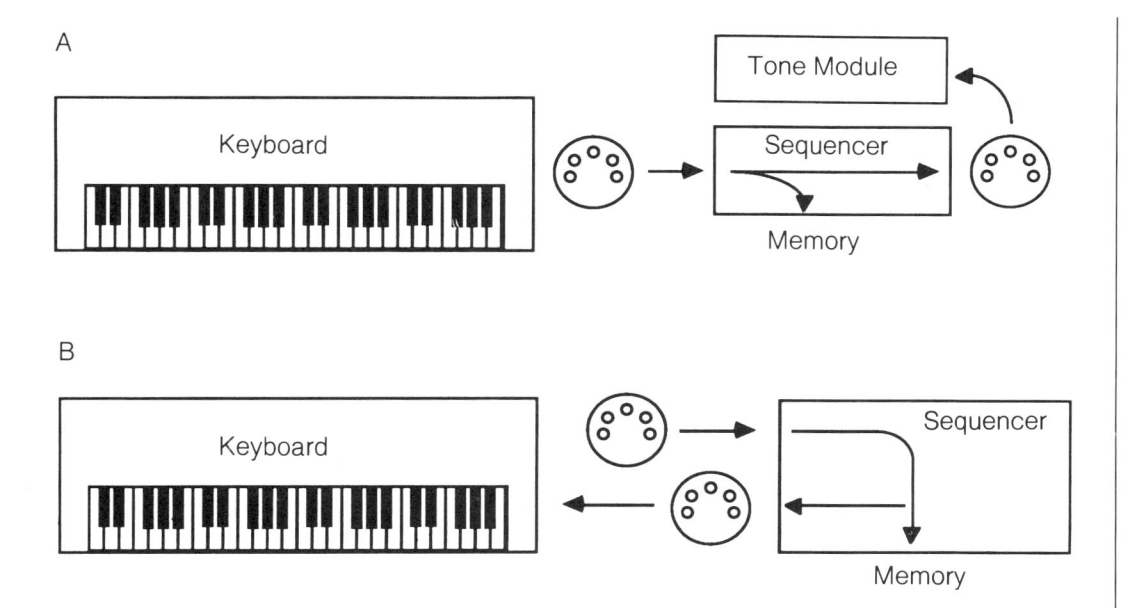

Figure 14. Sending the incoming MIDI signals through to the output using the in/thru (echo) feature is useful when the master controller, sequencer, and tone module are hooked together in series (a), as it allows us to hear the tone module during recording as well as during playback. But if a single keyboard is serving both as master controller and tone generator (b), in/thru will cause two of the keyboard's voices to sound each time we play a key (unless the keyboard has a local-off switch).

by separate modules don't end up being irretrievably jumbled together.

The other main type of input processing is *quantizing*. Quantizing on input is the norm with drum machines, but not with other MIDI sequencers; the reason is that most pop drum parts sound best when quantized, so there is no reason to record the small rhythmic irregularities that might make a keyboard or wind controller performance much more expressive. We'll discuss the various types of quantizing more fully in the section on editing.

Quantizing can also be done on playback. The idea here is that the sequencer records all of the rhythmic nuances of the input (subject to the limitations of its clock resolution) and allows the user to switch among various playback quantization settings (eighth-notes, sixteenth triplets, or whatever) without actually changing the data stored in memory. This is convenient if you want to try out different quantization settings, and don't want to be constantly making backup copies of a track in order to avoid destroying the original rhythmic inflections. But quantizing, like other data changes made during playback, takes up more processor time, and can cause poor rhythmic performance in dense passages. Also, this option will generally force you to quantize an entire track to a single rhythmic resolution, whereas the edit process may allow you to quantize smaller regions within a track to various resolutions. A few sequencers offer both edit quantizing and quantize on playback, but if they offer only one type, the first is preferable.

Other tricks can be performed on data as it is being played back. Many sequencers let you assign a channel number to each track, and rechannelize the track's data on output. Some will let you choose which MIDI output jack to send a track to, or even let you send a single track out on several channels simultaneously. Velocity scaling (adding or subtracting some increment to all of the velocity values) and pitch transposition of tracks are also quite common playback features. In a good computer-based (as opposed to dedicated-hardware) sequencer, the track sheet display will indicate what channel, transposition, and velocity scaling values have been given to each track. You may also be able to set a program number for each track, so that a patch change message will be sent out whenever the track starts playing from the top.

When playback is started in the middle of a song, we specifically don't want to hear the notes before the playback start-point. There may be other types of data,

Sequencer Features 33

however, which it would be nice to have the computer send out as it is fast-forwarding to the start-point. In particular, we would like it to search for and send out program changes, so that all of our instruments will be playing the right sounds. A few sequencers do this.

If we are using controller 7 (volume) to change our instrument output levels for a little automated mixing during the song, we would also like the sequencer to scan for controller 7 messages during the fast-forward. (Good luck finding a sequencer that does this.)

Scanning for other controllers would be pretty silly, unless we're using the sequencer specifically to control a MIDI mixing/fading module, in which case we need a sequencer like the JL Cooper MAGI/SAM system, which will scan all of its mix-controlling events in fast-forward.

The most important playback option is *track muting*. Track muting operates exactly like the muting of mixer channels or tape tracks. The data on a muted track is simply not played back when you hit the play button. Some sequencers may force you to mute or unmute tracks before starting playback, but a good sequencer will let you mute or unmute any track "on the fly," while playback is proceeding.

A sequencer that didn't mute tracks would be nearly useless for practical work. Quite often in the process of recording a tune, the musician accumulates several versions of a piece of material—a chord accompaniment pattern, for example—and isn't sure which version to use. By storing each version on its own track and then muting all but one of the alternate tracks, the player can listen to each of them in the context of the entire arrangement. A few sequencers make this process more convenient by offering *mute registers*. A mute register stores a programmable combination of muting and unmuting for all tracks, and any of the registers can be recalled with a single command.

Track soloing is, again, an idea borrowed from audio mixing. A solo switch allows you to mute all but one of the tracks with a single command.

Some sequencers offer a very large number of tracks. But it takes time for the processor to search through the tracks for the data that is to be sent out next. Because of this, some sequencers place an upper limit, such as 12 or 32, on the number of tracks that can play back simultaneously. The other tracks can be used for data manipulations, but not simultaneous playback. Other sequencers will let you play back as many tracks as you like, but they may begin to perform sluggishly as the number of active tracks rises.

One method of making the playback process more efficient, and thus more rhythmically precise, is to mute all but the tracks you are currently using. This might happen during a recording session, for example: If you're recording a sequenced bass part on a tape track by itself, you could mute all the sequencer tracks except the bass, and get a tighter rhythm. There are probably some sequencers out there, however, with which this trick won't help. It won't help if the sequencer is programmed to look up the data on a track first and *then* check to see whether the track is muted or not.

A final question is what happens when playback stops. If we happen to hit the stop button while some notes are sounding, we would like the sequencer to send note-offs for them. This is obvious enough that most sequencer programmers have taken care of it. Problems can arise, however. If we change the transpose value on a track in the middle of a note and then mute the track, for example, the wrong note-off might be sent, leaving the note ringing on forever. Problems of this sort are commoner than you might think. What if you've got a sustain-pedal-on message in a track, and stop playback before the corresponding sustain-pedal-off message? You guessed it—stuck notes.

Some sequencers include a *panic button* as a feature. This command sends an all-notes-off message. Sad to say, some very widely used MIDI instruments (the DX7, for example) don't recognize all-notes-off messages. Some sequencers deal with this problem by incorporating a panic button that sends a separate note-off for every MIDI note on all 16 channels. This takes several seconds, but it is guaranteed to shut off all of your stuck notes—except for the ones being held by the imaginary sustain pedal. To clear those, you'll probably have to switch your master keyboard to the correct channel and then stomp on the real sustain pedal and release it.

The Many Faces Of Editing

If all a sequencer did was record incoming MIDI data and play the data back on demand, it would be moderately useful. What lifts sequencers into a whole new realm is their ability to make changes in data once it is in their memory. These changes are called, collectively, *editing*.

There are no inherent limitations on the editing process, other than those imposed by the nature of MIDI data itself, the size of the computer being used as a sequencer, and the amount of time the programmer has to develop the editing software. Editing can do absolutely anything we can imagine that it might do. Existing sequencer software falls short of this ideal, but that's not surprising considering how new the field is.

Certain basic editing tasks are implemented in some form on virtually every sequencer. Beyond these is a vast gray area where sequencers differ widely from one another, and where the terminology becomes a bit hazy. At the high end are some specific, complex data manipulations that can make life far easier in a few rare musical situations, but that most of us wouldn't miss if our sequencers weren't equipped with them—a good thing, because most sequencers aren't.

Basic Editing Tasks. Looking at the characteristics of a MIDI note, we can see immediately what an editing operation might be able to do to it. The note has a pitch (MIDI note number), velocity, channel, start time (in relation to the beginning of the track), and duration (the number of clock ticks between the note-on and note-off). All of these, as they appear in the computer's memory, are simply numbers, and numbers can be added to or subtracted from.

In this section we're going to make an assumption made on virtually all sequencers: The assumption is that edit operations will be applied to all of the notes on a given track in the region between two *markers* called the edit start-point and the edit end-point.

These markers are usually definable by the user, but they may not be called markers. Often the punch-in and punch-out points do double duty as edit markers. In a sequencer with poorly designed regional editing software, edit markers may have to be at bar lines—and the machine may insist that the piece of music has bars of the same length throughout, whatever our musical intentions. A better approach lets us specify our markers at any clock tick within any bar.

At this point, we're going to assume that the region to which the edit operation will be applied will be contiguous and linear: No notes will be skipped over in the middle of it. Later on, we'll take a look at some more interesting ways of defining regions for editing.

To perform an edit, we must first define the region where we want the edit to be done: We select a track, and also set the start-point and end-point markers if we don't want to edit the entire track. Then we select an operation (such as transposition) and a value that we want used in the operation (such as +12, if we want the notes in the region to be transposed up an octave). And finally we command the computer to carry out the edit.

Maybe the most fundamental edit operation of all is *copying*. In copying, the group of notes within the region is duplicated in some other region (such as on a previously empty track). For the sake of the novices out there, maybe we should explain that copying is different from *moving*. When you move material from one place to another, it is no longer in the place where it started. In copying, you end up with two identical blocks of data, one in the original location and one in the new location you have specified.

Nearly as fundamental as copying is *erasing*. Erasing is used to clear out areas of memory that contain notes we don't need any longer, so as to allow us to put new material into those areas (or simply to tidy up the loose ends in our data). Two types of erasing have to be distinguished. Assuming that we're erasing material from the beginning or middle of a long track, what will happen to the timing of the events further along in the track? Either they can stay where they are in relation to the other tracks, in which case our erase operation will have opened up a hole in the selected track—or they can be shifted backward in time, so that the hole is closed up (see Figure 15). An ideal sequencer would offer both types of erase operations. Some sequencers only perform one of the two directly, but allow you to get the other musical result by time-shifting the material following the erasure forward or backward in a separate operation.

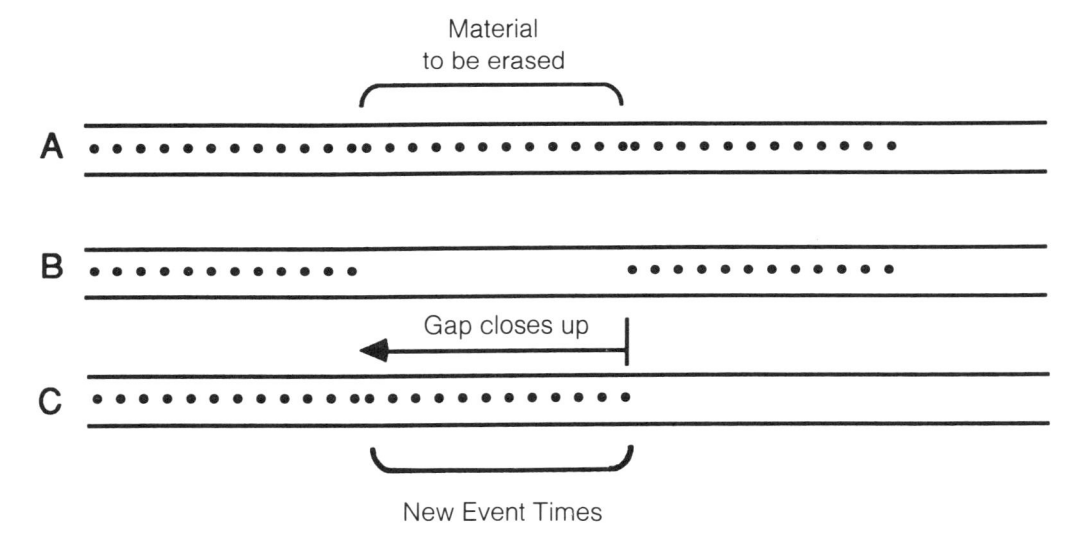

Figure 15. Two types of erase operations. (a) The original track, containing material that is to be erased. (b) An erase operation that preserves the original timing of events following the erased passage. (c) An erase operation that deletes the empty bars and beats from the track. The gap is closed up, and the event times of all events after the erased passage are now earlier than they were before.

Programs that use standard Macintosh edit commands have slightly different terminology: A *cut* operation removes the data from a region while making a copy of it in a special buffer called the *clipboard*. The contents of the clipboard can then be *pasted* into a new spot. If we want to put the contents of the region into the clipboard without erasing it from its original location, we use the *copy* command, followed (as with cutting) by a paste command. To delete the contents of a region without copying it into the clipboard, the *clear* command is used.

In copying, the region into which we place duplicates of the original notes starts out empty. In fact, the computer may be programmed not to let us perform the copy operation unless the destination region is empty. In merging, however, the contents of two regions are combined into a single region—not end to end but interleaved with one another like the fingers of two hands or the gears of a clock. (Obviously, the strict one-to-one alternation of elements from the two sources that this image might suggest would not generally be musically useful; their final ordering must leave their timing intact.) Depending on how the sequencer is designed, the merge operation might erase the two regions that we started with, or it might leave them intact.

Another important edit operation is called *time shifting*. When an entire track is being shifted, it's called *track shifting*. In time shifting, the notes within the region maintain their original rhythmic relationship to one another, but the group starts earlier or later in relation to the rest of the piece. Most sequencers won't let you shift a track or region back to a point before the beginning of the piece; you have to shift all the other tracks forward.

Time shifting can be used in conjunction with copying to rearrange the various sections of a piece into a new order. Shifting an entire track backward or forward by one or two clock ticks can also be extremely helpful—so helpful that some sequencers include a "track shift menu" that lets a shift amount be set individually for each track. When two MIDI tone modules are being played by separate tracks and one of them responds to incoming messages noticeably faster than the other, we may be able to get the sounds to lock up tighter rhythmically by shifting one of the tracks. Since such timing differences can be quite subtle, this sort of track shifting works best on sequencers that have a fairly high clock resolution (96 ppq or more).

Changing the pitch of a group of notes is called *transposition*. Transposition causes all of the notes in the region to be moved up or down by the same number of half-steps. Musicians have been transposing for hundreds of years, but in case you're still hazy on the concept, it's illustrated in Figure 16.

A problem can arise if the transposition operation takes some of the notes beyond the permissible range for MIDI notes—in other words, if the MIDI note number goes below 0 or above 127. Some sequencers will automatically transpose the offending notes back up or down by an octave so that they keep the correct harmonic relationship to the rest of the region while falling back into the permissible range. We've also run into a sequencer or two that couldn't deal with the out-of-range problem, and crashed when the user made this "impossible" request. The same kind of crash can occur with other edit operations, if the software is written poorly.

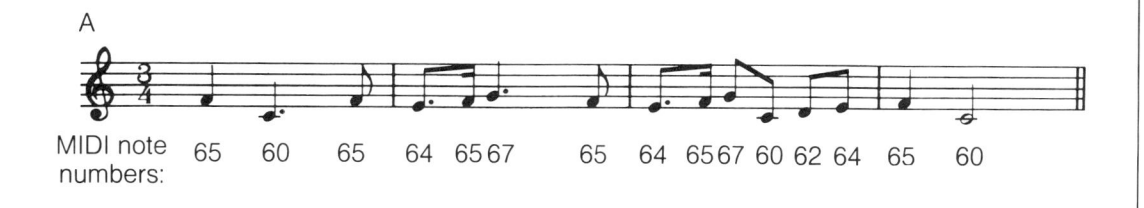

Figure 16. When a portion of a track is transposed, all of the MIDI note numbers are increased or decreased by the same amount, causing the pitch of the notes to move up or down by some number of half-steps. Here, bars 2-4 have been transposed up by two half-steps.

Rechannelizing is a simple process: We change the channel designation of the group of notes, so that when it is played back, a different tone generator (one that is switched to the new channel) will make the sounds.

There are several ways of editing the note velocities within a region. The simplest is *velocity shifting* (also called *velocity transposing* and *velocity scaling*). In this procedure, all of the velocities are adjusted up or down by the same amount. The concept is illustrated in Figure 17. Usually, velocities that would go beyond the lower or upper limit (1-127) during a velocity shift operation are assigned this limit value. If the lower limit for the operation is 0, the receiving tone module will interpret the note-on as a note-off, and not play it.

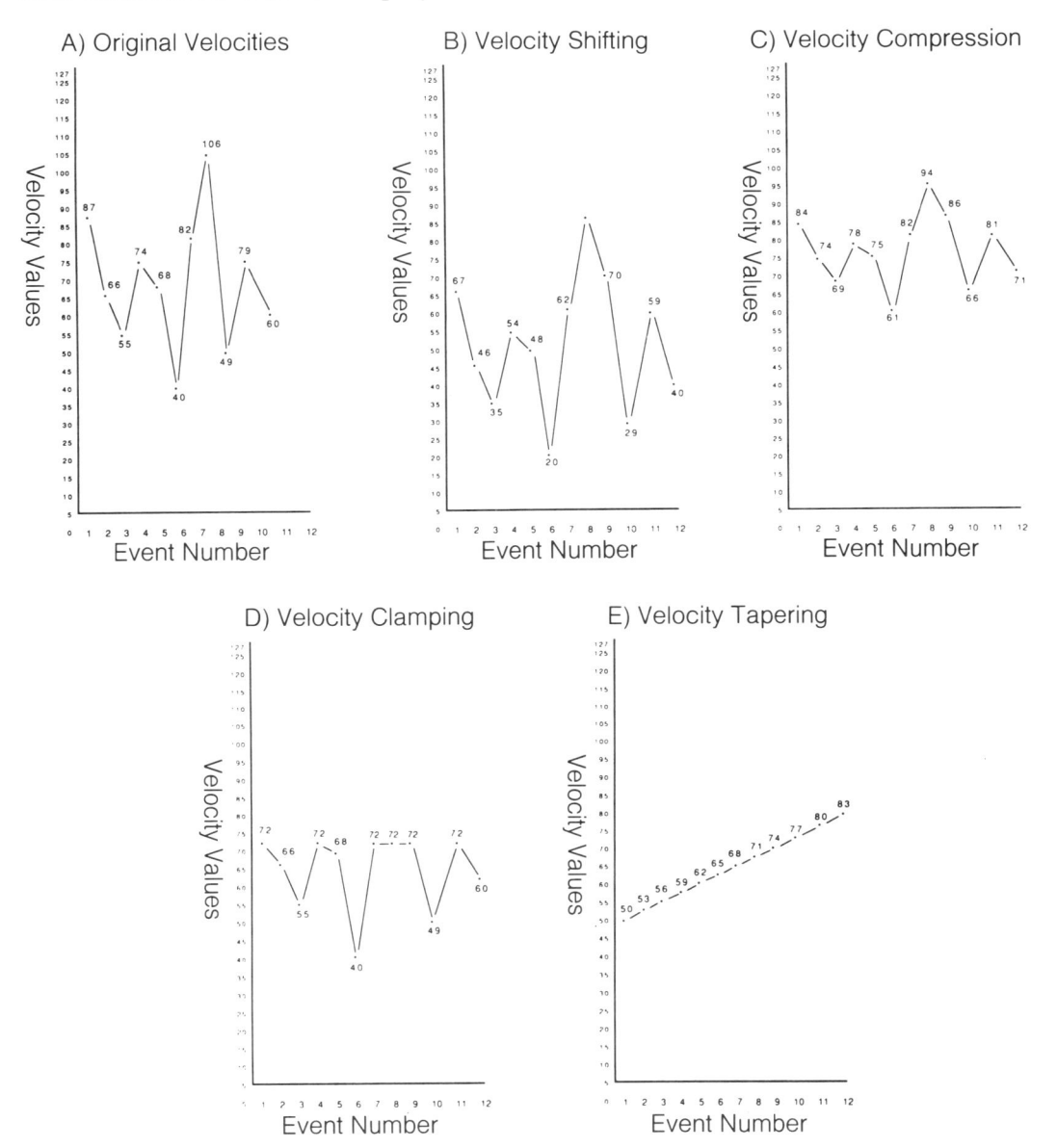

Figure 17. Five common velocity edit operations. (a) The original velocities of 12 notes. (b) A linear velocity shift of -20. (c) Velocity compression around a center value of 80 with a compression factor of 0.5. (d) Velocity clamping of all values over 72. (e) Velocity tapering with a starting value of 50 and an ending value of 83.

A *set velocity* operation strips off the recorded velocities of all the notes in the region and replaces them with a single new value. *Velocity tapering* (which is also called *velocity scaling*, unfortunately) replaces all of the velocities in the region, but not with a single value. Instead, values are assigned in an ascending or descending pattern. Velocity tapering is very useful for controlled crescendos and diminuendos (assuming that your synthesizer is using velocity to control loudness).

Moving into the realm of the mildly esoteric, we reach *velocity clamping*. In velocity clamping, no change is made in the velocity of a note unless it falls above (or below) a specified limit. Normal clamping, which is roughly analogous to the action of an audio limiter, lowers the velocity by some user-specified amount if it falls above the limit. Negative clamping would raise the velocity if it falls below the limit.

Velocity inversion flips the velocity values around a specified center-point, with higher velocities becoming lower and vice-versa.

Velocity compression maintains the existing contour relationship among the velocities, but brings them closer together or pushes them further apart. Compression requires that two items be specified—a center-point that all the velocities will move toward or away from, and an amount by which the difference between their current value and the center-point will be multiplied. (With some software, the center-point might be fixed at 64.) Compression is a very useful form of editing, because it maintains the expressive contours of a performed line while bringing it into a velocity range where it sounds best when playing the chosen synthesizer patch. Unfortunately, not many sequencers offer compression.

Sometimes the musician has to perform two or three separate operations like those just described in order to get the desired musical result. For example, you might perform velocity clamping so as to reduce the spikiness of the accents in your phrase, and then scale all of the velocities up or down by some fixed amount to get the desired overall brightness. Also, the set velocity operation might not appear on a menu, but might be available as a form of tapering (with identical start and end values for the slope) or compression.

Quantization. All sequencers offer some type of *quantization* (also called *auto-correct*). Quantizing is a way of getting notes that were played with irregular rhythm to fall precisely on the beat. All drum machines and some sequencers quantize on input, as mentioned earlier, which means that the material stored in memory will always be quantized. In this case, there may be no separate "re-quantize" edit operation. Some sequencers, again, let you choose between quantizing on playback, which leaves the material in the track unaffected, and quantizing as an edit, which changes the material in the track.

In quantizing, the user selects a rhythm value, and tells the computer to adjust the starting times of all the notes so that they fall on multiples of this value (that is, on the points of a grid whose nodes are separated by this value) with relation to the start of the bar, the start of the region, or the start of the piece. Since we're trying to be rigorous here, this definition sounds more complicated than the process of quantization actually is in practice. In practice, you simply select, for example, an eighth-note as the rhythm value, and the computer aligns all of the notes in the region so that they start at the same time as one of the notes in an imaginary pattern of perfectly regular eighth-notes that runs from the beginning of the piece to the end. Notes that were played close together may be quantized so that they are now precisely together, forming a chord.

Since most of the music that musicians are concerned with these days uses mainly duplet and triplet rhythms, a standard menu of quantization options may offer only duplets and triplets—quarter-note, eighth-note, sixteenth-note, and thirty-second-note, along with their triplet cousins. Assuming that our sequencer is running at 24 ppq, it's easy to see that we're really choosing quantization values that have some whole-number relationship to 24: A quarter-note is 24 clocks, an eighth-note triplet is 6 clocks, and so on. Figure 18 shows the relationships.

But what if we want to quantize to some number of clocks other than a factor of

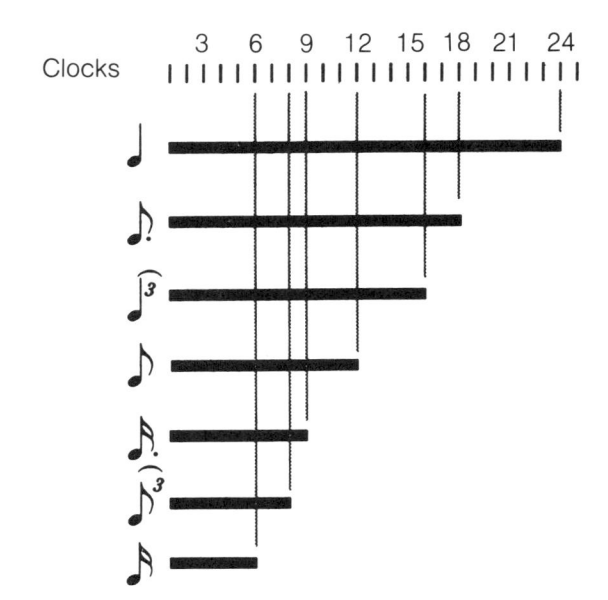

Figure 18. All note durations in a sequencer must be expressed in whole-numbers of clocks. Here are the durations of some common rhythm values at a clock rate of 24 ppq.

24? Some sequencers allow the user to enter any whole number as the quantization value. This is not the kind of thing you'd be likely to do every day, but it's nice to be offered the choice. Instead of quantizing to a whole number of clocks, the sequencer might let you specify a metrical value (such as 7 in the time of four eighth-notes) and attempt to align the note groups as closely as they can to this value, given the limits of the clock resolution. In the example just given, four eighth-notes at 24 ppq occupy 48 clocks, so the sequencer might divide 48 by 7 and produce a quantization grid with notes separated by 7, 7, 7, 6, 7, 7, and 7 clocks. Some sequencers, notably the Yamaha QX1, even let you specify nested quantizations—five equally spaced notes in the time of three of the septuplets just described. If you want to write like Frank Zappa, this feature is for you.

So far, we have been describing quantization as if it affected only note-on events. The most common type of quantization today is called *note-coherent* quantization, because the note stays the same length when the note-on is moved. Either the duration value stays the same, or the note-off (if this is stored separately) is moved the same amount as the note-on.

Other types of quantization are possible, however. In a few early sequencers, notably the Korg SQD-1, note-offs were treated as isolated events just like note-ons. When you quantized a track, all the note-offs would be moved so that they fell on the nearest "corrected" rhythm value. In other words, if you played a line of staccato eighth-notes and then quantized the line with an eighth-note resolution, all of your notes would either be legato (if the note-off got quantized so that it fell on the following eighth-note) or nonexistent (if the note-off got quantized backward so that it fell at the same point as the note-on). The violence that this did to the musical phrase was unacceptable, and nobody that we know of is offering this type of quantization any more.

With a smarter sequencer, we may be able to shift note-ons without shifting note-offs. This may change the length of the note slightly, but it can be useful musically in some situations. At least one sequencer (48 Track PC II for the IBM PC) features what might be called an "approximate" or "humanized" quantization, in which each note is shifted *halfway* from its starting position to the theoretically perfect alignment of the quantization grid. The commoner possibilities for quantization are shown in Figure 19.

Figure 19. Four possible types of quantization. (The sequencer's clock rate is 24 ppq.) (a) Six notes as originally recorded. (b) Quantized to sixteenths in a note-coherent manner—that is, note durations are unchanged. (c) Quantized to sixteenths with note-offs also quantized to sixteenths. (d) Note-ons quantized to sixteenths, note-offs not affected. Durations are changed. (e) Duration quantized to sixteenths, note-ons not affected.

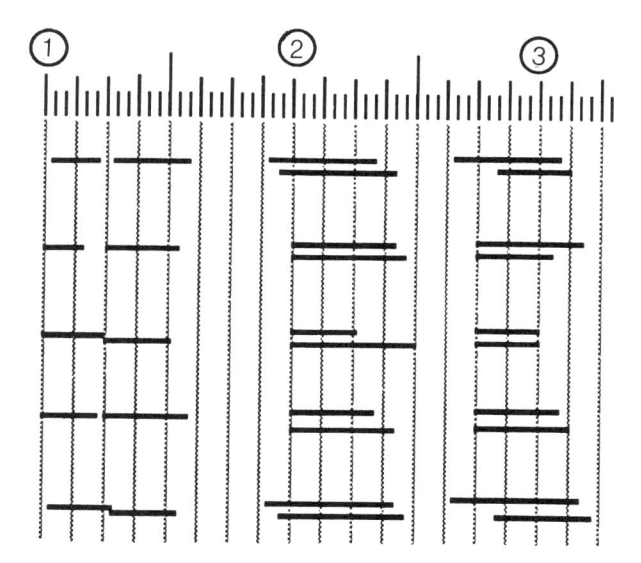

Finally, we can treat note duration as a separately editable parameter. Some sequencers allow all the durations in a region to be scaled up or down (that is, lengthened or shortened) in a fixed relationship to one another. A few allow duration to be quantized independently of note start time.

More About Editing. Editing can be fast and painless, or it can be a real chore, depending to a great extent on whether the programmer has given some thought to various convenience features. Here are a few:

We shouldn't have to start playback from the top of the song every time we make an edit somewhere in the middle. Most sequencers offer some form of regional playback or play-from-cue command.

Entering new values into data fields always takes keystrokes. For complex edits, it can take lots of keystrokes. So we would like these data fields to *default* to the most likely values. This way, we only need to type in new values if we need to change the defaults. For example, it wouldn't be surprising to see a sequencer whose quantization menu defaulted to sixteenth-note quantization, since this is probably the most often used value. In a good sequencer, data fields should always default to the last values we entered: It's fairly annoying to be writing a piece that uses triplets extensively, and to have to switch the quantization value from duplets to triplets every single time we want to quantize something, because the machine always defaults back to duplets when the edit operation is complete. A few highly developed sequencers even allow the user to define a default environment and save it to disk, so that it can be loaded at the beginning of every session.

An *undo* command is found on many sequencers. This command lets the user undo the last-performed edit operation if the results don't sound right. To be able to undo an edit, the sequencer has to copy the unedited region into an invisible area of memory called the undo buffer. The material usually stays in this buffer until the next edit is performed—or, if the undo buffer uses the same memory space as the record buffer, until the user records some new input.

Many sequencers use *alert boxes* to ask the user to confirm the operation before an edit takes place. This is especially useful if the sequencer doesn't have an undo command. Alert boxes do slow down the editing session, however. Some sequencers let the experienced user switch off the alerts, which speeds things up but does make mistakes a bit more likely.

When a region is being copied into an empty track, the user may be offered an opportunity to make multiple copies with a single command; the copies will be *appended*, each new copy starting at the end of the previous one. This is a quick, easy way of duplicating a two-bar drum pattern for 16 bars, for example. Someday we'll probably see a sequencer that will allow the time between copies to be specified, so as to allow for overlapping, and also perhaps a transposition factor by which each new copy is to be moved up or down. Someday.

Let's take a look at some other editing operations that are found on some sequencers:

Key-signature-coherent transposition may be offered on a program that "knows" what key your song is in. The transposition value will probably be specified in scale steps rather than half-steps, and the program will assign MIDI note numbers to the notes in such a way as not to produce any out-of-key notes. Whether it will "fix" accidentals in the source material or let them remain as chromatic notes in the transposed version depends on how the operating code is written.

Several operations can be applied to the timing of events in a region, including *stretching/compression* and *time reversal*. In stretching and compression, all of the relative time values are multiplied by some number, such as .5 to speed a track up to double-time or 2 to slow it down to half-time. You may be offered an option to multiply durations by the same value during the stretching/compression operation, so as to preserve the legato phrasing, or to leave them as they are.

Time reversal can be done in several ways. We can simply assign the pitch, velocity, and duration values of notes at the end of the track to the timing of notes at the head of the track, in reverse order. This will sometimes change a monophonic phrase into a polyphonic one because note overlapping will appear. Other types of time reversal result in different kinds of phrasing. For example, we might want to reverse the order of the pitches without reversing the velocities or durations.

Most drum machines and a few sequencers provide for *swing*, a rhythmic placement in which offbeats lag behind their expected placement by some factor. In our 24 ppq sequencer, quantizing to eighth-notes with swing might create a line with rhythm values of 13-11-13-11, 14-10-14-10, or 15-9-15-9, depending on the *swing factor* and on how the software operates. We could imagine a software routine that would quantize notes so as to align them with any user-specified grid, including such possibilities as different amounts of swing on different beats of the bar.

Event Editing. All of the operations we have just been describing are applied to groups of notes. But what if we've got a track that's perfect except for two or three scattered wrong notes here and there? Do we have to define each of these notes as a region by putting the start and end markers just before and just after it? On some sequencers this is the only way to fix individual notes. Even this method may not work if the note is in the middle of a chord: We might have no choice but to transpose or delete the whole chord as a unit.

Fortunately, many sequencers offer *event editing* environments. In event editing, the user is presented with a list that shows all the data in a track. A typical event edit screen is shown in Figure 20. Each event appears as a row of numbers (or note names or whatever); each of the vertical columns contains data of a different type. Each intersection of a row and column is called a *data field*. Dedicated-hardware sequencers sometimes have event editing as well, but because of the limited size of their visual displays they will typically show the data for only one event at a time.

Any of the data in the list can be changed by selecting the data field to be changed—moving a cursor to it, for example—and then typing in a new value or using an increment/decrement controller to change the existing value. For example, if one of the notes in our melody sustains a bit too long, we could change the duration from 47 to 45 without affecting any of the surrounding notes.

Event editing is inherently a somewhat cumbersome process. (How many musicians do you know who enjoy typing columns of numbers?) So it's important to consider how user-friendly the event editing environment of a given sequencer is. Here are some things to think about: Can you play back the track you're editing from within the event editing screen, or do you have to exit back to the main portion of the sequencer to hear your edits? Can you play only the portion of the track near the edits, or do you have to play the track from the start? Can you play a cue consisting of a portion of this track along with others? Can you switch back and forth between a multitrack cue and a solo playback of the individual track?

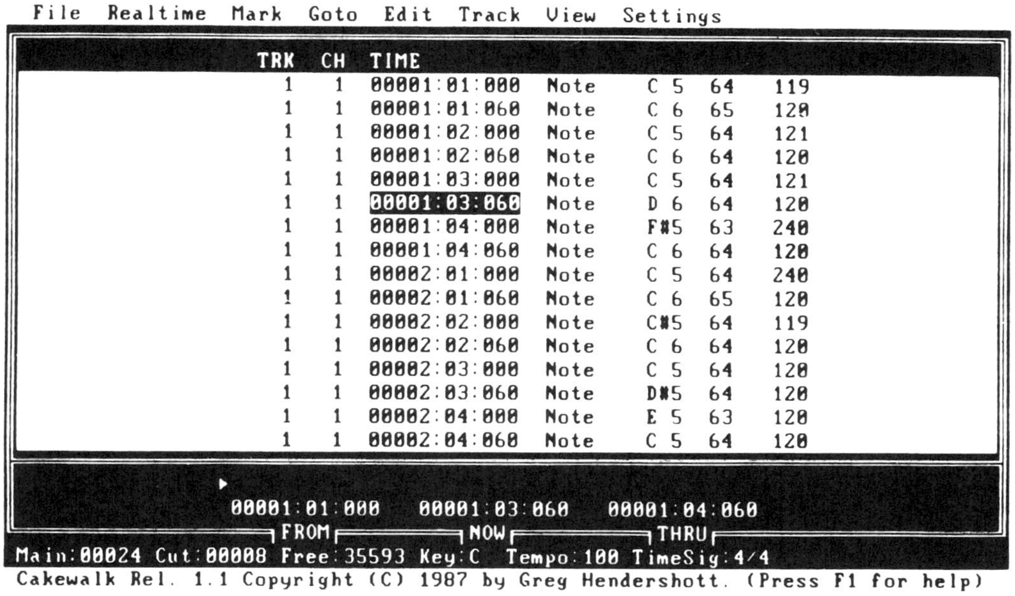

Figure 20. An event edit screen from Cakewalk, a sequencer program from Twelve Tone Systems for the IBM PC. The columns display (left to right) track, channel, event time in bar/beat/clock format, event type, and up to three data fields associated with the event type. For note events, the data fields are pitch (with octave number), velocity, and duration in clocks.

Does the sequencer automatically play a single note for you when you select one of its data fields, so that you can get audible verification that you're editing the right note? Does the event editing environment offer regional cut-and-paste operations? Does it let you scroll freely backward and forward through the data? Can you change the order of events, or do you have to delete a later event and then reinsert it manually earlier in the list? Can you change the selected data field by playing a MIDI keyboard, or do you have to type?

Defining Regions. The real fun in editing starts when you discover that there's no reason why you should have to apply the editing operation to *all* of the notes in a contiguous linear region of a track. This is software, after all, not audio tape. We can define our regions however we like.

Sometimes a sequencer won't let non-linear regions be selected directly for operations like transposition or velocity scaling, but will allow you to copy a non-linear region to a new track and erase it from the old track—after which you can perform the desired operation on the new track as a whole and then merge the new track back into the old one.

To start with, we can *split* a track just the way we split a splittable synthesizer keyboard. We can perform our edit on all of the notes above the split-point but not on those below it, or vice-versa. There's no reason in theory why the events on a track can't be split into two groups by velocity or duration value instead. Splitting events by channel assignment is called *unmerging*, because it is most often used after several tracks containing data on different channels have been merged onto a single track. If the sequencer offers unmerging, we can extract one instrument's data at any time and copy it onto an empty track for further processing.

Splitting is a simple *logical test*. For each event, the software asks the question, "Is this event's pitch higher than X?" If the answer is yes, the event will be edited; if the answer is no, it won't be. Computers are good at logic, of course, and programmers can devise logical tests they think musicians will find useful. Cakewalk, a sequencer program for the IBM PC, has a full screen of logical test criteria (see Figure 21) that can be invoked for edit operations. For example, we could select only the C's with a velocity greater than 80 and a duration less than 48.

Instead of specifying the absolute characteristics of a note, we might want to test logically for some aspect of its relation to the surrounding notes. For example, we might want to select notes that fall on the second beat of any bar, or notes that are more than an octave below the preceding note, or that fall on the same clock tick as some other note (that is, notes that are part of a chord). At this point we're talking about features that are not found too often on current software. If you think of something that could be useful in your music, you'll have to call manufacturers and bug them to find out whether their product has what you're looking for.

Once we have selected some notes with our logical tests, we might want to do something more imaginative to them than simply increase or reduce their values, or replace the values with constants. Why not allow the values to be replaced with similarly selected values from another track? This idea is implemented, along with some imaginative forms of logical testing, in Dr. T's Programmable Variations Generator, which is discussed more fully on page 80.

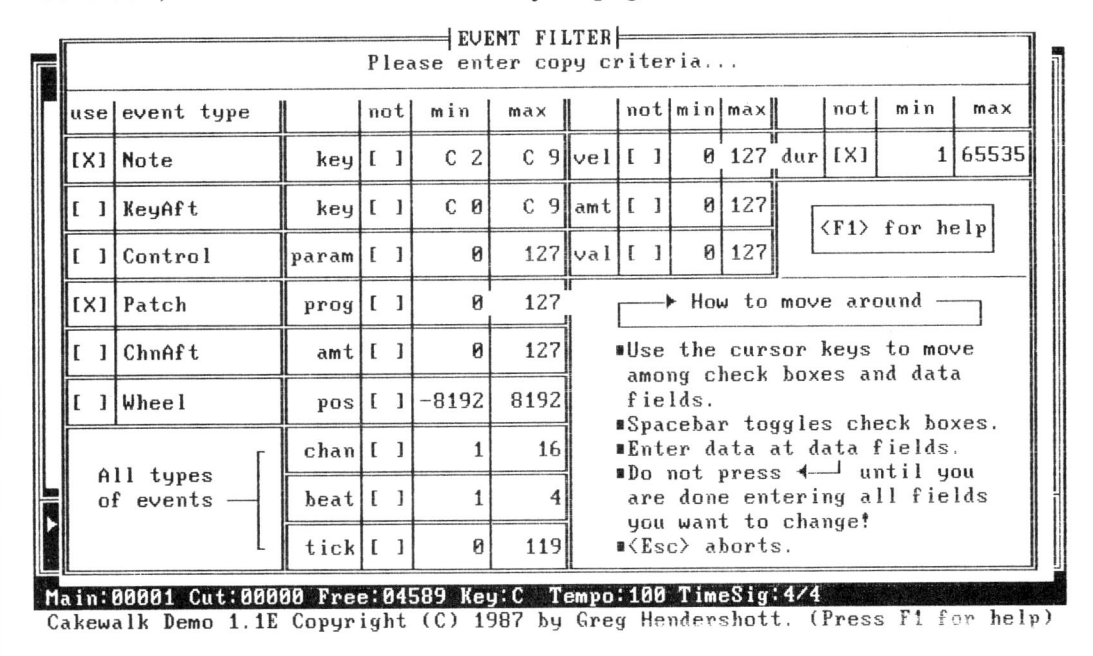

Figure 21. The event filter screen for Cakewalk (from Twelve Tone Systems, for the IBM PC). By entering an "X" between any pair of brackets, the user can select that type of logical test. For example, to edit only events on channels 3 and 4, you would enter an "X" next to "chan" and then enter a 3 under "min" and a 4 under "max."

Graphic Editing Environments

Computer screens are perfect for displaying information in various forms—pie charts, bar graphs, 3-D contour maps, you name it. So far there are two main ways of displaying sequence data graphically, both of which have antecedents in earlier musical traditions. These are notation displays (also called score or staff displays) and piano roll displays.

In a score display, MIDI notes are represented as conventional music notation on a five-line staff. The display will use most or all of the conventions of music notation, such as time signatures, rhythm values, and accidentals. New notes can be added to the score by selecting a rhythm value and then pointing and clicking—that is, guiding the on-screen graphics cursor to the point where you want the note to appear and clicking the button on the computer's mouse, or using equivalent commands on the computer's QWERTY keyboard. In systems that use a mouse, existing notes can be moved to new locations by clicking and dragging, and can be deleted by selecting an eraser icon, or by dragging the note into a trash can icon.

Most score displays are designed to interface with music printing software. A good program will let you select the number of staves to be bracketed together, the number of bars per line, and other printing parameters that have no effect on the MIDI data. You will be able to place standard musical symbols, such as accents, slurs, and even chord symbols and lyrics, on the score. Deluxe Music Construction Set (see Figure 11) is probably the best known of the score-oriented programs, since it is marketed to appeal to music hobbyists more than MIDI users. Its graphics capabilities are superlative, but its MIDI implementation is among the most primitive we've ever seen.

Editing a score is easier for many musicians to grasp than editing a column of data, because they are more familiar with the symbols. Unfortunately, score editing is not precise enough to deal with the complexities of MIDI sequencer data. For one thing, conventional scoring does not provide any way of indicating the lengths of notes accurately. If an eighth-note is 12 clocks long and a dotted eighth is 18 clocks, how do we notate a note that is 13 clocks long, or 17? By tying together a string of thirty-second-note triplets? If we try to do it this way, our score will quickly cease to be readable; it will become a tangled jumble of tied notes. And what if our clock resolution is not 24 ppq but 240?

Just as vexing is the impossibility of displaying velocity values. We can use conventional dynamic markings—*ff*, *f*, *mf*, *mp*, and so on—but these don't provide anything like the 127 different levels required. Besides, loudness is not the same as velocity. Maybe we ought to use dynamic markings to indicate changes in MIDI controller 7 (loudness). If so, we have no way to indicate velocity at all. Nor is there any way to show program changes, pitch-bends, controller changes, or other data that might be part of a track.

In sum, score editing can be useful for correcting wrong notes, but its main appeal will be to those who are looking for either score printing or educational software, not to those who need sophisticated editing of MIDI data.

The piano roll display (see Figure 22) suffers from some of the same problems, but it offers some significant advantages as well. In this system, notes are displayed as horizontal black bars, exactly like the long holes punched in player piano rolls. The difference is that the "roll" runs from left to right instead of up and down.

The piano roll display is a two-dimensional music graph, with pitch (MIDI note number) on the vertical axis and time on the horizontal axis. The event time (as in a notated score) gets later as you look from left to right. If the display scrolls like a piano roll during playback, there may be a line down the center of the screen that corresponds to "now," and events may begin as their left edge scrolls across the line.

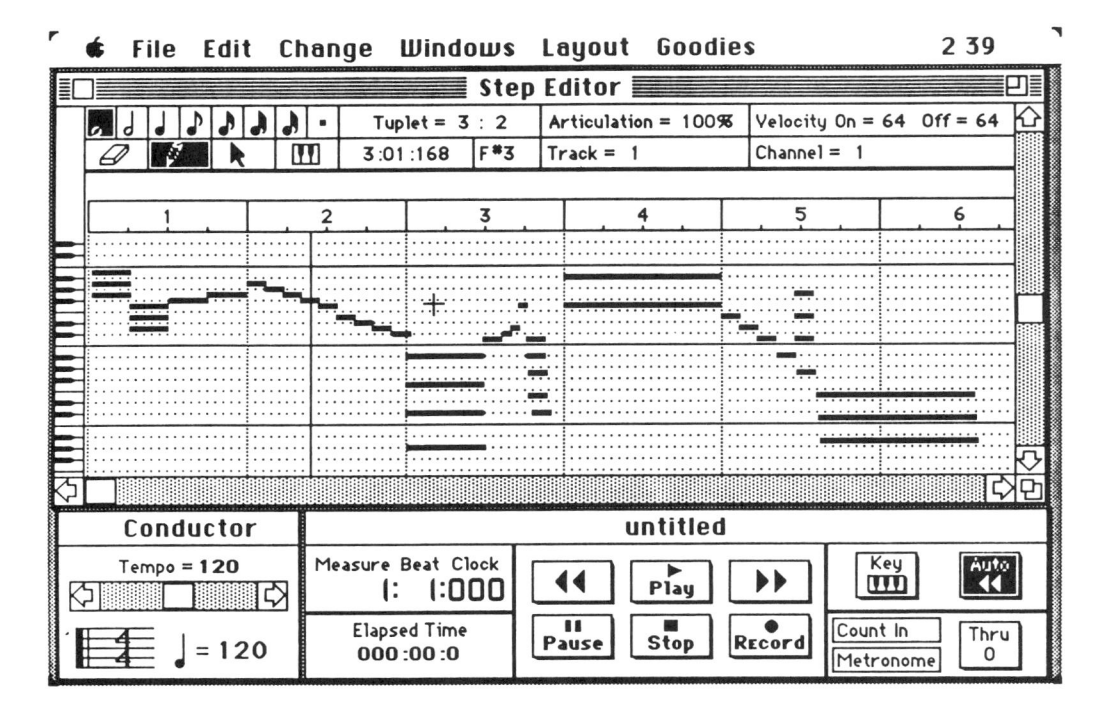

Figure 22. The bar-graph note display from Passport's Master Tracks Pro software for the Macintosh. The duration of each note corresponds to the length of the bar, while the pitch corresponds to the vertical position relative to the keyboard at left.

The advantage of a piano roll display is that it allows the exact lengths of notes to be displayed—subject to the graphic resolution of the screen. Also, notes can be displayed that don't start in conventional (quantized) rhythmic positions.

The piano roll display does not show note velocity values, nor does it show non-note data. Various ways have been devised to get around this problem. Some programs have a velocity window, for example, that displays the velocity for the currently selected note and lets you edit this value.

Piano roll displays are ideal for cutting and pasting groups of notes graphically. Because the graphic display is two-dimensional, the software can easily be designed so that the region is limited vertically (in pitch) as well as horizontally (in time). Thus you can isolate an element such as a bass line by dragging the mouse cursor across it, without including other notes that may be occurring at the same time but higher or lower in the pitch range.

Editing Non-Note Data. Since most MIDI sequences consist mostly of notes, it's not surprising that most sequencer programmers spend most of their time developing routines for dealing with notes. Currently, other types of data are still getting short shrift when it comes to editing tools.

The requirements for editing non-note data are somewhat different. Quantizing pitch-wheel messages wouldn't make much sense, for example, because a lot of these messages usually occur close together, and it's important that the pitch-bend sound smooth. Quantizing would pile up dozens of messages on each eighth-note or sixteenth-note, resulting in a jerky-sounding bend. Ideally, a sequencer should allow us to quantize the notes in a track without quantizing non-note data.

Other types of editing changes, however, should be allowed for either notes or non-note data. It's quite annoying, for example, to have a sequencer refuse to rechannelize controllers because it is programmed to edit only the notes.

If a sequencer does nothing else, it should allow us to strip non-note data out of a region. In other words, we should be able to erase a program change, a sustain-pedal-off message, or a whole bunch of mod wheel movements that aren't in quite the right place without affecting the notes themselves. Then we can record some new non-note data on an empty track and merge it with the previous recording.

Event editing environments can be quite handy for editing non-note data. Inserting and changing the values of program changes one at a time, for example, is by far the easiest way to deal with them. It would be hard to imagine wanting to make a global "transposition" of a bunch of program changes. With controllers, pitch-bend, and after-touch, on the other hand, dozens or hundreds of events are usually recorded at once, and having some global way of working with them is far preferable to entering new values by typing.

One procedure peculiar to controllers is *thinning*. It sometimes happens that playing back hundreds of controller events in a short time interferes with the rhythm of other parts, or that those events are using up memory that we would rather use for notes. But the synthesizer itself may not be changing its sound audibly in response to the extremely minute difference between one controller byte and the next higher one. A thinning procedure "combs" the event list, removing every second, third, or fourth controller event.

Compression and expansion, both vertically and horizontally, are also highly useful procedures for controllers. A pitch-bend that is timed right but goes a little past the mark can be compressed so that its highest values just reach the right pitch. A pitch-bend that reaches the right pitch but gets there a bit early or a bit late can be stretched out or shortened. Not many sequencers offer these options yet, but they're important enough that they're sure to become more common.

Another basic idea for controllers is *translation*. Maybe we'd like to do some expressive playing on a DX7 by sending it some breath controller data, but we don't have a breath controller handy. We ought to be able to record the data into the sequencer from a modulation wheel (controller 1) and then edit the data so that it can be sent out as breath controller bytes (controller 2). A few sequencers offer controller translation in some limited form.

The Master Tracks Pro software for the Macintosh from Passport Designs provides graphic input and editing for controllers (see Figure 23). This feature lets the user draw the controller contour on the screen with a mouse, which is undoubtedly the most intuitively meaningful way to deal with such data. We could imagine a system that would display several such contours simultaneously, so as to let you see the differences among them—but nobody is offering this feature yet.

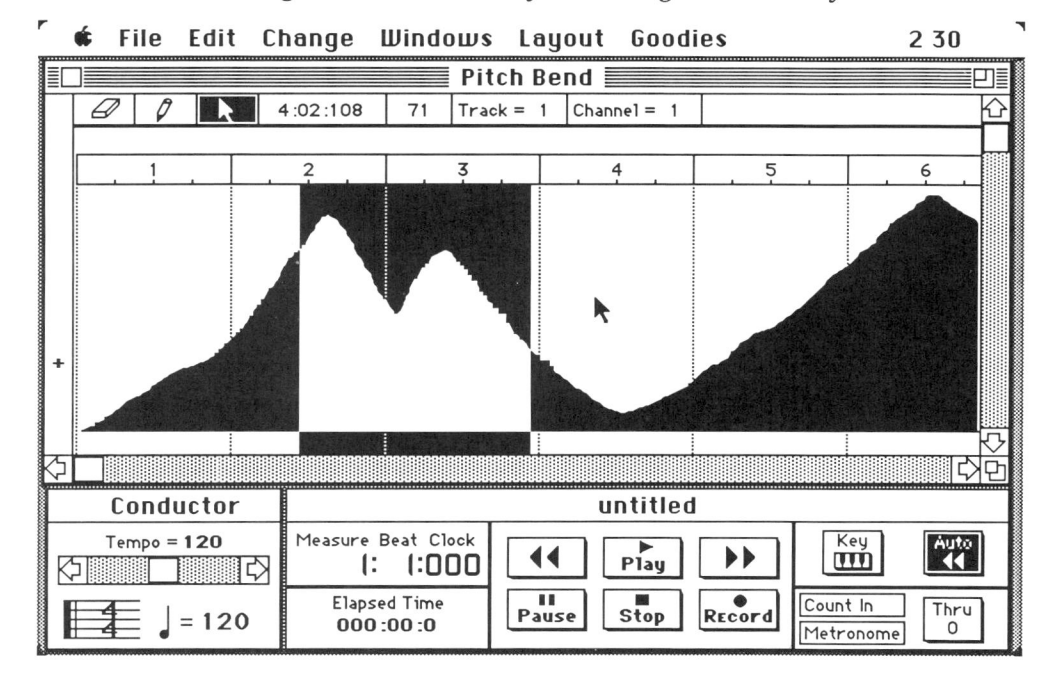

Figure 23. The graphic controller editing screen from Passport's Master Tracks Pro. A contour like the one shown can be created or edited by clicking on the pencil icon at upper left and then dragging the mouse across the screen. The region highlighted in inverse video has been selected for editing.

Synchronization

Because music is a time-based art, every sequencer has to run with reference to a source of clock signals. This source can be inside the sequencer itself (an *internal clock*) or it can be a clock signal arriving from somewhere else (an *external clock*). During any given playback run-through, the choice of internal or external sync is an either/or choice. There is no way to switch back and forth without stopping the machine—and probably no need to.

Only a few early sequencers ran strictly on internal sync. These days, just about all of them are equipped for external sync as well. Both hardware-based sequencers and computer MIDI interfaces usually have sync in and out jacks. If a sequencer has no sync jacks, it should still sync to MIDI clocks (or even MIDI Time Code). When a sequencer is running on internal sync, it should automatically be sending clock signals of some sort, so that other devices can be synced to it.

External sync is used for making sure that two devices stay perfectly in time with one another as they play. Without some common timing reference, the two would be bound to get out of step sooner or later. Incidentally, we've run into one sequencer (which shall remain nameless) that is advertised as having "SMPTE sync" when there is no SMPTE input to the machine. It lets you compute the elapsed time of your sequence in terms of SMPTE clocks—but the sequencer runs on its own internal clock during playback; it isn't actually synchronized at all.

Internal sync is different from external sync in that the sequencer itself may be able to control the internal clock in various ways while playback is proceeding. External sync tends to be brutally simple: The sequencer starts when the sync signal starts, speeds up when the sync signal speeds up, slows down when the sync signal slows down, and stops when the sync signal does. When we reach the level of SMPTE and other time-stamped sync signals, this is no longer true. But we're getting ahead of ourselves. Let's start by looking at internal sync.

Even the simplest sequencers allow the user to change the tempo of playback. The tempo change may have to be entered while the sequencer is stopped. A slightly more flexible design would allow the tempo to be sped up or slowed down during playback.

Some sequencers allow a tempo to be stored as part of the definition of each song. With this feature, a song can be loaded from disk and played immediately: No need to manually reset the tempo.

But what if we want to change the tempo during the course of the song? Professional-level sequencers offer various ways of doing this. If the sequencer is designed so that a song is built out of a list of "sequences," each sequence might be programmable with its own tempo, and the user might be able to make tempo changes only at the junctures between sequences.

Another type of design includes a *conductor track* as part of each sequence. This track contains no notes or other MIDI data, only timing information—principally tempo changes and time signature changes. Tempo may be specified in absolute bpm values, or as a percentage of the initial tempo. The latter system comes in handy if the musician decides that the whole tune is a bit fast or slow. Only one new tempo—the initial one—need be entered, and all subsequent tempo changes will keep their existing relationships.

On some sequencers, tempo changes must occur on bar lines. Others allow a tempo change to occur on any beat or clock, but all tempo changes must be entered manually. Some sequencers allow precisely defined rubatos to be programmed. The user might say, "Begin at 100 bpm. At bar 29, beat 3, begin slowing down gradually and evenly, so that by bar 36, beat 2, the tempo is 85 bpm." Still other sequencers will memorize and replay the tempo changes created by the user during playback. Sequencers designed with an eye toward audio-visual production may have utility procedures that let the user specify the location of selected beats in SMPTE seconds and frames. The sequencer will then calculate the tempo changes.

Time signature changes are not audible in themselves, of course, but programming them can be useful for two reasons: The sequencer's metronome output may be able to follow them, which will make it far easier to record parts with shifting meters. And if the editing environment is oriented toward working with entire bars of material, being able to redefine the length of the bar in the middle of the piece lets you easily find and specify the bars you want to work on. You might run into a conductor track somewhere that must be programmed with the time signature changes for the entire song while the song is empty, and that cannot be changed once the recording process has started; most, however, can be reprogrammed at any time without affecting the music. Changing the bar lines after some recording has taken place could cause computer bugs to show up in some programs.

When one of the 'dumb' types of external sync is chosen, internally programmed tempo changes become irrelevant. The sequencer will lock up to whatever drum machine, tape track sync tone, or sync box is sending the sync signal. That is, it will lock up if it is equipped to read that particular type of sync signal. Sync signals come in a bewildering variety of shapes and sizes, each of which has its own advantages and disadvantages. In order for the sequencer to read a sync signal, it has to have the right type of input jack, and also the right operating software to understand the signal. With a computer-based sequencer, the sync jack will generally be found on the interface box.

Sync signals come in two flavors—smart (also known as absolute) and dumb (relative). A dumb sync signal just says "...now...now...now...now..." over and over. This has the advantage that it's easy to decode. No logic is required. The sequencer's reference clock is advanced by one tick every time the sync input gets a clock message. The disadvantage is that if one of the clock messages gets lost for some reason, or if a bit of static on the line creates the false impression of an extra clock message, the receiving sequencer will get out of sync with the sending device, and will have no way to get back in sync, short of the user stopping the machine and starting over at the beginning of the song.

A smart sync signal deals with this problem by *time-stamping* the messages. Every message reveals the current clock time—usually in hours, minutes, seconds, and fractions of a second. A sequencer that understands a smart sync signal can't get lost. If one of the timing messages is garbled, the next one will immediately alert the sequencer that it has a little catching up to do. The disadvantage of this scheme is that the sequencer has to do more work to understand the clock signals, which means more expensive hardware and software.

Another advantage of smart sync—and it's a big one—is that we can start our master timing device (such as a multitrack tape deck) in the middle of a tune, and the synchronized device will *chase-lock* to the correct point in the music. In other words, the sequencer will fast-forward silently until it reaches the same beat that the master timing device is currently at, and then start playing back at the correct speed.

Recording A Sync Tone On Tape. Many forms of sync tone, including dumb signals like FSK and smart ones like SMPTE, can be recorded as a *sync track* on a multitrack tape deck. When the sync track is played back, any device that is synchronized to it will automatically stay in time with the music already recorded on tape (assuming that this music was also recorded using the same sync track as a timing reference).

MIDI clocks, like other MIDI data, cannot be recorded on tape, because the frequency of their transmissions (31.25kHz) is so high that tape recorder electronics can't handle it. If your sequencer has only MIDI for external sync and you want to sync to tape, you'll need to buy a sync interface device of some sort. This could be as simple as the Yamaha YMC-10, which does nothing but translate MIDI clocks to and from FSK. Or it could be as complicated as the Garfield Master Beat, which puts out clock signals, including SMPTE, suitable for many different types of hardware, and can be programmed with tempo maps for entire tunes.

MIDI Clocks. Most sequencers these days will read MIDI clocks. In fact, some of them will *only* sync to MIDI clocks or their own internal clock. The MIDI clock is a simple one-byte message (a dumb clock signal) that is sent down the MIDI cable at a rate of 24 ppq. Some sequencers, such as the Sequential Studio 440, are designed with a special MIDI in jack which is intended to receive only MIDI timing data, not incoming notes and other performance data. Other sequencers may let you specify which jack they are to look for the timing data on. This segregation is done to keep the timing more accurate, as a MIDI clock byte could easily be delayed by several milliseconds if the transmitting device is busy sending out some other message when the appropriate moment rolls around.

Some devices send out MIDI clocks only when they are playing; when the stop button is hit, the flow of clock signals ceases. Other devices, however—notably sequencers and drum machines from Roland—send out clock signals at all times, whether they are running or stopped. The reason for this is to allow you to slow down or speed up the clock on a master device while it is stopped, and have all of the slave devices be ready at the new tempo when you hit the start button.

In order to keep the slave device from running forever, though, we need some special commands, which are also defined in MIDI—*start*, *stop*, and *continue* commands. A start command tells the receiving device to begin from the beginning of its current song, while the continue command tells it to start from wherever it last stopped. In order to set the "last stopping time" of a slave device to the middle of a song without actually advancing the clock from the beginning of the tune in playback mode, we need to use MIDI *song position pointer*. This special command tells the receiving device how far into the song to start, measured in sixteenth-notes.

Roland devices use a similar stop/start/continue command structure with their non-MIDI FSK clock signals, by the way, so don't plan on syncing a Roland sequencer to non-Roland gear using the sync jacks, unless you've got a sync interface box handy.

SMPTE. Back in 1967, the Society of Motion Picture and Television Engineers found themselves in need of a standardized timing reference, so as to be able to synchronize film and videotape to one another and to audio tape. They adopted a multipurpose digital sync signal, or *time code*, that now goes by the acronym of the name of the Society—SMPTE (pronounced "simp-tee"). Since sequencers are now being used extensively in producing film and TV scores, it makes sense that SMPTE sync is implemented on a number sequencers. One unusual sequencer, the Q-Sheet software for the Macintosh from Digidesign, organizes its sequenced events in terms of SMPTE times rather than with reference to beats and bars.

We don't have space here to go into the details of SMPTE sync. Suffice it to say that SMPTE time code is a smart signal, time-stamped with the time of day in hours, minutes, seconds, frames, and sub-frames. Because the SMPTE engineers were faced with several different standards of film speed (24 frames per second, 25 frames per second, etc.), there are actually four different types of SMPTE signal, which are referred to as 24, 25, 30, and "drop-frame." If a sequencer has SMPTE at all, it probably has all four, so all you have to do is make sure that your sequencer is switched to the same option as what your VCR is sending, and you're in business.

When a sequencer is synced to SMPTE, it will start playback at whatever time the user has designated, and will stop when the SMPTE signal is interrupted. But unlike a dumb sync signal, SMPTE *doesn't* tell the sequencer how long a quarter-note is supposed to last. The sequencer has to figure this out for itself, based on its internal tempo settings. If you're used to using dumb sync, you can easily get confused into thinking your SMPTE interface isn't synchronizing properly, when all that's happened is that you've inadvertently changed the tempo setting of the sequencer. The sequencer will start on cue, just as it would with dumb sync, but will run too fast or too slow. Or, if you've changed the start time by a frame or two, it could start just perceptibly early or late and stay that way—again, a musical disaster caused by user error, not by the failure of the sequencer to synchronize properly.

MTC. MIDI Time Code (MTC) is a new form of time-stamped sync signal that is defined as part of the MIDI Specification. It was developed by the people at Opcode and Sequential to allow devices without special sync jacks to send and receive time-stamped sync code based on SMPTE time designations over a MIDI cable. MTC uses up quite a bit of the bandwidth in a MIDI cable (that is, it occupies about seven percent of the total available time), so some manufacturers prefer to send and receive it via special MIDI input and output jacks that are not used for notes and other data.

Other Time-Stamped Signals. Several companies are now offering lower-cost alternatives to SMPTE synchronization. These are not suitable for locking up to video or film; SMPTE is still the standard in this part of the industry. But if you're simply planning to sync your sequencer to tape and want to be able to chase-lock to the middle of a tune, you have several options—none of which, unfortunately, are compatible with one another. Hybrid Arts uses a tone that they call HybriSync in conjunction with their Atari software sequencers, and both SynHance and JL Cooper have recently released sync boxes that read and write similar tones. There may well be others by the time you read this.

These sync signals have some real positive uses—such as saving musicians hundreds of dollars a pop—but it's hard to avoid the feeling that the whole area of synchronization is as disorganized today as digital keyboard buss signals were before the introduction of MIDI. To paraphrase Frank Zappa, "Just what the world needs—another synchronization standard."

FSK & Pulse Sync. These older forms of sync are dumb (no time-stamping), but they are inexpensive and widely used. FSK (Frequency Shift Keying) is a sync tone in which two pitches an octave or so apart alternate with one another at the clock rate (usually, but not always, 24 ppq). If you listen to FSK, it sounds rather like a sustained synthesizer tone being modulated by a very fast square wave LFO. Several different types of FSK tone have been used by different manufacturers over the years. FSK is easier to record on a tape track than pulses, but if tape playback speed is varied too widely, the receiving sequencer can lose the ability to track the tone.

By the way, various manufacturers use different pitches for their FSK tones, so don't plan on syncing two devices together directly just because they both use FSK.

A pulse sync tone is simply a low-frequency square wave; if you listen to it, it sounds like a buzz or fast click, because the rising and falling edges of the waveform have a lot of high-frequency audio content. Pulse sync can be tricky to record on some tape decks, because its fundamental frequency is often below 20Hz, and these extremely low frequencies are sometimes rolled off by built-in filters in the tape deck to avoid rumble. But it has the advantage that you can swing the tape playback speed all over the yard and the sequencer or sync box will follow it like a charm.

Clicks & Audio Input Sync. The most dumb form of sync imaginable is one in which the sequencer sends or receives a single click on every quarter-note. The problem with this sort of sync is that the sequencer has to perform some guesswork in order to figure out when the clock ticks ought to fall between quarter-notes. If the transmitting device happens to speed up or slow down between clicks, the receiving device has an unappetizing choice. It can advance the internal clock a number of ticks instantaneously if the next click arrives early, or it can step through the required number of internal clock ticks and then wait around twiddling its thumbs if the next click arrives late.

Even at this, some internal logic is needed for the sequencer to make an educated guess about how fast those between-the-clicks clock ticks ought to be going, and interpolate the missing pulses. You're more likely to find such internal logic on "smart" sync boxes like the Garfield Time Commander and Kahler Human Clock, which are specifically designed to track input signals like eighth-notes and quarter-notes—either clicks or actual audio signals from a drummer or equivalent. These can be tracked even when the tempo is varying.

Clock Divisors. Various devices run at various internal clock speeds, and each of them may want to send and receive external signals at this speed. So what are we to do if the device we want to use as our master clock is sending at 96 ppq and the slave device prefers to run at 24 ppq?

One option is to use edit operations to multiply all of the note times and durations in the slave sequencer by four. It will think it's playing a whole-note every time the master advances by a quarter-note, but the whole-notes will be incredibly fast, and the two devices should sound right together. The bad news is that many sequencers don't offer this kind of time-stretching as an edit option. However, they may very well offer something easier and just as useful: They may let us divide the incoming clocks by some integer value, such as four. In this situation, the slave sequencer ignores three incoming clock pulses and then advances its own internal clock by one tick on the fourth one. The musical result is the same: Every time the master plays a quarter-note (sending 96 clocks in the process), the slave plays a quarter-note (because it only "sees" 24 of the clocks).

If your sequencer doesn't offer a clock divisor option, you can buy a sync box that will perform the necessary magic.

Data Storage

There were one or two early digital sequencers that had no data storage capability, but they've gone the way of the dodo. Most sequencers these days allow you to store the contents of their memory on computer disk, so that you can build up a library of arrangements and load them into the machine as needed. A few sequencers use other types of storage media, such as RAM cartridges or cassette tape.

Mostly, the process of storing and loading data is pretty straightforward, and should be explained in your owner's manual. There are a few things that it pays to be aware of, however.

First, when buying disks, check what kind you're getting. The difference between 5¼" and 3½" disks is obvious when you pick them up, but you'll have to read the fine print to find out whether the disks are single-sided or double-sided, and whether they're single-density, double-density, or high-density. Buy the type recommended for your machine.

Second, disks can and do become unreadable. This can happen because they've come into proximity with a stray magnetic field (even a paper clip that's been in one of those magnetic desktop paper clip holders) or because of physical damage from excessive heat, moisture, or a stray dust particle. Treat your disks with care, and they'll reward you by taking good care of your music. But never, never trust them. *Always* make a backup copy of your work at the end of each work session. Store the backup disk in a different place than the main copy.

Some computers these days, and even a few instruments with built-in sequencers, are coming equipped with *hard disk drives*. A hard disk holds much more data than a standard floppy disk, and accesses this data much faster. A hard disk drive is also somewhat more fragile than a floppy drive. A hard disk would be ideal for loading sequences during a live show because of its speed—except, of course, that its inherent fragility makes most people nervous about taking one on the road. (And by the way, if you've got a hard disk, back up your work on floppies even though it takes annoying amounts of time. There's nothing like a hard disk crash for wiping out weeks of work.)

RAM cartridges load just as fast as a hard disk, and they're less fragile, but they're also more expensive. Not too many sequencers use cartridges for storage; this is probably going to become an obsolete form of memory within a few years, just as data cassettes have all but disappeared except among a few diehard Commodore 64 users who have never bought disk drives, and owners of non-MIDI drum machines.

Disk Operations. The simplest type of disk operating system does two things: It lets you save your music to disk as a disk file, and it lets you load disk files into memory. Hopefully it also lets you name your disk files before saving them—they're much easier to find that way—and lets you look at a directory that lists what's currently on the disk.

When it loads data from disk into memory, the sequencer may automatically clear the current contents of memory, or it may let you retain the current contents (provided there's enough space available) while loading the new file into a vacant track or sequence. The latter system is far preferable, because it allows you to take snippets of material from one sequence, save them to disk, and load them into another existing sequence. Some sequencers let single tracks be saved and loaded. If the memory is always cleared completely during a load operation, the only way to combine two pieces of music into one is to completely re-record some of the material from scratch.

Most, though not all, sequencers let you combine material from several disk files. Some of them will also let you store and load special files, such as default screen layouts, separately from your music files.

Dedicated-hardware sequencers normally include a disk-formatting command, so that new disks can be prepared to receive data. If the sequencer (hardware or software) is well designed, it will allow you to format disks without losing the current contents of memory. If it can't do this, you'll have to be sure to have a disk handy at the beginning of each session that has the necessary amount of blank space to store the work you're about to do.

Standard Disk File Format. Sequencers, as you've probably figured out if you've read this far, are not all alike. Different ones are optimized for different tasks. So let's say you're running a software sequencer on a Macintosh, and you've recorded a piece of music that could benefit greatly from a bit of data tweezing that your sequencer doesn't happen to let you do. Are you up a creek?

Not necessarily. Opcode Systems has introduced a standardized disk file format, which was ratified by the MIDI Manufacturers Association in June 1968. The idea is that any sequencer can be programmed (if its designers have gotten around to it) to read and write MIDI files from disk—unlike normal sequencer data files, which all use different formats. If you've created a piece of music using an interactive program like Jam Factory and want to edit it using fancy editing features that Jam Factory doesn't have, you can store the piece on disk as a MIDI file, close up the Jam Factory program, boot up the sequencer, and read the music into it from disk (assuming that you've got a Macintosh sequencer handy and that it reads MIDI files). A word of warning: Software has been released by several companies that reads and writes 0.3 or 0.4 rev MIDI files. The trouble is, the two revs are incompatible with one another. If you need MIDI file compatibility, make sure that the program you buy has or can be updated to rev 1.0.

MIDI files were first implemented on Macintosh software, but software for other computers is now making use of them. Even though disks can't be swapped between one type of computer and another, it's still useful to have a common format, because MIDI files can also be sent from one computer to another over a *modem* (telephone link). Want to trade MIDI arrangements with musicians across the country and around the world? MIDI files are the way to do it.

Direct Data Transfer. Assuming that you can't use MIDI files, it should still be pretty easy to transfer a sequence from one sequencer to another. All that's necessary is to sync the two devices and then have one play back while the other records. The receiving sequencer doesn't know whether there's another sequencer at the other end of the MIDI cable, or 16 keyboard players! It records the MIDI data in either case.

Special Applications

As computers get more powerful and software gets more sophisticated, programmers are coming up with more and more fun things that musicians might find useful. Some of these are discussed in "Beyond Sequencing" on page 72. Before we leave the subject of sequencers, however, we need to say a word or two about system-exclusive data storage and multi-tasking computer environments.

Multi-tasking is a fancy word for running two or more programs at the same time on the same computer. They don't actually run at the *same* time (remember, a computer only does one thing at a time), except in computers that have parallel processing—a technology that is still pretty much beyond personal computers.

In a multi-tasking environment, several programs can be residing in memory at once. Why is this useful? Well, maybe you're recording a sequence, and your synthesizer doesn't have the right bass sound for the bass line. You've got an editor/librarian program for the synthesizer, but it runs on the same computer, and you'd rather not go to the trouble of saving the sequence to disk, shutting down the sequencer, switching disks, booting up the editor/librarian, and so on. Multi-tasking allows you to use the editor/librarian without exiting the sequencer.

The hitch is, you need a lot of computer memory to hold all of the programs you might be using, and you need to be using programs that are smart enough to let you shuffle back and forth without bumping into one another and crashing. In the Macintosh, a program called Switcher can be used to put one application program into the background while a second is running. Switcher keeps track of what sections of memory each program is occupying; the programs themselves are entirely self-contained. In a more flexible multi-tasking environment, such as that being developed by Dr. T's Music Software for the Atari ST, the various music programs will be able to communicate with one another. For example, the user will be able to play the unmuted sequencer tracks from a command within the editor/librarian. The catch is that this type of interaction isn't likely to work unless all of the programs come from the same manufacturer.

Musical applications of multi-tasking are only beginning to be explored. We'll be seeing more and more of them in the next couple of years. Ultimately, the sequencer will be only one facet of a complete *digital audio workstation*.

If you don't own an editor/librarian program, you might still be able to use your sequencer for patch storage. Some sequencers will record system-exclusive data dumps (containing synthesizer patch data, for example) and let you store them on disk. While you won't be able to edit the patches with a sequencer program, you'll be able to store them on disk. You should also be able to include patch data as part of a sequence. This could be useful if the sequencer is playing a synthesizer that stores a limited number of patches in its internal memory. You could play as many different sounds as the music required by storing new patch data as part of the sequence.

Bugs, Crashes, And Revs.

By Jim Aikin

A bug is a piece of improperly written code within a computer program that causes problems when the program is run. If you give the computer a command to carry out a specific operation and it either does nothing or does something different from what you requested, you have encountered a bug. For example, you might have instructed the program to quantize a track to a triplet value, and found when you listened to the result that it had quantized to a duplet value instead.

When a program does something unexpected, it's often tough to tell whether a bug was at fault, or user error. Take a deep breath, consult the manual, and try the action again.

Virtually all software of any complexity contains bugs, but if the software has been thoroughly debugged, they will be minor. They can be hard for the programmer to spot, because they lie hidden quietly until some specific operation is called for. A bug that causes irreversible damage to recorded music is definitely not minor. If you encounter a major bug, write down exactly what actions you performed and what the computer did, and call or write to the manufacturer.

Bugs can be catastrophic or non-catastrophic. After a non-catastrophic bug has shown up, the program will still operate normally. A catastrophic bug causes the program to crash.

A crash is when the computer gets hopelessly boggled trying to carry out the programmer's and user's instructions. A crash will take one of two forms. The sequencer may lock up completely, refusing to respond to front-panel input. The only thing you can do in this case is shut the machine off and start over. Or (a more sinister possibility), the sequencer may continue to chug along, responding in some fashion to user input but producing gibberish.

Once a crash has occurred, there is usually no way to save your work to disk. Whatever was in the machine's memory is gone.

Why does software have bugs? Can't we expect it to work perfectly? Well, a sequencer program contains untold thousands of lines of code, so many that it's impossible to test every routine to be sure it works smoothly with every other routine. Computers, being incredibly stupid, can only do what they're actually told to do in completely explicit terms. When the instructions are incomplete, contain internal contradictions, or don't allow for all the possibilities, the computer is in trouble.

Good programmers include error-trapping routines in their code, so that if you try to type in values that the computer doesn't know how to interpret (such as a start time that's later than an end time), it will issue a warning and do nothing, or reinterpret your input as a permissible value. But programmers can't possibly think of all the silly things that a user might ask their software to do: After all, *they* know how to use it properly; it never crashes for them.

Most programs and hardware devices undergo *beta testing* before their commercial release: Beta testers get a free copy of the product to work with, in return enduring the bugs that pop up and giving the programmers feedback on how the program can be improved.

When a software or hardware sequencer is put on the market, it will probably still contain some bugs. As the manufacturers learn of these from users and rewrite the software to fix them, they issue new *revisions* (revs). Revs may also appear when new features have been added. The first official release of a product is usually considered rev 1.0. A completely overhauled product would be rev 2.0. Minor revisions are notated by changes to the right of the decimal place—rev 1.1, rev 1.15, rev 1.3, or whatever number the manufacturer feels is appropriate.

When buying any product that contains digital electronics, always ask what the manufacturer's *update policy* is. Some software makers will send a free disk containing updates (revisions) to registered owners; others charge only a nominal fee. Updating a hardware unit is a bit more difficult, because it generally means opening up the box to install a new ROM chip. ROMs are more expensive than disks, and more easily damaged.

As always with software-based products, though, I recommend that you never buy a product on the basis of the features that you're promised will be in the next rev. Begin with the assumption that you're going to be working for an extended period with the version (bugs and all) that is actually in the store. The music software field contains a regrettable amount of vaporware—software that is being spoken about in glowing terms but that doesn't exist. Be wary of salespeople who assure you that a rev will be out "in two weeks." (You could always suggest to them that you take the current version home now and write them a check "in two weeks.")

Most music software is wonderful stuff, and will open up whole new worlds of creativity. But the other kind does exist.

MIDI Basics

By Jim Aikin

Without MIDI, sequencers would still exist, but they would be a lot less common and a lot less well developed than they are. MIDI is the glue that holds a sequencing system together.

Developed between 1981 and 1983 by a group of electronic instrument manufacturers, MIDI (the Musical Instrument Digital Interface) was initially intended simply to allow the keyboard of one synthesizer to play the tone-generating circuitry of another. But it quickly became clear that lots of other applications were nearly as important. Following an extended dialog in which data types and logical procedures were defined, the first MIDI-equipped synthesizers appeared in late 1983. The period of initial confusion among manufacturers lasted for another year or two, however. Instruments built during this period exhibit some quirky behavior. Most of the rough edges have been sanded off by now. If you buy a MIDI-equipped instrument from a reputable manufacturer in 1988, you can be reasonably sure that it will interface properly with other MIDI gear.

You don't need to understand MIDI thoroughly in order to use it for sequencing. All you need to do is buy a couple of MIDI cables, plug your synthesizer into your sequencer, and start playing (with or without reading the sequencer's owner's manual). But music stores are still getting calls from people who ask, "Can I buy a MIDI?" So let's run through the concepts that will help you the most if you're just getting into this area for the first time.

What is MIDI? MIDI is not a piece of hardware. It is a communications protocol. It is a group of definitions. The definitions have been agreed on by the manufacturers in the MIDI Manufacturers Association (MMA) and the Japan MIDI Standards Committee (JMSC). The agreement is not binding, but it is in everybody's interest to adhere to it. All aspects of the communications protocol are defined by the MIDI

Specification 1.0 (and the addenda that have since been attached to it). A manufacturer who belongs to the MMA or JMSC and puts MIDI jacks on a device does not agree to implement *all* of the aspects of the Specification, but he or she does agree not to send anything out the MIDI output jack that violates the protocol.

Digital data. MIDI data is digital, and is designed to give commands to a receiving device that understands the MIDI language. It is not audio: You cannot listen to it. There is nothing in a MIDI command that says what sound or change in sound it will trigger. The nature of the sound (if any) depends entirely on how the receiving device interprets the MIDI command.

Connections. When MIDI devices are hooked up, out plugs into in. In plugs into out. Thru plugs into in. A thru jack on a unit transmits a duplicate of whatever arrived at the same unit's in jack. A thru jack does *not* transmit any data generated inside the unit itself. A MIDI cable carries data in only one direction.

Routing. You cannot mix the data from two MIDI outs and send it to a single MIDI in by building a Y cord. In the event that both transmitting devices are sending data at once, the messages will become hopelessly garbled. A special device called a *MIDI merger* is required for this task.

Channel and system. There are two types of data within MIDI—*channel* information and *system* information. Channel information consists of things like note-on and note-off commands, pitch-bends, after-touch, and so on—music performance commands, in other words. Generally speaking, sequencers record only channel information. System information is everything else in MIDI—things like start, stop, and continue commands, timing clocks, active sensing, song position pointer, and tune request, which have more to do with how the system is operating than with the music it is playing.

Status and data. Do not confuse the system/channel distinction with the distinction between *status bytes* and *data bytes*. Every byte sent down a MIDI cable is either a status byte or a data byte: A status byte defines the type of message being sent (including whether it is channel or system information), and may be followed, depending on what sort of status byte it is, by no, one, two, or more data bytes.

The reason for defining two types of bytes is that only 256 different eight-bit bytes can exist (see Bytes And Hex, page 62). If we set one group of 128 aside as status bytes, each of which has a unique definition, then we can use the other 128 to mean many different things. The meaning of a data byte depends entirely on what the last status byte was.

Channels. MIDI defines 16 channels through which music data can be transmitted. Unlike mixer channels, these are not simultaneous separate parallel signal paths. They are merely data designations that exist within a single digital signal. Every musical event must be transmitted on one of the 16 channels. Generally, a receiving instrument will be set to respond to incoming data on one channel, or perhaps three or four channels if the instrument is multi-timbral. It will ignore everything on the other channels. This is how we get the devices in a MIDI sequencing system to play different parts when they are all receiving data from a single sequencer output.

Modes. A set of four *modes* were originally defined for receiving devices. These modes have nothing to do with the nature of the data being transmitted, and it has become apparent that far more imaginative modes of reception are possible. Due to some initial confusion among manufacturers, a mode (mode 2—omni-on/mono) was defined that is almost completely useless. Modes are not terribly relevant from the point of view of sequencing, except that you will normally want to set your receiving tone modules to some sort of omni-off mode. If they are set to omni-on mode, they will all play all of the notes the sequencer sends out.

Notes. Every MIDI note-on message contains a status byte followed by two data bytes. The status byte contains the information that this is a note-on event, as well as the number of the channel (1 through 16). The first data byte contains the note number. MIDI defines 128 note numbers, though a five-octave C-to-C keyboard normally transmits only notes 36 through 96. Middle C is note 60. The second data byte contains the *key velocity* of the note, which has a range from 0 through 127.

Note-offs. MIDI provides two ways of turning off an individual note. A type of event called a note-off event is defined; like the note-on event, the note-off has two data bytes associated with it, one for note number and the other for key velocity. A variable *release velocity* value is only transmitted by a few keyboards, and is only recorded by a few sequencers. Instead of sending a note-off, a master controller can turn a note off by sending a note-on for that note with a velocity of zero. This is defined by MIDI as equivalent to a note-off.

MIDI also contains an *all-notes-off* command, which can be useful if a note-off has gotten garbled or lost in transmission, causing the note to ring endlessly. Not all instruments understand the all-notes-off command.

Running status. The reason for using a note-on with a velocity of zero as a note-off is to save transmission time when *running status* is being used. Running status is a shorthand method of data transmission in which one status byte is sent, followed by a whole string of data bytes. Until a new status byte is received, the receiving instrument is to understand that all of the data bytes are data of the same type. This speeds up the transmission somewhat, because the status byte only needs to be sent once, until a message requiring some other status byte is to be sent. If the status byte says "note-on, channel 3," the transmitting device can switch notes both on and off on channel three by using a note-on with a velocity of zero to switch them off.

In most situations, you shouldn't need to worry about whether or not your equipment is using running status.

Program changes. A program change message can be sent on any channel. The data byte can have a value from 0 to 127, but many receiving instruments do not have 128 different programs in memory. MIDI does not define how they will respond to program changes outside their range; some instruments ignore them, while others "wrap around." A program change message simply says, "If you're listening on channel nn, switch to your program number xx." The transmitting device does not attempt to specify what program xx actually is. If the synthesizer receiving this command has a trumpet sound stored in patch number xx, it will start playing that trumpet sound.

Pitch-bend. This is a channel message with two data bytes, a least significant byte and a most significant byte (see Bytes And Hex, page 62). Most instruments and many sequencers ignore the LSB, so the practical resolution of MIDI pitch-bend messages is 128 steps, with the center position of the pitch wheel or other bender at 64. The actual musical range of the pitch-bend is not defined by MIDI; it must be set in the receiving device. If you are using MIDI pitch-bending to bend two instruments that are set to different ranges, they will go out of tune with respect to one another at each bend.

After-touch. MIDI defines two types of key pressure—channel pressure and polyphonic pressure. Again, it is up to the receiving device(s) to determine what the pressure data will mean musically. Channel pressure contains only one byte of data

(0-127), while polyphonic pressure contains two bytes, one for the key number and another for the pressure value.

Controllers. A controller message is a type of channel message. In theory, a total of 128 controllers are available, but some of these have been defined by the MMA and JMSC, in such a way that there are 32 continuous controllers, 32 switches, and some other miscellaneous stuff. The modulation wheel is always controller 1, and volume changes are sent as controller 7, but most of the controllers are still undefined, and can be used for anything that you and your synthesizer manufacturer happen to like.

Some people (including manufacturers) tend to refer to various types of MIDI data, such as pitch-bend and program changes, as controllers. This is incorrect.

System-exclusive. In order to keep MIDI an open-ended system, its designers created a data type called system-exclusive. All system-exclusive messages begin with the sys-ex status byte ($F0) and end with the end-of-exclusive (sometimes abbreviated EOX) status byte ($F7). The data bytes between these two messages can be defined by any manufacturer in any way that may be required by their own products. Each manufacturer is given a system-exclusive ID number, which is used at the beginning of the sys-ex data. Most manufacturers also define their own instrument ID numbers. An instrument that receives a sys-ex message with the wrong ID number will ignore it. If the ID is correct, the instrument will do whatever it has been programmed to do upon receipt of this particular message. System-exclusive messages are used for transmitting the internal parameter settings of synthesizers and for many other purposes. Most sequencers ignore system-exclusive data, but a few will record it.

MIDI Data

The MIDI specification defines exactly how MIDI data is to be sent. The transmissions are digital, which means that they consist of two electrical states, one corresponding to the number 1 and the other corresponding to the number 0. MIDI messages, like other digital transmissions, are made up entirely of 1's and 0's strung together in various ways. A 1 or 0 is called a *bit*.

MIDI is a *serial* interface, which means that messages must be sent down a single wire, one bit at a time. (In a *parallel* interface, a whole packet of bits can be sent simultaneously, one bit on each of several parallel wires.)

The transmission rate (baud rate) of MIDI is fixed at 31,250 bits per second. In the computer industry, the term *baud* means "bits per second." A thousand bits per second is a *kilobaud*. So 31,250 bits per second is 31.25 kilobaud. This is far higher than the rates used in many types of data transmissions: In modem (telephone link) communications, rates of 300 to 1,200 baud are common. But 31.25 kilobaud is barely fast enough for music.

A MIDI byte begins with a *start bit* and ends with a *stop bit*. These bits are used to keep receiving devices from getting confused, and have no musical meaning. Between the start and stop bits are eight bits of MIDI data. Thus an entire MIDI byte consists of ten bits. A maximum of 3,125 of these bytes can be transmitted per second. Since many MIDI messages require three bytes, it is easy to see that about 1,000 complete messages can be transmitted per second—slightly more under optimum conditions, such as when running status is used, or when some of the messages consist of only a single byte such as the clock timing byte. When 1,000 three-byte messages are being transmitted per second, each message lasts 1/1,000 second, or one *millisecond* (abbreviated *ms*).

MIDI status bytes always begin with a 1, while data bytes always begin with a 0. Thus there are 128 possible status bytes and 128 possible data bytes.

Bytes And Hex

Unless you're a programmer, you may never have to deal with bytes or hexadecimal notation directly. But sooner or later, unless you flee back to the land of the piccolo and the dulcimer, somebody is going to start talking to you about running status, controller LSBs, and other concepts that will make very little sense unless you understand what bytes are all about.

Most electronic music equipment these days is digital, which means that the electronics handle everything in the form of *binary* (base 2) arithmetic. In our everyday decimal (base 10) arithmetic, we have ten different symbols to represent numbers; larger numbers are represented by stringing the ten symbols together in a specific order. Binary arithmetic can represent all of the numbers that decimal arithmetic can, but it does so using only two symbols—1 and 0. These are the binary digits, or bits. Binary is convenient for electrical devices, because they can perform complex operations using only two electrical states—on and off, 1 and 0.

Here is what counting looks like in binary (Figure 1).

binary	decimal
1	1
10	2
11	3
100	4
101	5
110	6
111	7
1000	8
1001	9
1010	10
1011	11
1100	12
1101	13
1110	14
1111	15
10000	16

As you can see, a lot more digits are needed to represent numbers the same size as the equivalent decimal number, but the counting process is very similar.

All computers handle bits in the form of eight-bit packets called *bytes*. Each byte consists of two four-bit packets that are sometimes called *nibbles*. There are 16 possible nibbles, starting with 0000 and continuing with 0001, 0010, and so on, as in the binary counting table above, until we reach 1111. So there are 16 x 16, or 256 possible bytes.

Binary numbers aren't easy for humans to read. When representing digital data on paper or on a computer screen, we would prefer something more compact. For this purpose, bytes are often represented in *hexadecimal* (base 16) notation. For hexadecimal, we need more symbols than decimal arithmetic provides, so the letters A through F are pressed into service. Here is our counting table again, with hexadecimal equivalents (Figure 2).

binary nibbles	decimal	hexa-decimal
0000	0	0
0001	1	1
0010	2	2
0011	3	3
0100	4	4
0101	5	5
0110	6	6
0111	7	7
1000	8	8
1001	9	9
1010	10	A
1011	11	B
1100	12	C
1101	13	D
1110	14	E
1111	15	F

Larger numbers, as in decimal, are represented by combining the hexadecimal digits. In computer applications, hexadecimal numbers usually appear as two-digit numbers, with each hex digit corresponding to one of the nibbles in a byte. For example, byte 1001 1100 is hex 9C.

In order to avoid confusing hex numbers with decimal numbers, a special symbol—usually an H or $—is often used before or after the number.

If a number is too large to be contained in a single byte, two or more bytes must be used. With two bytes, we can specify integers as large as 65,535. One byte contains the large part of the number, and is called the most significant byte (MSB), while the other contains the small part, and is called the least significant byte (LSB). Only a few MIDI messages require both an LSB and an MSB.

The Sequencer In A Music System

By Jim Aikin

By itself, a MIDI sequencer makes a dandy doorstop, paperweight, or bookend. Its reason for existence only becomes apparent when it is hooked up to other devices in a MIDI studio or stage environment. Given the right equipment in the right configuration, and given the right operating software, a sequencer can be used to create music of great complexity and subtlety. Here we're going to take a look at how a sequencer fits into a music system.

The simplest possible MIDI sequencing system consists of a sequencer and a single instrument—usually a keyboard synthesizer or sampler—which is used both for inputting data into the sequencer and for playing back what the sequencer has recorded. (Of course, an audio amplifier and speaker—or headphone—system of some sort comes in handy too.) This bare-bones setup is illustrated in Figure 1. In an extreme case, the sequencer might be built into the instrument itself, as in the Ensoniq ESQ-1 synthesizer. If no other equipment is involved, MIDI isn't being used,

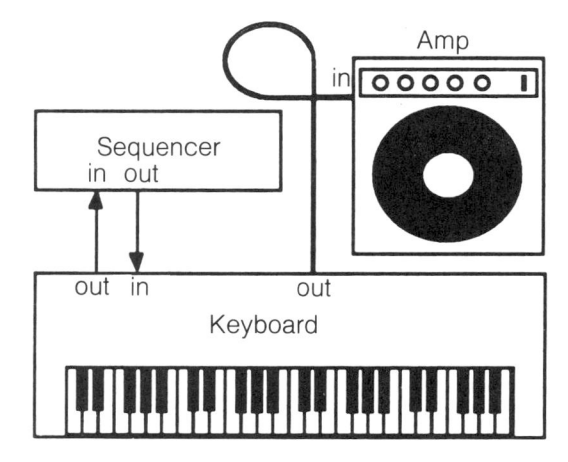

Figure 1. The simplest possible MIDI sequencing system contains only a single keyboard instrument, which functions as both a sound source and a master controller (input device) for the sequencer.

64   Theory And Application

so an ESQ-1 by itself isn't technically a MIDI sequencing setup at all. But it amounts to the same thing musically. Besides, all built-in sequencers these days will send out MIDI data, so a MIDI sequencing setup can easily be built up around a single self-contained keyboard/sequencer unit.

A sequencer can't make any noise by itself. It can only play whatever electronic voices are available in the instrument(s) it is hooked to. If it is hooked to a synthesizer that will generate up to eight notes at a time, then sequences with up to eight-voice polyphony can be created. We can store as many more simultaneous musical lines as we'd like in the sequencer—but the poor eight-voice synthesizer will run itself ragged trying to play them all back at once. If the synthesizer is capable of playing only one patch (sound program) at a time, then all of the sequencer's notes will have to be played by voices that use this patch, and they will all have the same sound.

This point is sometimes not understood by beginners. Suppose they begin by recording a bass part into one track of a sequencer using a Korg Poly-800, whose voices must all share the same patch. Then they switch the Poly-800 to a string sound to record some string chords, and get terribly distraught when the bass part is played back with a string sound. "What am I doing wrong?" they cry. What they fail to understand is that the sequencer doesn't record the *sound* of the bass, only the keystrokes that were used in the bass part. Since the Poly-800 will only play one patch a a time, the sequencer's output must use this, whatever it happens to be at the moment.

In order to build up musical arrangements containing a variety of sounds, we need either a variety of synthesizers and tone generators, or (more economically) a single synthesizer or tone module that is *multi-timbral*. A multi-timbral instrument is one that can create multiple timbres (pronounced "tam-brz") at the same time.

If we have several tone modules, each can be set to its own MIDI channel. The sequencer can then send various notes to various individual modules, and each module will create sounds using its own current patch. This hookup is illustrated in Figure 2.

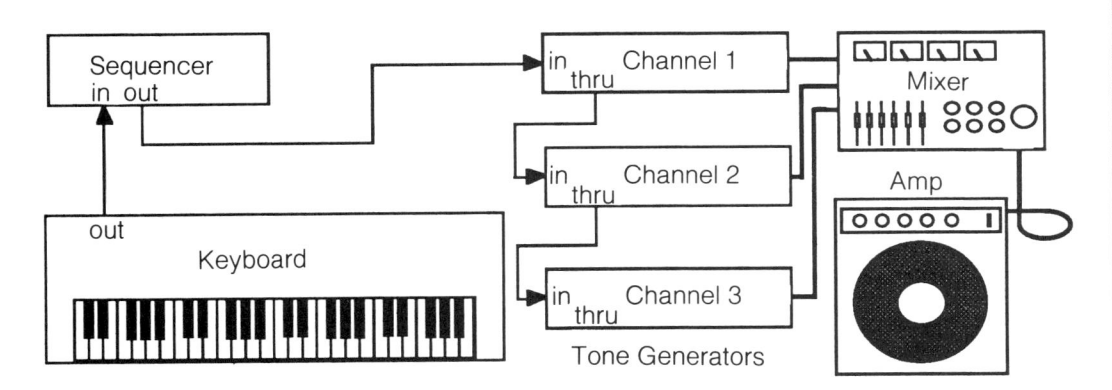

Figure 2. In a typcial small sequencer system, a master keyboard (which makes no sound by itself) sends MIDI data to the sequencer. The sequencer is configured so that its output is also a thru port, allowing the master keyboard to talk directly to any of the tone generators. At any given time, the master keyboard will probably be playing one of the tone generators while the sequencer plays the others.

But it's a waste of hardware to use an eight-voice or 16-voice device when all we want to play on that channel is a monophonic (one-voice) bass or lead part. So more and more manufacturers are building multi-timbral, multi-channel tone generators. Such a device is a single module with a fixed total number of voices (such as eight or 16) that can be assigned individually to any MIDI channel, and can use any of the patches in internal memory.

For example, we could assign three voices to channel 1 and have them play an electric piano sound, two voices to channel 5 with a distorted lead sound, one voice to channel 6 with a bass sound, and the remaining two voices (if this is an eight-voice module) to channel 11 with a chime sound. Now this one module can play sequencer tracks with music assigned to channels 1, 5, 6, and 11, and all of the parts will have their own sounds. We can send a program change command on channel 5 at any time, for example, and change the distorted lead sound to some other sound without affecting the sounds being played by any of the other voices. Thus a single eight-voice multi-timbral module can perform a number of different musical tasks in the course of a single arrangement. Alternatively, we could assign four voices to channel 1 with a piano sound, and another four voices also to channel 1 with a string sound. With this arrangement, each time a MIDI note arrives, two voices (a string/piano layer) will sound, but only four notes can be played at a time.

Multi-timbral keyboards include the Kawai K5, Casio CZ-1, and Oberheim Matrix-12. Multi-timbral tone generators without keyboards include the Oberheim Xpander, the Yamaha FB-01, TX81Z, and TX802, and the Roland MT-32. Most sampling keyboards and rack-mount samplers are also multi-timbral. Even more helpful when it comes to MIDI sequencing, many samplers use *dynamic voice allocation*. Instead of assigning some fixed number of voices to each sound/channel combination, they may allow any channel to use whatever voices are currently not sounding a note. If an eight-voice module has dynamic voice allocation, we could play an eight-note chord on channel 1 followed immediately by an eight-note chord on channel 2. Assuming that it has sounds assigned to both channels, the machine should play all the notes in each chord. The Ensoniq ESQ-1 and SQ-80 and the Kawai K5 are just about the only synthesizers that currently offer dynamic voice allocation, but it's sure to become more common in the future.

Our growing MIDI studio now has a master controller of some sort, a sequencer, and a couple of multi-timbral tone generators. But we're only getting started. Depending on our musical needs and the size of our budget, we may want to incorporate many other types of MIDI-controlled devices. Commands for these can be recorded into the sequencer as part of a song, allowing us an almost infinite variety of automated control over the finished arrangement. We may also need interface boxes of one sort or another in order to get all the parts of our system to talk to one another.

Every MIDI sequencing system is different, but they all include components in some or all of the categories below.

Tone generators. This is by far the largest category of MIDI equipment. Digital synthesizers, samplers, and hybrid designs can be found in all price ranges, from $250 or less for a used Casio CZ-101 or Yamaha FB-01 to half a million for a fully loaded Synclavier. As we mentioned above, a well-equipped MIDI studio will usually have at least a couple of multi-timbral synthesizers and a sampler handy.

MIDI controllers. Before the birth of a standardized digital music language, this whole class of devices would have been unthinkable. They don't make any sound of their own; all they do is generate MIDI data for driving slave modules and sequencers. If you're not a keyboard player, a guitar or wind controller can be the key to unlocking the world of sequencing.

A *master keyboard controller* like the Yamaha KX76 or Kurzweil MidiBoard has a velocity- and pressure-sensitive keyboard, along with a memory for storing keyboard setups that route various regions of the keyboard to various MIDI channels. Because the whole cost of the unit goes toward its performance attributes rather than toward sound-generating hardware, the keyboard may be somewhat better, and the MIDI convenience features more comprehensive, than on an equivalent synthesizer or sampler keyboard.

Acoustic pianos with MIDI sensors under the keys are found in some studios.

Many performance interfaces make use of *pitch-to-MIDI converters*. These devices sense the frequency (pitch) of an incoming audio signal by observing its waveform, and put out the corresponding MIDI note message. This is not an easy conversion to make, for technical reasons, and producing good data on a pitch-to-MIDI converter requires a clean performance technique. Pitch-to-MIDI converters like the Fairlight Voicetracker and IVL Pitchrider also sense the amplitude of the signal, which may be converted into velocity. Microtonal pitch variations may be translated into pitch-bend data.

Guitar controllers come in two forms: Some, like the SynthAxe and Casio MG-510, are designed specifically to generate MIDI data, and make no acoustic sound. Others use a hexaphonic pickup mounted under the strings of a conventional acoustic or electric guitar; the signals from this pickup are run through a bank of six pitch-to-MIDI converters.

Alternate controllers, which may use almost any imaginable physical motion, whether it happens to be "musical" in a conventional sense or not, are beginning to make inroads. Some of the more exotic devices, like Michel Waisvisz' Hands are available only on a custom-made basis. Others are sold commercially. The Palmtree Airdrums are a pair of sticks, shorter and thicker than drumsticks, with built-in motion sensors that generate MIDI when moved horizontally, vertically, or rotationally. The Fast Forward Designs MIDI Step is a one-octave organ pedalboard.

Why worry about a pedalboard when the subject is sequencing? Isn't that a live performance interface for somebody who has their hands full? Sure it is—but maybe you'd like to do live improvisation to a sequenced accompaniment, and you happen to have a sequencer that will transpose its playback in real time in response to a MIDI note input. Just step on the pedal, and you're in a new key.

Computers. Often, the computer will be functioning as the sequencer. But they're useful for many other things, such as patch storage and editing, and there's no law that says you couldn't use a hardware sequencer for sequencing and keep the computer around for other things—even video games.

Drum machines. A drum machine is a sequencer that is optimized for playing its own built-in percussion sounds. Most drum machines these days will both send MIDI notes when they play a sound and play and record their own sounds in response to incoming MIDI notes. By sending MIDI notes from a drum machine, you can layer the internal sounds with other sounds or record the drum part into another sequencer.

And because the drum machine will receive MIDI notes, you don't need to use its internal sequencer at all. In many cases, recording the drum part as one or more tracks within your main sequencer is a better approach. This lets you store the entire song on a single disk and load it at the next session, rather than having to deal with two different devices' memory. The drawback is that many sequencers aren't as slick at recording typical drum patterns as a drum machine is. One, the Roland MC-500, has a special drum pattern mode that gives you the best of both worlds—single disk storage along with some drum machine recording and song-building features.

Assuming that the drum machine sends and receives MIDI clocks, it can also be used as the master timing reference in the studio. This can be especially helpful if the drum machine will generate its own tape sync tone while the sequencer won't. You can sync the drum machine to tape and use its MIDI clock output to keep the

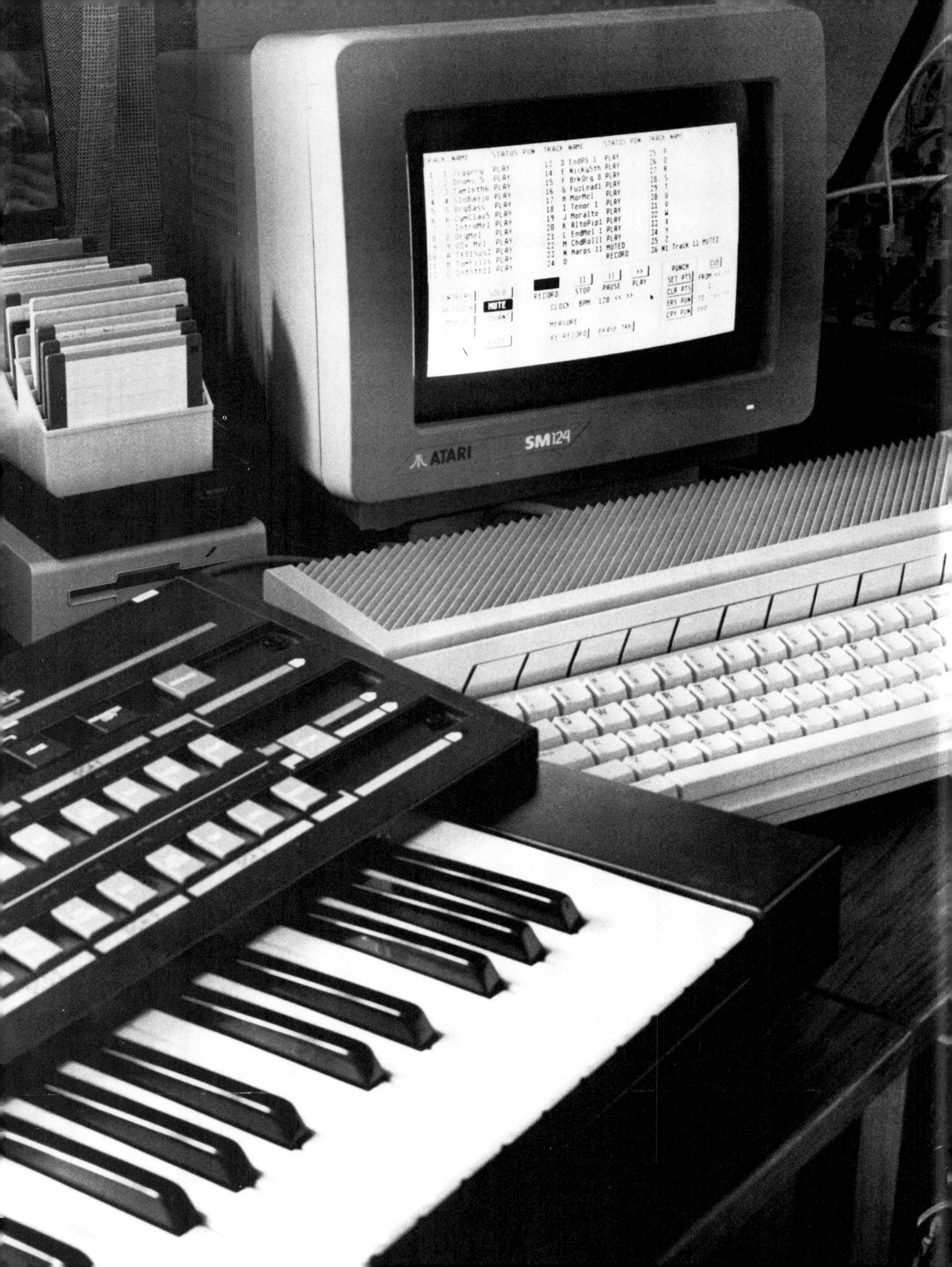

ATARI
SM124
RECORD
STOP
PAUSE
PLAY
PUNCH
CUE

sequencer locked to the tape, whether or not you use the drum sounds. A few drum machines won't transmit MIDI clocks while synced to tape, however, so if this application is important to you, you should learn exactly how the sync functions operate on the drum machine you're looking at before you buy it.

Audio effects. Two types of MIDI audio effects devices must be distinguished —*programmable* and *real-time controllable*. A programmable device has an internal memory in which it stores configurations of front panel settings. These can be recalled instantly by sending the device a MIDI program change command. In a real-time controllable device, the front panel settings can be changed one at a time by sending MIDI controllers or other data to the device. (Most real-time controllable effects are also programmable, and can respond to MIDI program changes.) Real-time controllable effects like the Lexicon PCM-70 tend to be a bit more expensive than straight programmables like the Yamaha SPX90, because more internal operating software has to be developed to run them. But lower-priced units like the Korg DRV-2000 reverb, in which some (though not all) parameters can be controlled in real time, are becoming more common.

The advantage of MIDI-equipped audio effects in a sequencing environment is that automated changes can be made in the sound processing; these changes, being part of the sequence, can be edited and stored on disk. This lets the musician do all kinds of neat tricks, like adding a longer reverb time to the last high note in a phrase, or suddenly cuing in a delay line to add echoes to a single drum hit.

The MIDI effects that are now available do not always respond to program changes or control changes in as smooth and silent a manner as musicians might prefer. It's quite normal, for example, for a digital reverb to "shut off" the reverberant sound while switching to a new program. Because of this, some care must be used to make changes in the effects at moments when the sound will not be disrupted.

Automated mixers and attenuators. Until a couple of years ago, automated mixing was exclusively the domain of megabucks studios. MIDI has changed all that. For the first time, a musician working in a home studio on a relatively modest budget can do detailed automated mixes using MIDI. The convenience that this affords to musicians is inestimable.

Two types of devices are currently available in this category—MIDI mixers and MIDI attenuation systems. The difference is that a mixer accepts a number of audio inputs (such as eight or 16) and provides a two-channel stereo output. An attenuation system provides MIDI automation, but not mixing. If it has eight inputs, it also has eight outputs; these must then be patched into an ordinary audio mixer. Other factors being equal, attenuation systems tend to be less expensive than mixers.

As with effects devices, some mixers and attenuators are programmable and some are both programmable and real-time controllable. A programmable mixer may have a programmable cross-fade time, during which the controls will move from their old values to the ones required by the new program. Cross-fade time may be global (that is, all the programmable settings will be governed by it), or it may be programmable on a per-patch or per-input-channel basis.

Automated mixing poses some special problems in sequencer design. When a tune is started in the middle, the sequencer must be able to update all of the mixer or attenuator channels to the settings that they were given after the last control change, or the music will sound drastically wrong. Nevertheless, just about any MIDI sequencer can be used with any MIDI mixing/attenuation system, as long as you're willing to do a certain amount of fiddling with the data.

MIDI-to-computer interfaces. Only one computer, the Atari ST series, comes equipped with its own MIDI jacks. All other computers must be equipped with a MIDI interface of some sort in order to be used for sequencing. In general, you should find the sequencer software you want, and then buy whatever interface is recommended for it. Not all interfaces that are designed for a given computer will work with all of the software that runs on that computer, so beware. Some computers have no MIDI interfaces built for them, and thus no MIDI software either.

Some interfaces are very simple, consisting of no more than a couple of MIDI jacks wired into whatever connector will plug into the computer. Others have a variety of features, such as tape sync or SMPTE sync in and out jacks, multiple output jacks to which individual tracks can be assigned, and built-in metronomes. The IBM Music Feature, an interface card that plugs into the IBM PC, even has its own eight-voice synthesizer (a Yamaha FB-01) built-in.

MIDI routing devices and data massagers. As long as you've only got two MIDI-equipped devices, you can connect them with a single pair of MIDI cables and never have to worry about where the MIDI data is being routed. But once you get five or six instruments, you're liable to spend almost as much time peering at their back panels with a flashlight as you do playing music, trying to figure out which jack is the in and which is the thru, and cursing the idiot who thought it was cute to mount the jacks sideways.

A whole host of handy devices has been developed to make life in the MIDI tangle easier. Many of these are programmable; that is, you can reconfigure your MIDI routings by sending a single patch change command to the routing box. A *switcher* has several inputs and several outputs, and lets you send any in to any out. An out can only be fed by a single in, however. To send two ins to the same out, you must have a *merger*.

In addition to straight merging and switching, many of these devices perform secondary tasks, such as rechannelizing (also called *channel bumping*, because the number of the channel is "bumped" up or down) and data filtering. Some designs go even further. The Yamaha MCS2, for example, has built-in wheels and sliders for generating and sending controller information.

The Axxess Unlimited Mapper and Oberheim Perf/x series (Systemizer, Navigator, and Cyclone) all perform many types of data translation, including things like turning a single MIDI key into a programmable chord.

MIDI-to-CV interfaces. Remember all of that old analog synthesis gear you've got stashed on the shelf in the garage? Want to do a little MIDI sequencing with it? Several items of equipment are available that convert MIDI data into a form that a Minimoog or ARP 2600 can use.

One of the most versatile is the Roland MPU-101, which will receive monophonically on four channels or polyphonically on one channel and put out control voltages, gates, and key velocity values for each of four notes, as well as global voltages (one each for the whole unit) for pitch-bend amount, modulation amount, and channel pressure. It can even be used to divide MIDI clocks by various factors to sync up an arpeggiator or analog sequencer.

Built-in MIDI modifications are available for some older instruments.

Synchronization devices. If routing MIDI data, which is all in a single electronic format, poses occasional challenges, getting devices to talk to one another when each sends and receives a different type of sync signal is often a nightmare. If your sequencer and drum machine don't speak the same language, and the tape deck won't listen to either of them, or if you're trying to sync the sequencer to something *really* weird like a human being, you'll need a sync box.

The simplest sync boxes are devices like the Yamaha YMC-10, which does nothing but translate FSK into MIDI clocks and vice-versa. If your sequencer (like many Atari ST software sequencers) only understands MIDI clocks, you'll need something of this sort to get it to sync to tape. Nearly as affordable, and lots more convenient, are newer units like the JL Cooper PPS-1 and SynHance MTS-1, both of which send time-stamped FSK tones that let the sequencer chase-lock to the middle of a long tune (assuming that it can receive song position pointer).

Garfield Electronics has specialized in synchronization interfaces, from their first Doctor Click to a whole line of devices with specialized uses. The Garfield Master Beat and the Kahler Human Clock are both designed to translate an audio pulse, such as the sound of a snare drum played into a microphone, into MIDI clock data. More sophisticated devices like the Master Beat, the Garfield Time Commander, and the Roland SBX-80 allow the user to define a "tempo map" of tempo changes, or to generate one themselves by memorizing an audio pulse coming from a tape track. And then there are the SMPTE sync machines....

Synchronization is far too complex an application for us to deal with it in detail here. It's beginning to look as if time-stamping of some sort is going to become nearly universal within a couple of years, but that doesn't mean that older, simpler systems are useless. It's still possible to make fantastic music with simple means; you just have to put out a little extra effort.

Beyond Sequencing

By Jim Aikin

T he sequencer is a passive beast. It faithfully records our input exactly as we play it, or as close to exactly as its timing resolution allows; and it performs on the stored data exactly the manipulations we request, no more and no less—assuming that it's working properly.

But there are other musical tasks that we might want a computer-based device to execute. We might, for instance, want it to become an *active* participant in the process of generating notes.

What do we mean by 'active'? That's up to the programmers who create this revolutionary software. Each of them has his or her own ideas about what the computer might be called on to do.

Usually, people think of computer-generated music—if they think of it at all—as a highly abstract sound sculpture created by having the machine select pitches, rhythms, and so on entirely at random. Randomness is an important ingredient in some machine-generated music, true, but the randomness needn't *sound* random. In fact, the software is probably working better (or the musician is using it better) if the randomness is controlled in very specific ways.

A computer doesn't create music entirely on its own. The musician specifies the large-scale features of a musical passage, and then lets the computer fill in the details, drawing on random number tables and other mathematical sources and processes, which are applied to the human-supplied source material in various ways.

If we don't want to go this far, if we don't want the machine to generate anything on its own, we can still use it in various ways to carry out our wishes in an automated fashion. Here again, the musician provides the large-scale features, such as a chord played on a MIDI keyboard or a movement of some controller, and the machine fills in the details according to whatever guidelines it has been provided. Most of us have seen a simple version of this concept at work in the lowly arpeggiator. The musician, in this case, provides an input by holding down the keys of a sustained chord, and the computer fills in the details by playing the chord notes one after another in some predetermined pattern and with some predetermined rhythm.

Whether we control the computer's output more or less strictly, the audible result—usually a string of notes—is a joint effort of human and machine. The question, then, is this: How do we teach the machine to do mechanically what we ourselves do so effortlessly? How do we teach it to create passages that will sound meaningful to our listeners rather than sounding like machine-generated gibberish? If we're going to ask it to spit out all these notes, how do we teach it to choose notes that we'll like?

We can approach answering this question in at least three ways: First, we can ask, What patterns of notes do listeners find meaningful? What exactly constitutes a 'musical' as opposed to 'unmusical' result? This is a question of esthetics, and composers and music theorists have been examining it for hundreds of years—often disagreeing vehemently with one another, too. An easier approach is to ask, What kinds of alterations or augmentations of our input can we manage to get the computer to execute in a reasonably expeditious manner? If we're adventurous, we can look beyond the first two questions to ask a third: What new kinds of satisfying music might we discover using the processes that the computer makes available to us, that we would never discover otherwise?

Taking too narrow an esthetic view—that we only want the computer to perform data manipulations that we have already identified as being used by composers and meaningful to listeners—is bound to be restricting, as well as difficult to teach to the computer. But going in the opposite direction, simply accepting as musically satisfying whatever passagework the computer happens to come up with during its oh-so-sophisticated data-shuffling routines, is an invitation to triviality. The goal is at the apex of the triangle that has those two points at the corners of its base.

The first generation of music-generating software tips its hat in the direction of identifying musically meaningful parameters and operations, often with startlingly beautiful results, but a lot more development remains to be done. If you're willing to throw together some code that you think musicians *might* find meaningful, and toss it out into the marketplace to see if anybody likes it, you're more likely to finish writing your program in a single lifetime. The question of what might *become* musically meaningful is up to the users of the software, of course, and to their listeners, not to the programmers, though programmers rely on feedback from users, and may have some shrewd esthetic ideas of their own as well.

If programmers' musical predilections are important in sequencer design, they become a central issue in software that goes beyond sequencing. The programmer and the composer/performer are collaborators, and it is going to get harder to determine which of them makes the more important contribution to a finished piece.

Christopher Yavelow makes some trenchant observations about this fact in his paper "Composition Or Improvisation?" in *The Proceedings Of The AES 5th International Conference*. "Fifteen years ago," he observes, "Music Mouse would have been considered an aleatoric composition by Laurie Spiegel, albeit of indeterminate length, orchestration, and melodic contour.... But this is 1987 and she chose to release the program as a software composition tool. In creating this new type of interrelationship between composer, software author, and performer, she has made a dramatic statement about the definition of music composition...." He mentions the idea that composers will develop their own "style templates" in the form of disk-stored setup configurations for particular music software programs.

But if it takes ten years to learn to play the violin in a deeply expressive way, it may take ten years to learn to play Jam Factory with as much virtuosity. We're not there yet; we're still twiddling with a lot of exciting possibilities whose expressive implications are still unclear.

The programs we'll be looking at here will all spit out endless streams of fresh-sounding notes. (A lot of the initial excitement of working with an interactive music program comes from the unpredictability of its sound.) Except for Music Mouse, they'll also do lots of intriguing high-level data manipulations that may or may not ever produce musical results that anybody will care about listening to. We're still investigating the question, "What can we get a computer to do by way of generating music?" The question, "What might we *want* the computer to do?" involves such tangled questions of musical form and substance that it may be years before we see software that addresses it effectively. Rumors are flying, about new programs with even more exotic capabilities. Rather than make any more generalizations—since we don't have enough of a base at this stage to draw valid ones—let's just take a look at some of the leading programs for generating music.

Music Mouse. Once a computer was equipped with a free-floating two-dimensional controller—the Macintosh mouse —it was probably inevitable that sooner or later somebody would think of playing music directly through mouse movements. Music Mouse (written by Laurie Spiegel and currently marketed by Opcode Systems) does precisely this. It's a simple, easily learned program, and lacks the kind of user-definable parameters that would make it truly open-ended. Even so, it's a kick to play, and it has some surprisingly original options that point the way (we hope) toward bigger and better things to come.

The Music Mouse screen is simply a two-dimensional grid with a piano-type keyboard along the X axis and an identical keyboard along the Y axis. The position of the mouse cursor is always somewhere on this grid. When the mouse moves to a new position, the notes corresponding to that position are sent out over MIDI.

Actually, that's an oversimplification, because Music Mouse generates four notes

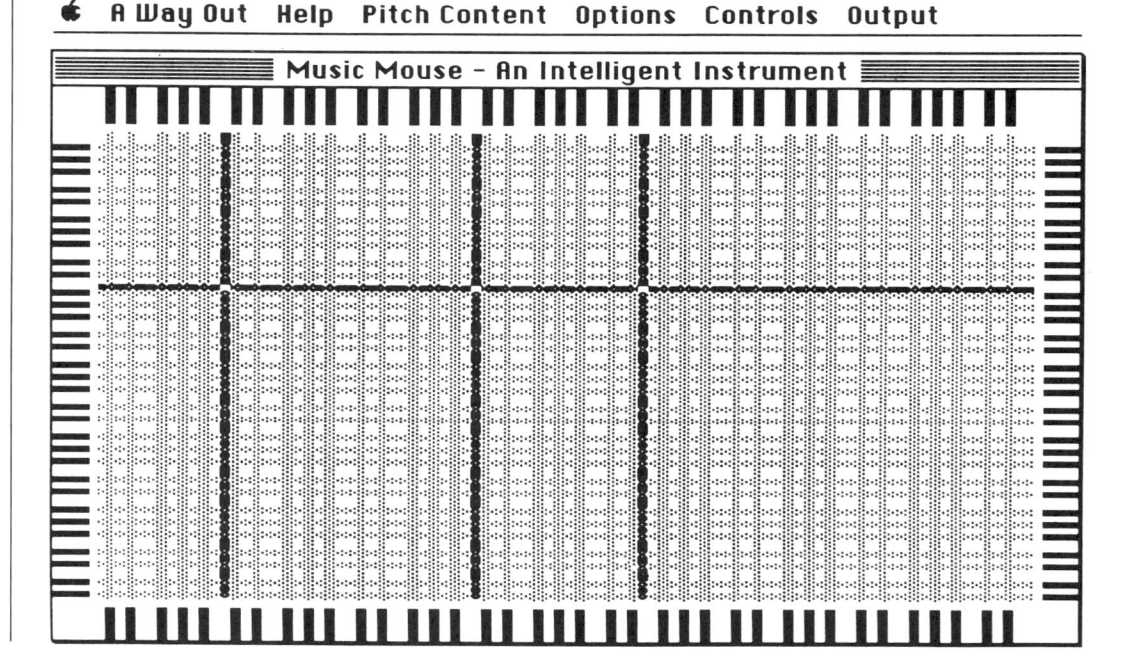

Figure 1. Opcode's Music Mouse, for the Mac.

at a time, not two. The relationships among these are preset: either three notes on the horizontal axis, arranged in an open-voiced root-position triad, or two notes each on the horizontal and vertical, arranged in intervals of a fifth and sixth. Instead of parallel intervals, you can switch the program to play lines in contrary motion. But, as with many parameters in Music Mouse, there is no way to assign your own intervals for parallel playing.

A grid in which all 12 tones of the scale were available at all times would be good mainly for highly chromatic and frankly atonal music. To get around this problem (or maybe we should say over the top of it), Music Mouse offers a set of six harmonic grids—full chromatic, a diatonic scale (the white keys), a pentatonic scale, a continuous cycle of open fourths, and a scale described as "Middle Eastern." Some user-definable harmonic grids would be a dynamite addition to the program.

If you move the mouse continuously, notes will be sent out in a steady rhythm. The pitch played will depend on what point in the grid the mouse happens to be at when the software "reads" its position. The rhythm can be sped up or slowed down using the computer's keyboard, but there is no way to synchronize the Music Mouse clock to any other clock source.

Quite a number of performance options can be selected from the computer keyboard with one hand while "playing" the mouse with the other. You can increase or decrease the MIDI velocity of the notes (all four will have the same velocity at any given time, however), as well as MIDI mod wheel, breath controller, after-touch, and foot controller values. You can change from legato to staccato articulation (only two values here). You can step up or down through MIDI program change numbers, and transpose the output in half-steps or return it to C. Using the computer keys to adjust these values is easy to learn, and adds a great deal to the expressiveness of the music.

You can also tell Music Mouse to send out notes even when you aren't moving the mouse. This wouldn't sound like much, of course, if the computer only sent out, over and over, the notes corresponding to the current mouse position. So a selection of ten melodic patterns is included. These are not defined in half-steps but in multiples of scale steps (which could be as wide as a fourth, if you've selected the fourths grid), so they tend to sound more interesting than you might think. As with the four "starting positions" of the note cursors, the filler patterns can move in parallel or contrary motion. Here again, the program needs to be developed so as to include user-definable fillers.

The idea behind Music Mouse is a highly general one—to have the computer spin out notes (whose patterns have been defined in advance) in response to real-time gestural input from the musician. A pair of large joysticks, track balls, or touch tablets that each put out different MIDI controller messages along their X and Y axes might be a better user interface than the mouse, and a program set up to respond to four (or more) controllers at once could do arbitrarily complex things. We might want to map one of the controllers to velocity instead of note choice—or to both. Or to the playback tempo of some pre-recorded material. The possibilities, as they like to say in music software advertising, are limitless.

Unlike the programs we'll be looking at in this article, there is nothing random about Music Mouse music. Nor is there any data storage. It is quite simply a performing instrument.

Fingers. Four monophonic voices seems to be about the lower limit for music of acceptable complexity. (Yeah, I know about the Bach *Suites* for unaccompanied cello. They're wonderful. They're also written with a great deal of implied polyphony.) Like Music Mouse, Fingers is a four-voice program, and it allows the user to interact with it while it is generating notes.

But there the similarity ends. Fingers lets the user specify the computer's source material in four areas: pitch, rhythm, duration, and velocity. To see how the system works, let's look at a single voice. The voice has four markers, one each for pitch, rhythm, duration, and velocity. The markers advance through on-screen lists of values. (Yes, it's a typical Dr. T program: The whole screen is filled with tiny numbers.) Each marker advances one step through a list each time the voice plays a note. When it reaches a loop (repeat) command, it jumps back to the top of the list.

What makes Fingers so interesting is, first, that the lists of values can all be of different lengths. That is, a voice could be cycling through a loop of four pitches, five rhythm values, three accents (velocity), and eleven different staccato/legato duration articulations, all at the same time. In this case, it would repeat the entire pattern once every 660 notes. And that's just one of the four voices.

Once you've got the voices going, there's no need to let them keep repeating without variation. You can enter new values at any time, either by typing them in or by playing them on a MIDI keyboard. You can open up and close off parts of the various lists, again interactively, while the music is playing, so as to guide a marker naturally into a new area of pitches or articulations, or move any marker instantly to any point with a single click of the mouse button. Voices can be muted, unmuted, and transposed individually. They can be assigned to separate MIDI channels, and new program numbers can be sent out.

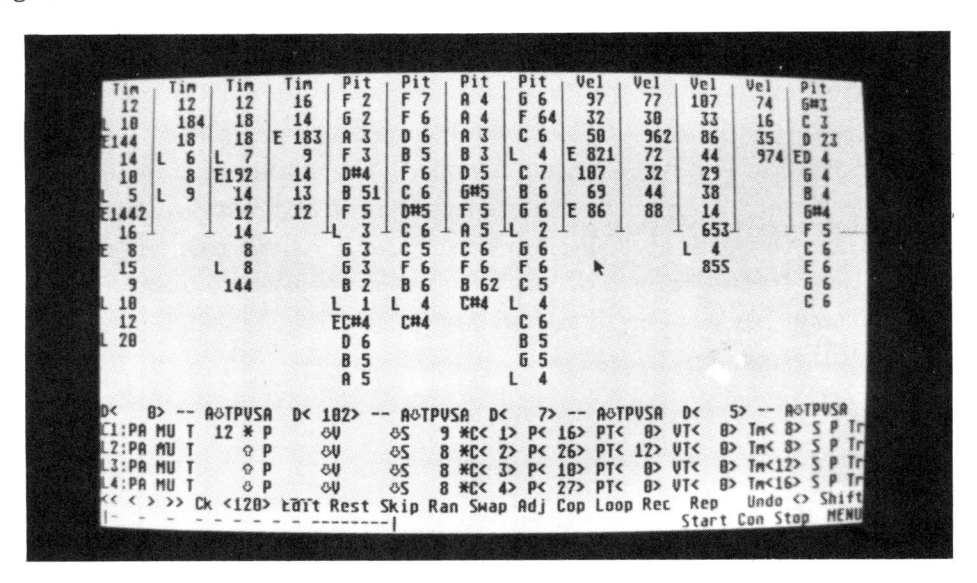

Figure 2. Dr. T's Fingers, for the Atari ST.

The program is not without limitations: The voices are monophonic, which lends Fingers a "note-y," meandering sound. The textures that are produced tend, at least in my halting preliminary experiments, to be longer on repetition than on broad, sweeping variation. Also, the rhythmic elements of the voices have a tendency to get out of sync with one another when you start doing much screen input.

Lists of values can be stored to disk. Just as interesting is the fact that Fingers is always recording its output in a format compatible with Dr. T's Keyboard Controlled Sequencer. By storing this output file to disk, you can turn your improvisations into editable sequencer music.

Jam Factory. A software company called Intelligent Music has become a leader in the field of real-time interactive improvising software by introducing no less than three programs for the Macintosh—Jam Factory, M, and Upbeat. They share some

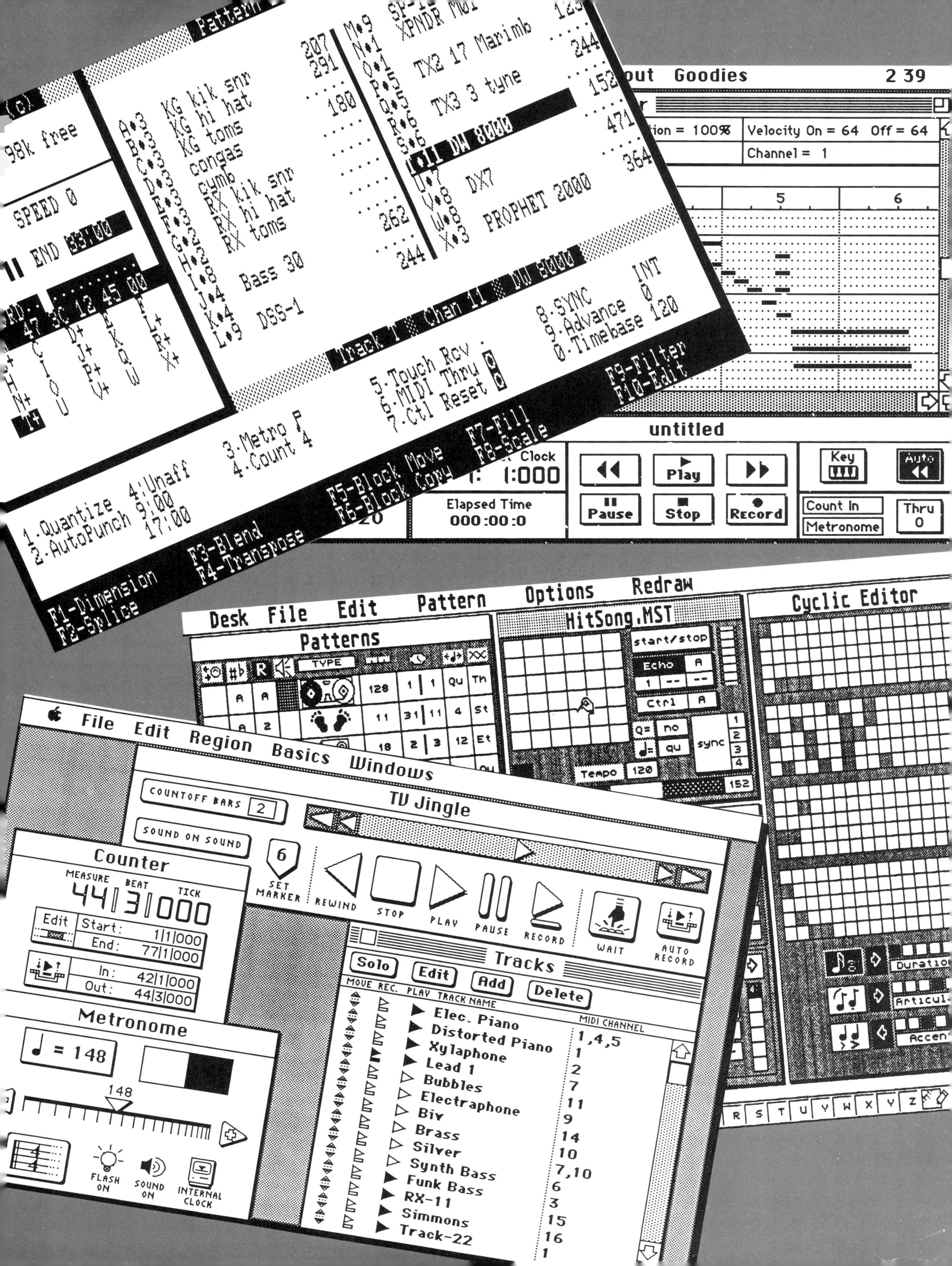

Pattern
98k free
SPEED 0
END
A•3 KG kik snr
B•3 KG hi hat
C•3 KG toms
D•3 congas
E•3 cymb
F•3 RX kik snr
G•2 RX hi hat
H•2 RX toms
I•8
J•4 Bass 30
K•4
L•9 DSS-1
XPNDR M01
TX2 17 Marimb
TX3 3 tyne
DW 8000
DX7
PROPHET 2000
Track 1
Chan 11
1.Quantize
2.AutoPunch
3.Metro
4.Count 4
4:Unaff
5.Touch Rcv
6.MIDI Thru
7.Ctl Reset
8.SYNC INT
9.Advance 0
0.Timebase 120
F1-Dimension
F2-Splice
F3-Blend
F4-Transpose
F5-Block Move
F6-Block Copy
F7-Fill
F8-Scale
F9-Filter
F10-Edit
Goodies
2 39
Velocity On = 64 Off = 64
Channel = 1
untitled
Clock
1:000
Play
Pause
Stop
Record
Elapsed Time
000:00:0
Key
Auto
Count In
Metronome
Thru
0
Desk File Edit Pattern Options Redraw
Patterns
TYPE
HitSong.MST
start/stop
Echo
Ctrl
sync
Tempo 120
Cyclic Editor
Duration
File Edit Region Basics Windows
COUNTOFF BARS 2
SOUND ON SOUND
TV Jingle
SET MARKER
REWIND
STOP
PLAY
PAUSE
RECORD
WAIT
AUTO RECORD
Counter
MEASURE BEAT TICK
44|3|000
Edit
Start: 1|1|000
End: 77|1|000
In: 42|1|000
Out: 44|3|000
Metronome
♩ = 148
148
FLASH ON
SOUND ON
INTERNAL CLOCK
Tracks
Solo
Edit
Add
Delete
MOVE REC. PLAY TRACK NAME
MIDI CHANNEL
Elec. Piano 1,4,5
Distorted Piano 1
Xylaphone 2
Lead 1 7
Bubbles 11
Electraphone 9
Biv 14
Brass 10
Silver 7,10
Synth Bass 6
Funk Bass 3
RX-11 15
Simmons 16
Track-22 1

broad outlines in common, but each has features not found in the others. Jam Factory was written by David Zicarelli.

Like Fingers and Music Mouse, Jam Factory is designed to send a MIDI output from up to four "players" at a time. These are not monophonic, however; each player can play chords. The raw material that each player will use is entered from a MIDI keyboard, and is then varied in whatever ways the user specifies using the on-screen controls. These controls are live at all times, so the musician can generate a piece of improvised music that changes in a number of precisely controlled ways, while allowing the computer to choose the actual order of the notes and a few other things. Among other performance parameters, duration and velocity cycles of up to 16 steps can be defined by the musician, as can the probability that notes will be skipped instead of being played.

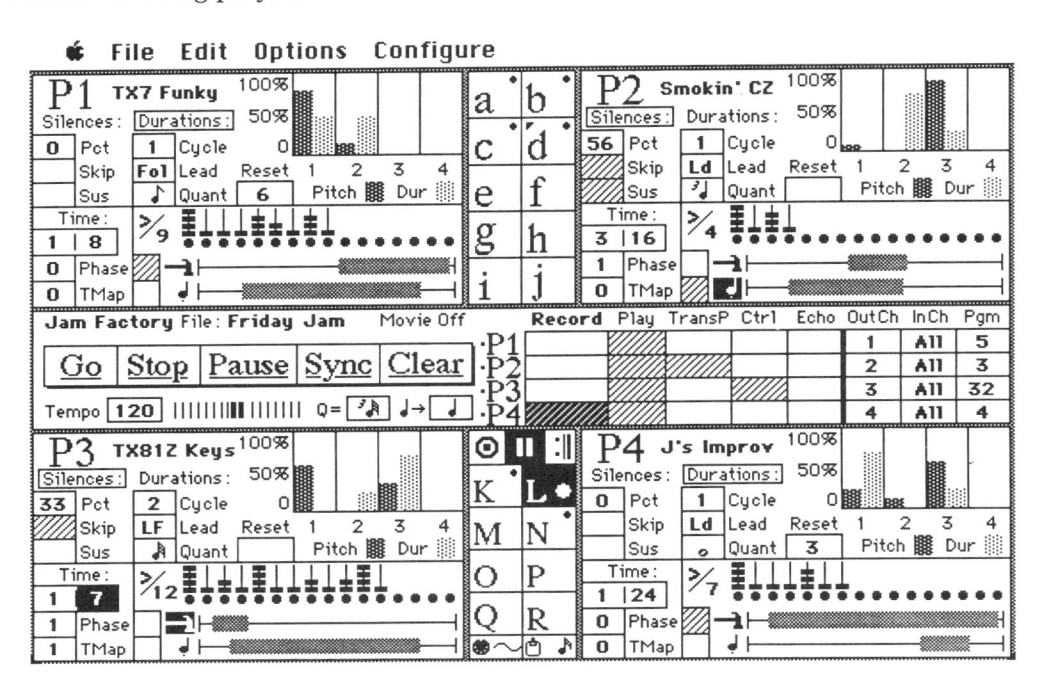

Figure 3. Intelligent Music's Jam Factory, for the Macintosh.

At a higher level, Jam Factory lets you store up to ten presets, each of which contains all of the current front panel settings. Any preset can be recalled during playback. You can also use any of the eight "macros" to record control changes as you're making them. Playing back a macro will recall all of your moves (even calling up presets or changing the transposition from a MIDI keyboard), complete with their timing. Macros don't contain notes, however, so a macro may sound different each time you use it, depending on what notes the players are choosing. An entire Jam Factory performance can be stored on disk as a MIDI file and edited in any sequencer program capable of reading these files.

A player in Jam Factory selects notes not randomly but using a mathematical algorithm called a transition table. The table stores all of the transitions made by your input between one note and another, and how often each transition occurs—for example, how often you went from C to D as opposed to from C to G. Explaining transition tables in detail would take more space than we have here; suffice it to say that you can have the player's output resemble your input quite closely, or be fairly jumbled, and that the transition table algorithm will help the program make note choices that are somewhat sensible in terms of how humans understand melody.

You can set up time distortion maps, which result in a wide variety of irregular rhythms, and scale distortion maps, which cause transpositions to be non-linear. You can also program eight "control presets," which will change the state of certain buttons for the four players whenever a user-specified MIDI event is received. For example, you could switch players 2 and 4 out of playback mode and into record mode by moving the pitch-bend wheel on your MIDI keyboard.

M. At first glance, M appears to be quite similar to Jam Factory. Each of them has four "players" and provides large-scale control over variations in velocity, duration, and rhythm, together with some output controls such as transposition and the ability to send patch changes.

But in place of Jam Factory's global presets, which store every setting for all four players, M provides a set of six independent presets within each parameter area. For example, there are six transposition presets, each of which contains transposition values for all four players. Six note percentage presets store the likelihood (from 0 percent to 100 percent) that individual notes will sound or be silent during playback—and again, each preset stores a separate percentage for each of the four players. Other sets of six presets are found in areas like velocity range, randomness of note order, output channel, patch number, and non-random cyclic pattern of rhythm, articulation, and velocity.

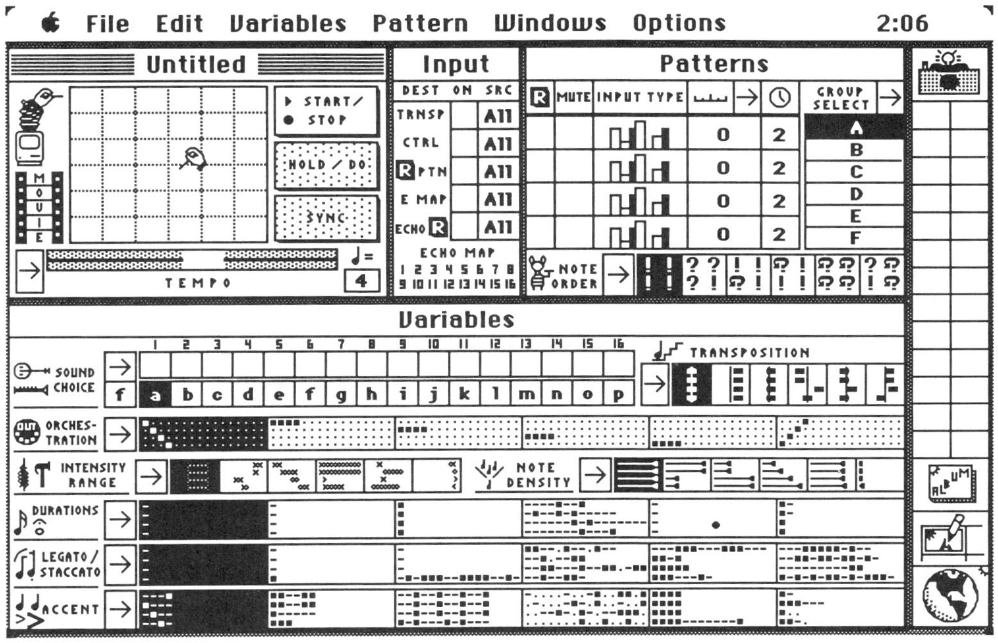

Figure 4. Intelligent Music's M, for the Mac.

The players themselves store not one set of notes but six different sets. All four players have to play from the same "bank"; that is, when the musician switches to bank B, each player starts using the notes that it has stored in its own area of bank B. The players don't share notes. But the user can switch from one bank to another at any time.

Each bank of notes for each player can be recorded in one of several different ways—with rhythms in real time, or in step mode, or in a repeating loop somewhat like a drum machine pattern. A MIDI file of notes can also be ported in as a single pattern. While a player is playing, you can shorten its pattern to just a few notes, or open it out to its full length. The note content of a pattern can be edited in some limited ways.

You can switch manually from one preset to another in any area, or you can manually edit the values in the current preset, all without interrupting playback. At a higher level of complexity, you can improvise a performance in M by moving the visual cursor around a "conducting grid." This 6 x 6 grid has no fixed meaning. Instead, you can assign any of the banks of six presets to any direction within the grid (up, down, left, or right). Thus the conducting grid lets you make sweeping coordinated changes in several aspects of the sound at one time. You could be moving simultaneously from more note randomness to less, while increasing the amount of velocity variation and selecting some rhythm patterns with longer cycles. Tempo can also be conducted from the grid, and the amount of change from lowest to highest tempo can be precisely controlled.

M does not record performances consisting of control moves like Jam Factory's macros. However, it does record the actual notes played and store them as MIDI files. It also has a global preset memory in the form of 26 "snapshots" of all screen controls, which can be stored and recalled at any time. Transposition from a MIDI keyboard is also possible.

The M conducting grid is a unique performance interface, and M lets more phrases of note material be recorded at a time. Its ability to do repeating cycles of various interlocking lengths is better developed than the cyclic features of Jam Factory. Having independent presets for each parameter type opens up far more combinations. And being able to send a single player out three MIDI channels at once, each with its own program changes, allows for much more complex orchestrations. So the fact that M doesn't have Jam Factory's time distortion, scale distortion, or macro features is probably an even trade.

Programmable Variations Generator. And now for something completely different. All of the programs we've been looking at so far are designed for real-time interactive music-making—in other words, for machine-assisted improvisation. The

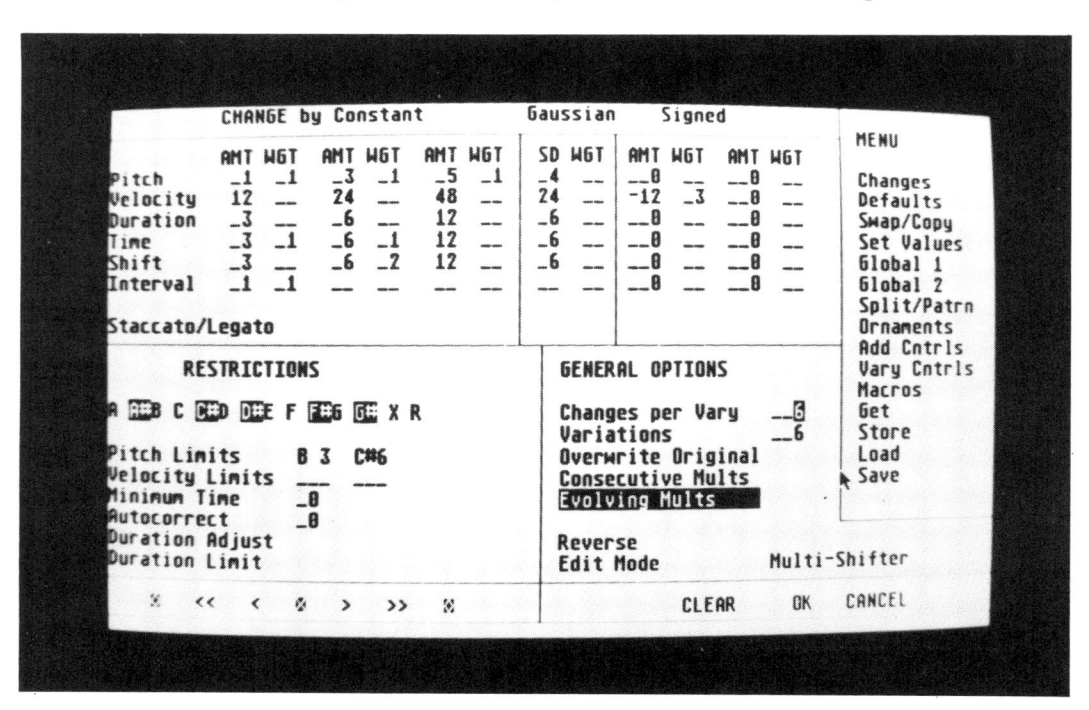

Figure 5. One of the screens from Dr. T's Programmable Variations Generator, an optional module for the Keyboard Controlled Sequencer for the Atari ST.

Programmable Variations Generator (PVG) from Dr. T's Music Software is a non-real-time program. It's an adjunct to Dr. T's Keyboard Controlled Sequencer (KCS) for the Atari ST. The PVG lets the user give the computer complex instructions for generating random (or non-random) variations on an already recorded track or sequence. The results of a PVG operation are stored onto a new track, just like any other material recorded in the sequencer, and can be edited or discarded as desired.

The PVG can be instructed to choose a certain number of notes at random within a track, while the user protects certain notes (puts them off limits) on the basis of their pitch, channel, duration, position at the beginning or end of the track, etc. For each randomly selected note, changes can be made in pitch, duration, velocity, channel, or several other parameters. These changes can be of specified interval size, or the size can be left random as well, or the change can consist of assigning the note to some user-specified value.

The program can swap values from one note to another within a track, rotate values "around the circle" of a group of consecutive notes, reverse selected values in a region, all while choosing the region for itself randomly, or import whole chunks of data from other tracks and insert them at random points. It can select notes at random to erase. Wholly determined changes can also be made to all unprotected notes, which falls more in the domain of editing than of random music generation.

The PVG contains an ornament generator, which will add new notes (whose relative pitch and time can be specified) to randomly selected notes in a track, or to all unprotected notes. It can make a number of different variations at a time, storing them one after another on the same track so that a continually evolving phrase is generated. It also contains a powerful macro feature, which can perform either random or determined actions on notes based on where they fall in the beat or in the bar. For example, you could set up a track containing a continuous sixteenth-note drone on a single pitch, and instruct the PVG to replace the sixteenth-notes on beats two and four of every bar with randomly selected notes. A macro can perform a number of separate operations on the entire track, or perform them sequentially on parts of the track. It can even select some operations at random from the macro list, and perform these.

Unlike the real-time programs, the Programmable Variations Generator can probably yield effective musical results long before the user learns all of its features, because its primary application is not creating music from scratch, but making changes in music that the composer has already created. You could compose a whole piece note for note and just use PVG for adding a few unpredictable accents to a hi-hat rhythm, for example.

What makes it more difficult to use, aside from the sheer number of operations that are possible, is that it is not optimized, the way Jam Factory and Music Mouse are, to produce an "acceptable" output. Improvising programs pretty much have to be able to generate plausible music "out of the box," while PVG operations, which have fewer built-in restrictions, seem often to lead to more exotic-sounding phrases.

============================ Note Edit ============================

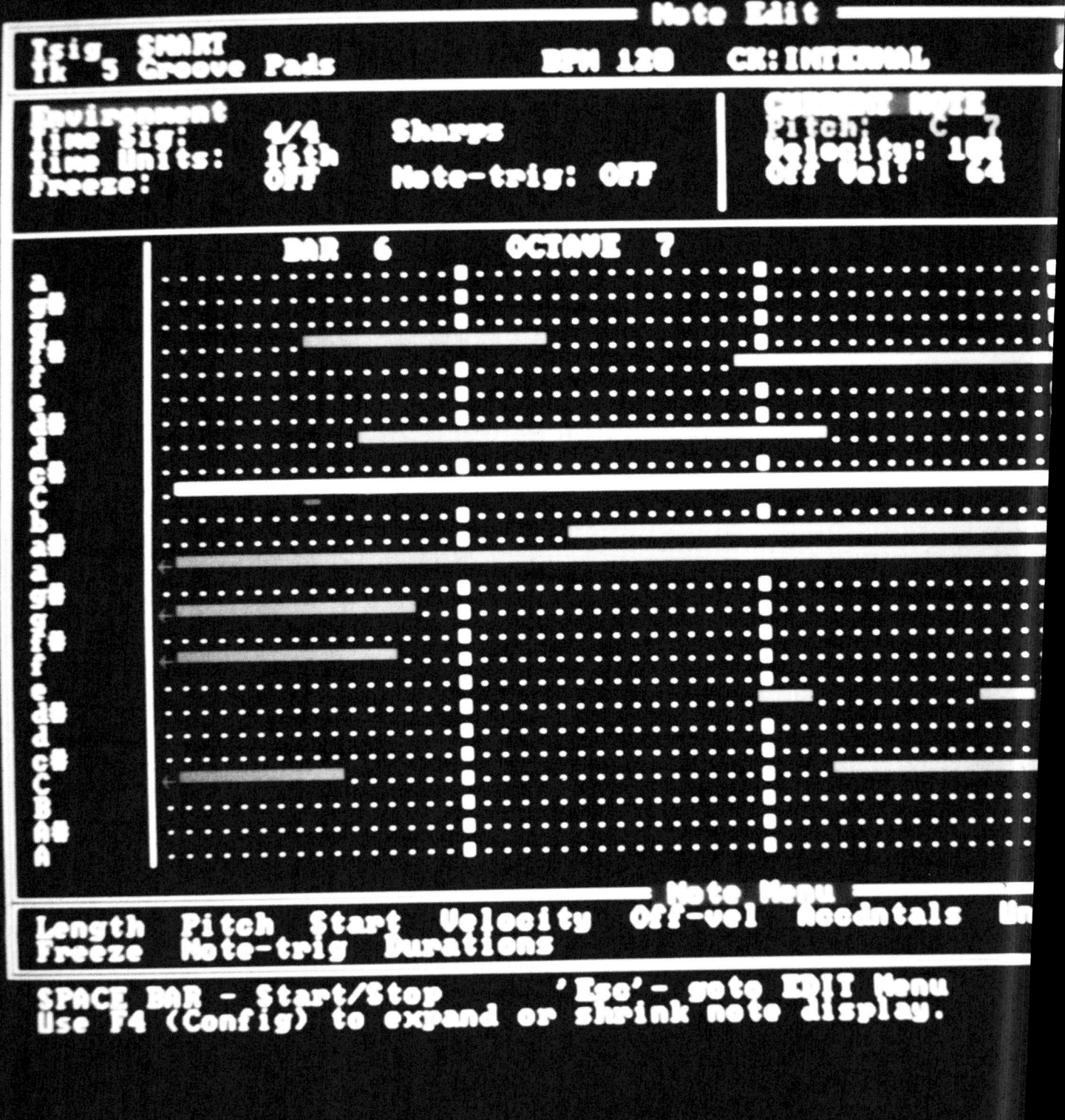

Tsig SMART
Tk 5 Groove Pads   BPM 120   CK: INTERNAL

Environment   CURRENT NOTE
Time Sig: 1/4   Sharps   Pitch: C 7
Time Units: 16th   Velocity: 100
Freeze: OFF   Note-trig: OFF   Off Vel: 64

              BAR 6   OCTAVE 7

============================ Note Menu ============================
Length   Pitch   Start   Velocity   Off-vel   Accdntals   U
Freeze   Note-trig   Durations

SPACE BAR - Start/Stop   'Esc' - goto EDIT Menu
Use F4 (Config) to expand or shrink note display.

Product
Reviews

Introduction

By Michael Marans

Back in the days before MIDI was king, deciding which sequencer to purchase was a simple matter. Either you wanted the one that was available for your instrument or you didn't. Nowadays, a fair number of hours can be, and for your own sake should be, spent before making a buying decision. The first consideration is whether your needs are best suited by a hardware device, or a computer-based software program.

Hardware sequencers have the advantage of being easily transported (making them ideal for live performance), and since they are designed for specific functionality, offer dedicated buttons and controls. Unfortunately, you may have to suffer with a small LCD display, limited editing parameters, and (in some cases) a lack of ability to upgrade the operating system. In addition, since a hardware sequencer is in essence a dedicated computer, you will generally pay a higher price for these devices than for a software program, though less than for software plus a computer.

If you already own a reasonably high-powered computer (Macintosh, Atari ST, Amiga, or IBM PC), a software sequencer can not only save you money, but may also provide greater power, speed, and functionality. A computer's video screen is ideal for displaying large amounts of sequence data, and if you're familiar with your computer, it's possible that you will be able to minimize the time spent learning the sequencing program.

Once you have decided which type of sequencer to purchase, it's time to start looking at the specific capabilities you need both for your present applications and future system expansion. Do you need extensive editing parameters? Do you need to have your sequencer synchronize to SMPTE time code for film and/or video work? What about multiple MIDI outputs for especially dense arrangements?

Less product-specific but equally important considerations include manufacturer support, service and update policies, and the best test of all: customer satisfaction. Ask your store salesperson to let you work with the sequencer before you buy it. It's one thing to watch an expert zip through numerous esoteric functions with seeming ease, and quite another to perform the same functions yourself. Any first-class music store should have no qualms about giving you time to test-drive a program before committing to a purchase.

There are numerous programs and hardware devices currently available, and with each passing day the number of choices increases. Space does not permit us to present all of the products on the market, but the few included here are typical of the wide assortment of sequencers you can expect to find at the local music store. A program's inclusion in this section should not be construed to be an endorsement, nor should an omission be considered a warning to avoid it.

We've included both hardware devices and software programs for the most popular computers and just for good measure, two programs that fall on the outer fringes of the sequencer realm: Finale, a music notation program, and Ludwig, an algorithmic composition program. You'll notice marked similarities among the devices and programs, but the differences will also be strikingly clear. Take note of the features you think will be essential for your particular applications, and also of those you find intriguing and want to know more about. This will help you make an educated, informed choice; the best way to ensure that you'll be getting the sequencer that's right for you.

C-Lab Creator: Sequencer Software For The Atari ST

By Jim Aikin

Rumors had been circulating for several months about the C-Lab sequencer, which was supposedly making quite a splash in Europe, where it originated. So as soon as the company lined up U.S. distribution (through Digidesign), we pounced on a review copy. Sequencers for the Atari ST are flying thick and fast these days, so we were naturally curious what would make this one stand out from the pack.

The rumors are true. Basically, Creator is just dripping with features. It offers (as an option) four MIDI output jacks, each with 16 channels for 64-channel operation. Its pattern/song playback architecture lets you play up to four independent lists of patterns at once—and if that doesn't provide enough structural complexity for you, you can set each of the tracks within each pattern to loop independently. The event editing utilities are among the best developed we've ever seen. The controller editing commands include both multiplication and translation. The program has a couple of exotic record modes and some unusual types of quantization. Operations are elegant, and visual feedback is maximal. We did have a few minor quibbles, but there's no question that Creator is a thoroughly professional sequencer. It has the kind of spectacular design that leaves your basic garden-variety sequencer looking a little green by comparison.

Overview. As we just mentioned, Creator is a pattern/song sequencer, with 99 patterns (each containing 16 tracks) that can be assembled into an "arrangement" list. The arrangement list is quite unusual in that it's four independent layers deep. This allows you to do things like recording a single long lead line in one pattern that flows across several other accompaniment patterns. Or you could load and store drum patterns to disk separately, and put them on a layer of their own. Naturally, Creator will let you record a long pattern while playing back several shorter ones in order from the arrangement list. In effect, then, you can record into any pattern while monitoring any combination of other patterns.

Only one arrangement can be in memory at a time. This might seem to be a limitation for those who need to have a whole set on call at once, but there are two ways around the problem. Essentially, you can slice the arrangement into chunks, so that a single arrangement list could actually contain a number of independent pieces of music. You can insert pattern 0 at any point within the list to serve as a stop mark, and continue with a new song at the next entry in the list. You could also set up four independent pieces in the four layers, since each layer can be muted or unmuted independently. And that's only the beginning of the goodies in the arrangement section, which we'll delve into more fully below.

One extremely nice point about Creator is that both the arrangement list and the track sheet for the current pattern are displayed on the screen at the same time. When an arrangement is being played back, the track sheet window will switch (unless you tell it not to) to whatever pattern is currently playing, so you can keep an eye on what's going on. And the arrangement list will scroll, with the currently playing pattern highlighted in inverse video. Screen updating is also going on at lightning speed in two elapsed time indicators (bar/beat/subdivision/tick and hour/minute/second/millisecond) and in key velocity bar graphs for all 16 tracks. With all this going on and the machine simultaneously spitting out sixteenth-notes through several MIDI outputs, we started wondering whether somebody had snuck in and installed a super-fast processor in our ST. Then we learned that Creator will load from disk while playing back music! Astounding. But somehow, C-Lab keeps it all happening without a glitch.

Pull-down menus are used for many commands, but the commoner items have both on-screen mouse buttons and keyboard equivalents (which are shown right on the buttons in little tiny letters for added convenience). We were especially pleased to see a prominent 'undo' button which can save you from just about any disaster, including accidentally punching in on the wrong track. Changing numerical values is accomplished by clicking either the left or right mouse button. Holding the button scrolls the values rapidly. One of our few complaints about the program is that you can't use the number keys to type in new data for a parameter. Most items have small enough ranges that they'll scroll to wherever you want them within a second or two. For large, rapid changes, you can press the control key with your other hand, which turns the mouse into a slider control.

Recording & Track Operations. Creator records real straightforwardly: Click on the record button and the whole screen switches into inverse video to let you know you're happening. At the same time, your programmed metronome countoff starts. For the metronome, you can use the Atari's internal sound, or you can send any single note, at any velocity, on any MIDI channel you like. This allows you to listen to a drum machine woodblock or whatever, rather than the Atari speaker. Curiously, the MIDI metronome output setting is not stored as part of a song, so you have to manually enter the data at the start of every session. (Don't confuse this with programmable tempo; Creator does have the latter.)

The recording will be stored on whatever track you have selected within the current pattern. If you make a mistake and want to re-record, you don't even have to click on the stop button. Just click on record again, and the count-in will start over.

Creator is one of the few sequencers we've seen (maybe the only one, come to think of it) that records during the count-in but doesn't adjust those early notes so that they pile up on the downbeat of bar one. It is quite capable of recording "time before zero" material. This may seem odd at first: If you want that slightly early note to sound at all when playing back an individual pattern, you have to go to the event editor and change its start time yourself, or quantize to whatever resolution is needed to shift it onto the beat. There is an important advantage in this system, however. You can build an arrangement where some of the patterns have upbeats rather than starting on the beginning of bars. Having done so, you can remove a pattern's upbeat or reinsert it into the arrangement by shifting a special parameter that determines where in the bar the arrangement will jump from the last pattern to the next one. But arrangement mode features belong in a separate section of the review. That's the trouble with software. everything interacts with everything else.

Auto-punch recording can be done between a standard pair of markers, or you can punch in and out manually. A cycle recording mode lets you layer additional material into your track without erasing the existing stuff. There's even a software safety key, which must be switched off before a destructive punch-in can take place. A cue button lets you use the mouse as a slider to scroll quickly to any point in a long pattern or arrangement.

Many of the standard types of data processing can be handled in Creator either as edits (which alter the stored data) or as output parameters for the tracks (leaving the recorded data intact). Quantization, transposition, channelization, velocity transposition, velocity compression, upper and lower key limit, track delay, loop length, and "ghost of" are all output parameters programmable for each track within each pattern. (There is also a parameter on the screen called "accent," but it isn't explained in the manual and doesn't do anything.)

What is "ghost of"? Glad you asked. When a track is set up as a ghost of another track, it contains no musical data of its own, but rather "looks at" whatever is on the master track. This might be in any pattern, not just the current one. The ghost track can have its own channelization, transposition, velocity shift, and even time delay, which allows for all sorts of interesting MIDI layering. If the material on the master track is later edited, the ghost track will still be identical with the new track. This could be useful if you want to keep an ostinato part going through several patterns.

Obviously, the screen isn't big enough to display all the parameter data for 16 tracks at once. An unusual and highly functional "double window" system lets you see, at any given time, all of the output settings for the currently selected track as well as the settings of the currently selected parameter for all 16 tracks. (See Figure 1.) A

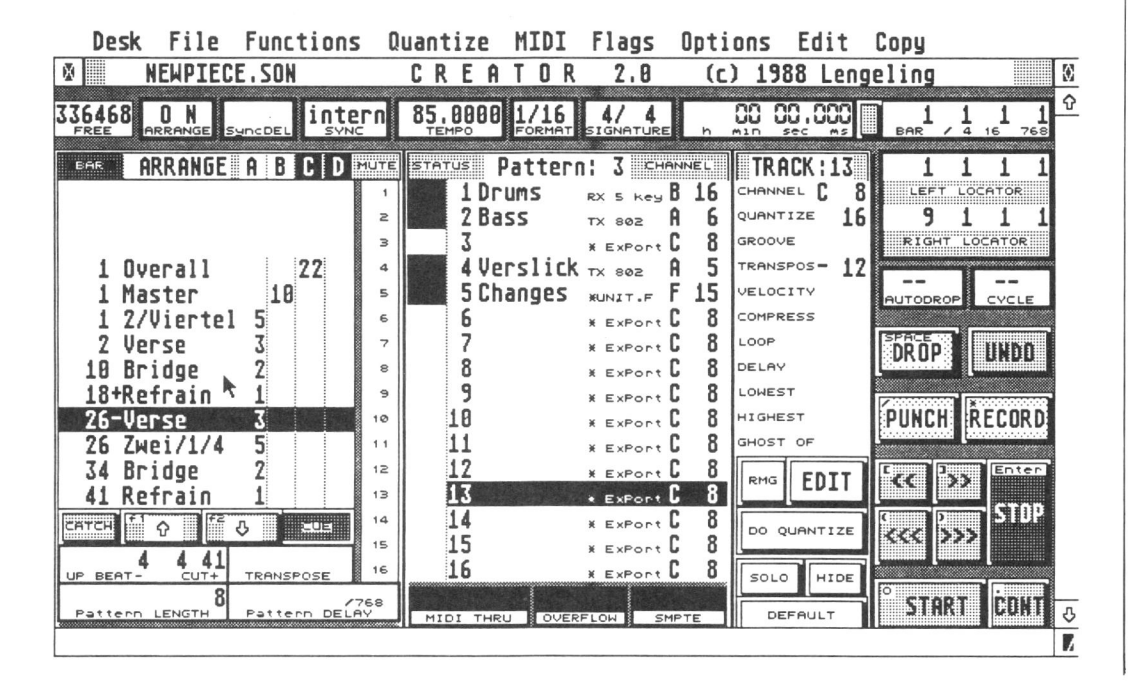

Figure 1. The main screen for the Creator sequencer. The arrangement list is shown at left, with the starting bar number, name, and number of each pattern. The window in the center shows track data for the currently selected pattern. When data has been recorded on a track, the block at the left side of the window turns black. Output parameter settings are shown in the column to the right of the track names. Currently, the loop length settings are being displayed for all tracks, while the box headed "TRACK:2" shows all settings for track 2.

track parameter window to the right of the pattern track sheet window has slots for all of the output controls listed a couple of paragraphs back. When you click on the slot for transposition, let's say, a column at the right side of the track sheet switches instantly to display the programmed transpositions for all the tracks. When, conversely, you click on a new track in the track sheet to make it the currently selected track, the values in the track parameter window all change instantly to tell you exactly what's going on in the output of that track. The values can be edited in either window, and what's more, they can be edited while the machine is playing back. You will occasionally get stuck notes if you scroll the transposition value during playback, but if you're silly enough to do something that weird during a gig, you deserve stuck notes.

The output parameter system is quite slick. There is a potential problem in the design, however—the only real gripe that we had with the program. The problem arises because all empty tracks, in all patterns, default not to a vanilla group of settings but to whatever settings you last programmed into any empty track. This is intended to be a feature, not a flaw: It lets you make a convenient use of MIDI echo (out/thru) while switching from one track or pattern to another, which is very considerate. The only time it will trip you up is if you record a track, set up some parameters for it (let's say, a transposition of −24, eighth-note quantization, and a 16-beat loop for a nice four-bar bass riff), and then decide that you don't like your first take. So you go into record mode and re-record this same track. When you enter record mode, the music data on the track is erased. Thus the track is, temporarily, an empty track—so the program cheerfully copies your transposition, quantization, and loop length onto every other empty track in the sequencer.

The quickest way to return the unused tracks to vanilla status is to store a vanilla "channel default" for some channel you don't plan to use, and then simply set an empty track to this channel. Channel defaults are another cool feature: Each channel can have its own set of default settings stored in a separate buffer, and you can restore the current track to the settings for its current channel with a single click. To return to our complaint, getting rid of a superfluous quantization value on empty tracks is especially important, because if a track is quantized prior to recording, the setting will be used by the program as an input quantization, eliminating all those little nuances you thought you were recording. If you re-record parts often, you'll find that this whole situation can get rather annoying.

Much more sensible is the track/channel naming feature. Each track can be given its own eight-character name. In addition, each of the 64 output channels can be given a separate eight-character name, which will be displayed in smaller letters on the track sheet. This second name would normally be used simply for a tag to show what module is listening to that channel. It will be loaded automatically into the appropriate spot(s) on the track sheet of any pattern, whenever that output channel is selected. This makes it a bit easier to keep track of what is on what track—though frankly, that second set of letters is tiny enough to be hard to read at a glance.

Don't be misled by this discussion of channelization into thinking that Creator is a one-channel-per-track sequencer. The track channelization can be switched off, in which case each track can play back on any combination of 16 channels. Each track must be "channelized" to transmit only to a single output jack, however.

Editing. Creator has a full array of regional editing commands and a powerful event edit screen. It also offers, throughout the program, a convenient way of dealing with the large numbers that can be generated by its 192 ppq resolution.

Here's how this works: At the top of the main screen you can set not only a time signature (numerator 1-99, denominator 4, 6, 8, 12, 16, 24, 48, 64, or 96) but also a quantization value for the data displays. This quantization has nothing to do with how notes are played back, it's purely for convenience. Instead of displaying time values in bar/beat/tick form, as most programs do, Creator displays them in bar/beat/subdivision/tick form, where the subdivision corresponds to the display quantize value. If you set this value to sixteenth-notes, then the displays will roll over from 1/1/4/8 to 1/1/2/1, as the 49th tick corresponds to the next sixteenth-note. The result is that you never have to worry about how many ticks there are in your preferred metrical resolution, the way you do in most sequencers. The global time signature and quantization can be changed at any point during your work session, and all the displays and arrangement parameters will be adjusted accordingly. There is no provision in the program for creating a piece that shifts time signatures, unfortunately.

Most of the edit operations that are accessed from the pull-down menus will affect the entire current track; if you want to do regional editing between the start and end locator points, you have to use a less complete set of commands that appear in a separate dialog box. Not to worry, however: It's extremely quick and easy to make a copy of your track (by clicking and dragging it to a new location in the pattern) and then use "cut inside locators" and "cut outside locators" menu commands to slice the region out of the original track while slicing everything except the region out of the copy. After editing the copy, you can merge the two tracks. Several different copy commands are included, making it easy to append material to itself several times, copy tracks to other patterns, and things of that sort.

When it comes to actually quantizing the stuff in memory, Creator offers a number of options. To begin with, you can quantize note length by itself, with or without setting limits for the minimum and maximum length that will be generated. You can also set all the notes in your track to a fixed length, for that great robotic feel, or add or subtract a fixed amount from all their lengths. You can quantize (if you should want to) the times of all events, including pitch-bends and controllers. You can quantize both note-ons and note-offs, which can affect note length. You can

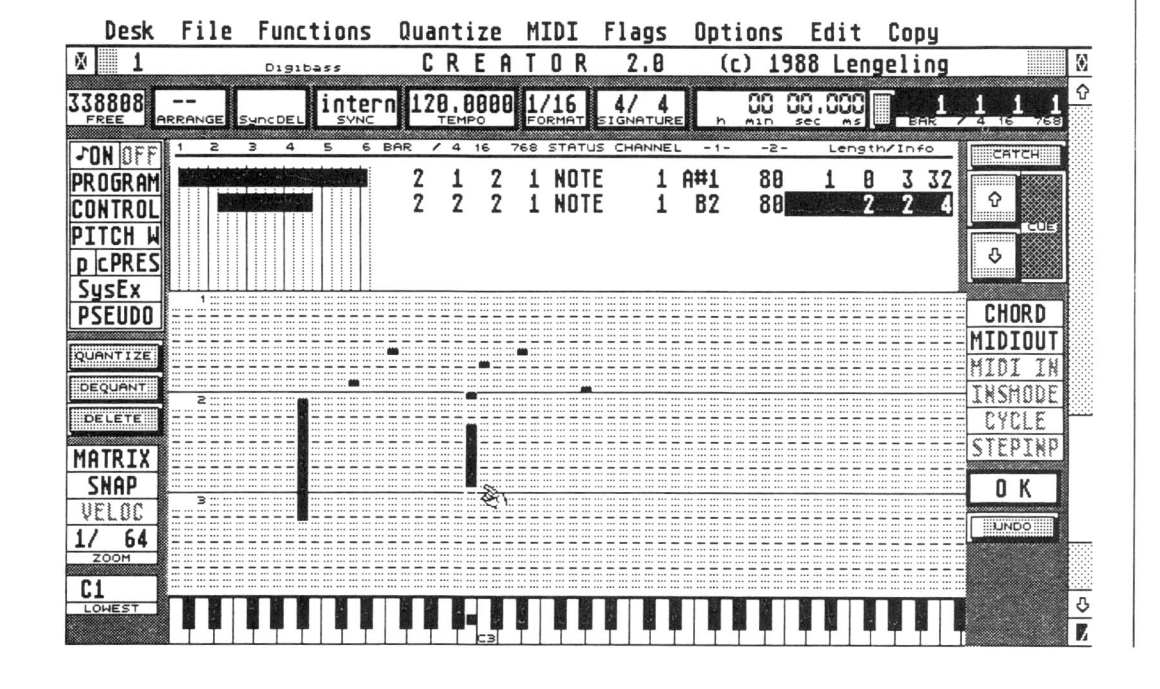

Figure 2. Event edit screen for Creator. Lengths of notes are displayed in the bar graph column at left. Individual event types are selected for display or insertion using the selection box at left. Cue buttons at upper right can be used to scroll through the list while listening to the notes, or a location can be selected using the scroll bar at the right edge.

quantize only note-ons without moving note-offs, or quantize notes so that they retain their length while starting at quantized times.

There is also a feature called "capture quantize," which has two parameters—the number of clock ticks around the quantization grid within which the program will look for notes to quantize, and the percentage of change that will be made in the note's start time. For example, let's say you set the number of clock ticks to 96 and the percentage to 50 percent, and ask for quantization to the nearest quarter-note. In this case, the program looks for notes that start within 48 ticks before or 48 ticks after each quarter-note beat, and then moves each note that it finds to a new position exactly halfway between its original position and the beat. We've seen this feature on a couple of other sequencers, but only with a fixed 50 percent adjustment, not with a percentage you can set yourself.

More complex operations can be performed using the "process data" and "transform events" windows. In the process data window, you can specify a region using a pair of bar/beat/subdivision/tick indicators, and then independently switch on or off a set of functions for changing MIDI channel, quantization, transposition, delay, velocity, velocity tapering, and velocity compression. Also in this box is a command for deleting notes above and/or below whatever pitch limits you may set.

In this window, velocity compression is performed only in ratios of two. You can select -1:4, -1:2, 1:2, 1:4, 1:8, or fixed velocity, just as with the track playback parameters. If you want to multiply all of your velocities by .9 to smooth off the accents just a tiny bit, then you want to use the transform events window instead.

This window is a complete search-and-replace utility, again with regional start and end point definition. You get to define the event that will be searched for within the track (or region) and exactly what it will be turned into. Three "variables" are provided, as is a wild card that says "accept any value for this byte." The variables can be used to shuffle values from one place to another. For example, if you've recorded something with channel pressure (monophonic after-touch) and later want to translate this into note pressure (polyphonic after-touch), the data byte signifying the pressure will be in a different place in the new event. The variable lets you move it. The same solution is used when translating pressure into mod wheel or vice versa.

One of the variables can undergo either addition or multiplication during the transformation. This is intended mainly for compressing and expanding controller values. Multiplication values run from –12 to 99.9, with negative multiplication being used to invert values. (Addition must also be used here to keep the values in range.) A tapering function in this window lets you move smoothly from one value to another between the start- and end-points. This would be most useful for making velocity and modulation curves.

If you want to do crazy things, like turning note velocity into pitch-bend amount or inverting the pitches in a track, the transform events window will oblige. We do have one minor gripe: When you enter this window from the main sequencer screen, the last set of values you entered will still be in place, so you can perform the same operation on several tracks without having to re-enter the values; unfortunately, when you call up the same window from the event editor screen, you'll have to re-input the settings manually, as they will be wiped.

A separate box allows you to delete or keep events that conform to the same kinds of criteria.

Event Editing. Creator's event editing environment is just about the slickest we've seen yet. Seventeen events, with all their associated data values, are displayed on the screen at any one time. The list scrolls during playback, and you can also scroll through it rapidly with the mouse. A pair of up/down mouse buttons can be used to scroll backward or forward through the list one event at a time, and notes will be heard (though at some fixed length) during this step-time playback, making it easy to locate to any spot. If you've got lots of chords in a track, you can click on a "chord" button, causing the scrolling to play your chords as simultaneous events rather than separate ones.

To edit an event, you click on the relevant data field and scroll the value up or down with the mouse buttons. If your time change moves the event to a different point in the list, the screen will update immediately to reflect the new order. You'll hear the event when you click on it to select it. If velocity is being edited, you'll hear the changes, as the machine will send out a rapid series of notes at the new velocities.

You can insert a new event of any type by dragging it onto the list from a resource box at the left side, or delete it by dragging it off to the side. The computer's insert and delete keys can also be used for this purpose. The resource box is also used to select which types of events will be displayed. This is a very convenient way to get pitch-bends out of the picture temporarily (they will still sound during playback, of course), or to look at the program changes by themselves. An undo button lets you get back to the original version of your track at any time, if you don't like the edits you've made.

Note-off events can be displayed separately, but the computer cleverly prevents you from editing their pitch, which would cause stuck notes, or their time, which must be edited in the note-on's duration field. You can edit their velocity, however, which is the purpose of the feature.

At the left side of the event list is a rudimentary bar graph representation of your data. This can be used to shorten or lengthen a note by clicking on the note's lower right corner and dragging, or to change its start time by dragging the whole thing left or right. A nifty little extra feature allows you to set a series of notes to the same duration by clicking on the lower right corner of the first one and then dragging down across the rest. This is good for editing chords and runs.

C-Lab has solved very neatly one of the chief problems of showing a bar graph side-by-side with an event list. The problem is, how do you deal with the fact that sometimes all the events visible in the list will occupy a quarter-note or less of time, while at other times they will stretch across ten or 12 bars? If you try to display all 12 bars, you'll run out of screen real estate, but if you confine yourself to a smaller region, some of the notes visible in the list may not appear in the graph at all. Creator's graph is a little more than five quarter-notes wide, but all the events in the list are always displayed. This is done by leaving the bar number undefined. In other words, any note that starts on beat 1 will appear at the left edge of the graphic area, no matter what bar it's in. The result is that a typical series of notes will run diagonally down the graph from left to right, just as you'd expect, but when it crosses the bar line the series will jump back to the left edge and start over. The extra beat (five quarter-notes of display rather than four) is to allow the durations of notes near the end of the bar to be displayed properly. Any note whose duration spills over into beat 6 appears to run off the edge of the graph.

If you don't find the graph useful, you can hide it simply by hitting the 'g' key on the computer. This speeds up the scrolling of the display somewhat.

Have we mentioned the MIDI insert features yet? While in the event editor, you can replace the pitch and velocity values of a note event by playing a MIDI keyboard.

There is no way of replacing pitch without replacing velocity or vice versa. Other Atari sequencers don't have this limitation, and they conveniently step to the next note when you use this type of input. This allows you to do a whole series of notes without touching the mouse. Creator isn't quite that slick. In most other respects, though, its list editing and graphic displays are distinct improvements over the rest of the pack.

Program change data and controller data can be input through MIDI in the same manner. Another mode lets you insert new notes (which will have the same start time and duration as the current event) from a MIDI keyboard. You can't insert new non-note events in this mode, however.

Creator has a whole class of pseudo-events. Many of these are currently undefined (a portent of things to come?). The current batch includes the loop point marker, mute and unmute commands for any track in the pattern, absolute and relative tempo changes, and MIDI song select. You can also send any MIDI byte you like (tune request, anyone?), or turn the MIDI clock output on and off automatically. Mutes and unmutes can be recorded in real time.

By editing the loop pointer's time value in the event edit screen, you can easily set up a loop whose length is a fraction of a beat. The mute and unmute markers are quite useful in conjunction with looping tracks. For example, let's say your pattern is 16 bars long, and has on one track a two-bar drum pattern that loops. By muting the drum track in bars 7-8 and 15-16, you could open up holes in which to record drum fills without having to worry about copying out the drum pattern the requisite number of times. This way, if you later want to change the drum beat, you can go back to its original two-bar-long track and edit it once, rather than having to edit bars 1-2, 3-4, 5-6, etc. individually.

We'd like to see a "number of times to play the loop" parameter added. Nested loops would be a cool addition, too. As it stands, all loops in Creator go on forever, except when the program is playing an arrangement. In this case, everything in a pattern, including the loops, stops playing when a new pattern begins in that layer of the arrangement. (Here we are talking about arrangement mode again. Arrgh!)

Relative tempo events will add or subtract some specified value from the metronome setting. Absolute tempo events will set the metronome to the specified value. Tempo events can be stored in any track, but you might want to devote one pattern specifically to them and run it by itself in layer D of the arrangement, creating, in effect, a conductor track. Creator will record absolute tempo events in real time, by the way. By clicking the mouse on the metronome display, you can scroll the values up or down, and tempo events will be recorded.

Building Arrangements. If you've been following along, you will already have picked up various tidbits about Creator's arrangement (song) functions, which are quite powerful. Basically, the 99 patterns can be assembled in any order in an arrangement list. This list is four layers deep, so up to four patterns can be playing back at a time. Each pattern can be given its own start time, and will play until a new pattern starts in the same layer, at which time it will shut off.

The manual doesn't say what the maximum size of the arrangement list is. We got bored after inserting 200 patterns, and stopped. It does say that the largest bar number the list will deal with is about 1,330 in 4/4 time. Pattern 0 serves as a stop marker, and can be used to split the list into several separate songs. Each pattern is used several times, it can be given a new name every time if you like. Curiously, there is no way to give names to the 99 individual numbered patterns.

Each pattern in the list can be given its own combination of track mutes. These are displayed in a narrow column next to the track sheet, so it's very easy to tell what you've muted. During playback the arrangement list scrolls, and the track sheet is updated to show the currently playing pattern. Even the mute display is updated.

Patterns can be added to the list by clicking and dragging or by hitting the insert key. They can be deleted by dragging them off the list or by hitting the delete key. It's all very intuitive—no messy commands to learn. If you change the starting time of a pattern so drastically that its position in the list is affected, the program reorders the list automatically.

Each pattern in the list has several parameters associated with it, in addition to mutes: number (1-99) and name, obviously, plus length, delay, transpose, and upbeat/cut. The length parameter lets you shut off a pattern after playing a portion of it, even if the next pattern on that layer of the arrangement isn't scheduled to start yet. By increasing the length setting of a pattern, you can push all of the subsequent patterns in the arrangement to later start times.

Delay and transpose operate about the way you'd expect. Upbeat/cut is unusual, however, as we mentioned earlier, this parameter lets you set the time when the program will shut off the previous pattern and start the new one, without affecting where the new one falls in relation to the beat. So if notes at a time before zero have been programmed into a pattern, they can be heard as upbeats in the arrangement when this parameter is used. The parameter can also be used to make the transition between patterns sound smoother. Normally, if notes are still sounding when the end of the previous pattern is reached, the note-offs will be generated by the program precisely at the point where it switches to the new pattern. But if this is the downbeat of a bar, the MIDI data stream can get a bit packed. By setting the cut point slightly ahead of the bar, you will be able to get the note-offs out of the way in a much more expeditious manner.

Disk Functions. As we mentioned earlier, Creator will let you load, save, or even format a blank disk while it's playing. We wouldn't recommend saving while playing, as it's always remotely possible that an error could be introduced into your file. Loading while playing is much more useful, because it lets you do nearly seamless live performance playback of a whole set.

You can load and save single patterns, songs (everything in memory is considered a single song), or "sequences," which turn out to be single tracks. These are given automatic filename extensions of PAT, SON, or SEQ by the machine. When you save a new version with the same filename, the last version you saved is renamed with a BAT, BON, or BEQ extension, so you'll always have two versions on disk in case either you or the computer does something horrible.

Other Stuff. There are too many features in Creator for us to list them all. We thought you might like to hear about a few, though. If you increment the real-time clock display by a single second or minute, the bar/beat display will be updated to show the equivalent spot in the music, depending on the current metronome setting. This could be real handy if you need exact timing hits. Any combination of the 16 MIDI channels can be transpose-disabled, a feature that owners of multiple drum machines will be happy to see.

Start, record, stop, pause/continue, and several other things can be controlled remotely from one octave of a MIDI keyboard. (You get to pick the octave.) A portamento footswitch (controller 65) can be used for punch-in-and-out. You can double or halve the speed of all the events on a track with a single edit command. You can use a "humanize" feature to randomize, slightly or drastically, the timing of events. Creator will both record and display sys-ex data dumps, and will let you assemble your own hand-shaking messages if these are needed.

A "MIDI data overflow" meter on the screen will show immediately if you're sending so much data so close together that some of it must be delayed in reference to its nominal time. Function keys F3 through F10 can be used for storing locator start and end times. Combinations of mutes can also be stored.

All of which is thoroughly impressive. Less impressive: Text events can be inserted in the event list, which sounds hip until you discover that your text will be displayed in a column that's a generous six characters wide. A freshman programmer in a good junior college could probably come up with a better way to display text in a track, so we're reasonably sure C-Lab will have something more appropriate up and running with the next revision. There's also a manual tap tempo key, but we couldn't get it to work worth a damn, so we aren't even going to mention it.

Creator uses a hardware key (which the Brits call a "dongle"). This plugs into the Atari's game port. You can make copies of the program disk, but the program won't run unless it sees its precious dongle in the port. This is probably the best system yet devised to combat software thieves, but it certainly isn't convenient if you happen to own and use several dongle-dependent progams. In order to switch from one to another, you can't just change disks. You have to switch the computer off, because it's not a good idea to plug or unplug the key while the electronics are active. We'd like to see somebody market a dongle-stacker, a little box that would let you plug several keys into one side and route the Atari's connectors to whichever one you prefer with a multi-position switch.

Conclusions. This sequencer is going to have the competition scrambling to keep up. If they make the mistake of assuming (as we've heard some manufacturer's representatives defensively claim) that the competition's design isn't better, just different, Creator is going to eat them alive. Of course, it's in the top price bracket for Atari software, so if you don't need all these features, a less expensive sequencer could still be the right choice for you.

The program is laid out logically, making it quite easy to learn, and the manual is far above average, especially considering it was written by a native speaker of German. The track output parameters allow you to do lots of operations, even up to the level of recording whole pieces, without getting into editing if you don't want to. On the other hand, the edit functions are quite comprehensive. In terms of both speed of operation and sheer number of features, Creator is an amazing accomplishment. It's not without its little quirks, of course: The empty track default business is annoying, and if you're going to store text in a track, you certainly want to be able to read columns wider than six characters. But in a program this complex, there are bound to be places where the programmer doesn't have time to sand off the rough corners. We were delighted to find out how few problems were visible, and how minor these were.

Head-to-head product comparisons are odious, because they're always incomplete, but we know readers like them, so we'll indulge in a bit of A/Bing of Atari sequencers, for the benefit of those whose local stores don't stock them all. The only Atari sequencer that can really slug it out toe-to-toe with Creator, in our opinion, is KCS Level 2. This contains a cornucopia of algorithmic randomizing and editing features not found in Creator. Building a long song out of short segments gives you more options in KCS, but the process is significantly easier to work with in Creator.

Creator also has a definite edge in terms of controller editing, and its event editor has more convenience features. Having multiple MIDI outputs has to be counted as a plus, too.

If you're shopping for a professional-level Atari sequencer, or if you're waffling between the Atari and the Mac for sequencing because you like the Atari's price but you like the Mac's reputation and its tough, no-nonsense graphics, you owe it to yourself to check out Creator on a black-and-white monitor. It looks like a Mac program, and it acts the way Mac programs ought to act. They don't always act that way, do they? Creator does.

C-Lab Creator

Description: MIDI sequencer software.

Hardware requirements: Atari 520 ST, 1040 ST, or Mega. Monochrome (recommended) or color monitor. Optional output expander (with three additional MIDI out jacks) plugs into RS-232 port.

Memory: About 106,000 events (53,000 notes). 99 patterns, 16 tracks each.

Features: Pattern/song architecture with four simultaneous patterns playable at once. Track playback parameters including quantization, transposition, velocity compression, and looping. Multiple quantization insertion. Controller editing and translation. 192 ppq clock resolution. Will load from disk during playback. Remote start/stop from MIDI keyboard. Compatible with GEM desktop accessories.

List price: $349.00. ExPort output expander, $175.00.

Contact: Digidesign, 1360 Willow Rd., Suite 101, Menlo Park, CA 94025. (415) 327-8811. In Europe: C-Lab Software, Postbox 70 03 03, 2000 Hamburg 70, West Germany

---

Keyboard, **April 1988.**

Voyetra Sequencer Plus Mark III: IBM Sequencer Software

By Michael Marans

Sitting down with Voyetra's latest incarnation of the Mark III sequencing program is like watching the season premier of your favorite television show. You know it will have all of the familiar faces you've come to know and love; the excitement, intrigue, and drama that got you hooked in the first place; and maybe, just maybe, a few surprises thrown in to keep you watching for the rest of the year. Well, version 2.0 is not going to disappoint you, and in fact, Voyetra seems hell-bent on winning the ratings sweeps.

Sequencer Plus was originally released in 1985 (when the company was known as Octave Plateau). Version 2.0 is available as an upgrade for owners of the Mark I, Mark II, and pre-2.0 Mark III versions of the program.

The Basics. The Mark III sequencer provides 64 tracks, each of which may loop independently and contain multiple time signatures. A wide range of editing parameters—cut/copy/paste for tracks (including multiple tracks), microscopic for notes and MIDI events, combine with a group of functions called "transforms" to facilitate utilitarian processes and pave the way for creativity and experimentation. Data is entered mneumonically (press R for Record, V for View, etc.); values are entered from the numeral keys and the plus/minus buttons. All information is clearly displayed on three main screens with assorted pop-up windows that are called into view whenever appropriate. A number of functions overlap from screen to screen, and the command syntax is generally (and thankfully) very consistent. A built-in librarian allows performance set-ups and patches to be stored and loaded with the sequences. (Patch Master Plus, Voyetra's universal librarian, is required to download sys-ex data into the Mark III.) On-line help is available at the touch of a button without leaving the current screen, so it is relatively easy to execute even the most complex functions regardless of your previous experience with the Mark III.

Voyetra provides a very informative supplementary booklet about DOS (Disk Operating System) and related topics for those who are new to the IBM world. They also include a comprehensive user manual, but even though it is divided into tutorial and reference sections, we thought it could have been better organized. We found ourselves chancing upon functions that were not listed in the index, and often had to jump from one section to another in order to find the information we needed to complete a given procedure.

Thrills And Frills. Version 2.0 includes a generous number of utilities such as keyboard macro support (which helps make the user-interface very friendly), and automatic MIDI channel assignment and multi-channel recording (both of which greatly simplify MIDI operations). Some of the utilities just plain make your life easier, like the "note pad" for text and the song list play mode. Clock and sync functions include real-time song position pointer defeat, dynamic tempo display, SMPTE calculator, and selectable 96 or 192 ppq. One of our favorites was the giant (three inches high) bars, beats, and SMPTE display screen, which allows you to monitor song status from anywhere in the room.

Who could enjoy meat and potatoes if dessert weren't available on the menu? Obviously the engineers at Voyetra have a sweet tooth extraordinaire, because they've included some really delectable goodies, known as transforms. Transforms duplicate a number of the functions that are accessible from the main menu (transpose, quantize, track offset), but transforms permanently alter the data, while the main menu functions are playback-only. Often it is useful to audition a quantization value in the main menu, and when you are satisfied, perform a quantize transform so that the computer does not have to perform too many real-time housekeeping chores. This helps maintain clocking and playback accuracy.

Transforms are divided into six groups: time, pitch, velocity, split, random, and miscellaneous. Each group offers a mix of utilitarian and creative functions, which may be performed on the region specified in the view page. Quantization, listed under time transforms allows the degree of quantization to be adjusted from one to 100 percent, and is performed without affecting other MIDI data. Note durations may also be quantized as well as adjusted by percentages or given fixed values. Feeling adventurous? Try the retrograde transform, and hear all of your notes and MIDI data played in reverse. The compress/expand transform proved to be very useful, allowing the timing of all events to be squeezed or stretched by defining a ratio of original length to new length. For example, we were able to record a complex drum fill over two bars, and by inputting a ratio of 2:1, have the fill play in double-time. A ratio of 1:2 returned our fill to its original length. One nifty trick is to copy a track and define a ratio of 200:201 on the new track, so that when the original and the copy track play together, a number of subtle phase and flange effects are created. Ratio values may be any number from one to 4000, so the possibilities are virtually endless.

Harmonic inversions, transpositions, and remapping of notes are all easily accomplished using the pitch transforms. Some "Let's fool the computer" tricks (like lying about the key signature of our composition), provided musically interesting and slightly bizarre, avant-garde results.

Velocity transforms feature an algorithm that compresses or expands velocities based on the average velocity in the specified range. We found the crescendo transform to be extremely useful for creating smooth dynamic transitions, and there is a negative crescendo.

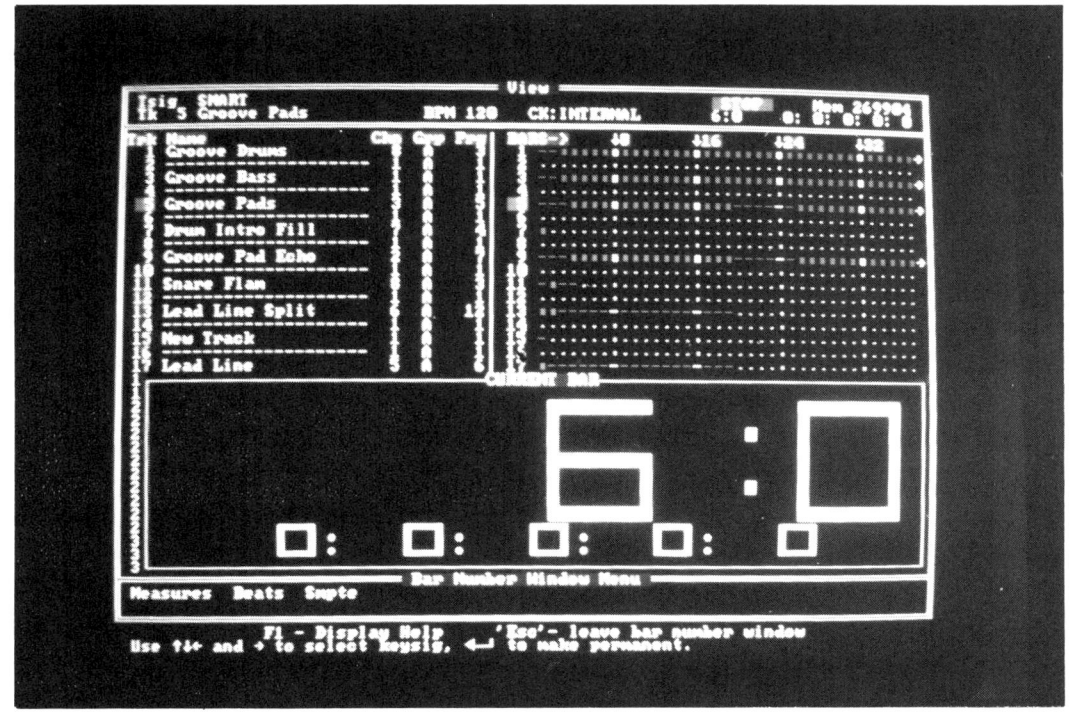

Figure 3. Sequencer Plus view screen (upper half). Measures containing music appear as squares, those with rests are dashes, and those not yet recorded are dots. The large pop-up box shows bar, beat, and SMPTE time.

Sequencer Plus also contains a number of split transforms, and this is where we give our highest compliments to the design engineers. Split tranforms allow the user to define criteria that split notes out to a new track while the other notes remain in the original. Normally this is done by defining a pitch range, but you can also split by quantize (all notes falling within a "time window" around a reference beat value), velocity (all notes within a specified velocity range), duration (notes longer than a specified duration), and our very favorite, modulus, which splits out every "nth" note starting on a specified note. We found the modulus transform to be invaluable for adding accents to drum tracks.

Multiple transforms may be repeatedly performed on the same data, or portions of the data. Here's a process you might want to try that combines the crescendo and

---

Pros & Cons

Pros: 64 tracks with independent looping and time signatures, multi-menu operation with pop-up windows, extensive editing capabilities, multi-channel recording, graphic note editing, on-line help, very user-friendly.

Cons: Step-recording not possible from MIDI keyboards, limited MIDI event edit display, single-measure display for note editing, limited track looping parameters.

modulus transforms to create interesting, human-sounding drum fills (in this case a snare roll), from absolutely rigid, computer-generated notes. Start by inputting two bars of sixteenth-notes from the edit page using the QWERTY keyboard. Each note will have a default velocity value of 64. (Unfortunately, the Mark II does not allow you to use your MIDI keyboard for step entry.) Next, set the parameters of the crescendo transform to start the fill at the barely audible velocity of ten, and smoothly increase over two bars to velocity 110. Now use the modulus transform to split out every fourth note, starting on the first note of the pattern. Give the split-out new crescendo values of 20 to 127, then merge the two tracks back together. The result: a snare roll crescendo with every fourth note accented.

While we're on the subject, if humanizing parts is your thing, you'll definitely want to check out the section of random transforms. Options include pitch, start time, velocity, and duration. Each of these allows the percentage of randomization to range from one percent (give me a little slop) to 100 percent (let the computer be the composer).

Miscellaneous transforms tend to be on the utilitarian side: track merge, track rebar (useful for viewing several bars of material in the edit window), and range rebar, which allows you to change the time signature for the specified range.

If We Could Only... Unfortunately, every silver lining has a cloud, and as much as we like this program there are a few things that we would love to see improved. Probably our biggest complaint is that edits above the level of single events must be performed in ranges defined by bar lines. This makes it a hassle if you want to cut from the third sixteenth of beat three to the second sixteenth of beat two in the next bar, or perform any other inter-bar edit. (This applies to punch-in recording as well.) You could perform the above example by using the track rebar transform to make all of the bars one sixtenth-note long, but whew, what an effort. To be fair, a number of sequencers only allow editing by bars, but when you've got 192 ppq resolution staring you in the face, it sure does make you want to get inside... This sequencer almost teases us with its power, because every time we are given a feature, it makes us want more. For example, tracks loop independently (or may be left unlooped), yet looped tracks may only loop from start to finish, and will always keep looping for as long as the sequence is running. We would have liked definable loop lengths, start-points, and the ability to program the number of repeats. Another case: group mutes and solos. We're enticed by the prospect of having recording console capabilities, but alas, the mutes and solos are not programmable, and cannot be turned off or on when the sequencer is running.

Two more minor complaints, both of which involve the edit screens. We would love to be able to expand the range of the note edit screen to show more than its current one-bar limit, and to be able to see more octaves at once. The other less than desirable edit screen is the MIDI event display. Complete data is displayed for only one event at a time: there is no event list screen. This is the one (and only one) part of the program where the information shown doesn't really tell you a whole lot, except that MIDI information is there. Editing it requires far more keystrokes than used anywhere else in the software. It would be a lot easier to replay a pitch-bend than to try to edit it from this screen.

Conclusions. Sequencer Plus has just about everything you could possibly want in a sequencer—lots of raw power, sophisticated editing, creative utilities, and the friendliest user interface this side of a mouse. It's also made by a company that stands behind its products and continually enhances them—without penalizing the user for buying an earlier version. Voyetra tells us that they are already working on a new update that will address some of our concerns.

The upscale price tag on the Mark III ($495.00), like that on its luxury car namesake, is justified by the performance, style, and overall capabilities found in the program. So slip behind the wheel, step on the gas, and go make some music.

Sequencer Plus Mark III
Version 2.0

Description: MIDI sequencer software for IBM PC/XT/AT or compatible.
Hardware Requirements: IBM Computer or compatible with minimum 512K RAM (640K preferred) and two disk drives, MIDI interface (Roland MPU-401, version 1.5 or 1.5a with IBM card, or Voyetra OP-4000, OP-4001, or V-4001 interface card). Supports non-MCA bus PS/2 models 25, 30, and 30286. Software available in 5.25" and 3.5" disk formats.
Memory: 64 tracks per song, about 60,000 notes with 640K RAM, songs up to 9,999 bars long.
Features: Multi-menu operation with pop-up windows, independent track looping, time signatures, transposition, and offset, cut/copy/paste editing with multiple buffers, microscopic event editing, punch in/out recording, selectable data filtering, group solos and mutes.
Suggested Retail Price: $495.00.
Contact: Voyetra Technologies, 333 Fifth Ave., Pelham, NY 10803. (914) 738-4500.

Keyboard, **January 1989.**

Kawai Q-80: MIDI Sequencer

By Michael Marans

Power. Speed. Convenience. Words that should be permanently etched into the brain cells of engineers before they are ever allowed to design a MIDI device. Power appears to be a readily attainable objective, given the level of sophistication found in the present generation of hardware and software. Speed and convenience? These are often sacrificed due to cost considerations, but more and more equipment under $1,000 attempts to address these issues by including features such as a built-in disk drive. Three cheers to those manufacturers who have made this handy item a standard feature. (Remember cassette tape interfaces? Ouch.) Another prime consideration in the design of any piece of equipment also happens to be the one most commonly neglected: *ease of use!* Sophisticated "power users" may be willing to swap user-friendliness for increased functionality, but entry-level users must often endure great frustration, a high price for gaining access to higher levels of technology. This problem is most likely to show up in sequencers, where powerful features are often implemented in a manner that impedes a composer's creative flow.

Kawai America has introduced the Q-80 Digital MIDI Sequencer, hot on the heels of several successful products, most notably their K1 synthesizer and R-100 drum machine. These instruments proved that sophisticated technology could belong to everyone, not just to a few elite individuals with disposable MIDIbucks. But while these products offered a large degree of power, they fell short in the speed and ease of use departments. So how does the mid-priced Q-80 sequencer fare in these critical areas? Well, it certainly offers a number of powerful and convenient features, including some, such as the disk drive, that are generally reserved for more expensive devices. But easy to use? Oh, well, two out of three ain't bad.

Overview. The Q-80 is rather beautiful to look at, with its sloping front panel complemented by the sleek drive housing. A total of 21 switches (enough to satisfy even the most hard-core fans of dedicated buttons), 22 LEDs, a 32-character backlit LCD, and of course the ever-present alpha dial, all manage to share space on the front panel without crowding. Abbreviated menus are printed directly above their corresponding function buttons, several of which have icons printed on them.

Figure 4.

The Q-80 borrows heavily from a number of tried-and-true schools of sequencer design, but some new nomenclature has been thrown in just to keep things interesting. Sequences are created as songs, each song consisting of up to 32 tracks and 15,000 notes (26,000 note total memory). Tracks are linear, similar to recording on analog tape, but they may also consist of "motifs," short drum machine-like segments which may be freely interspersed as events along multiple tracks. Tracks may be up to 999 bars long and loop independently, and each may contain multiple time signatures, real bonuses when creating polyrhythmic compositions. "Chain" mode is provided for linking up to ten songs. Information may be entered in real to step-time, the latter from the front panel as well as from MIDI devices.

The editing functions are surprisingly sophisticated, and include advanced features like note split and event extraction. In addition to the memory allocated for sequencing, 64K of RAM is available for storing system-exclusive data. This storage is divided into ten banks, each bank containing up to 16 tracks of data. Tracks can hold up to 999 blocks of sys-ex information, each "dump" occupying one block. This sounds like a great deal of storage space until you realize that dumping the internal single patches of the K5 synthesizer and the pattern and song data of the R-50 drum machine would fill the entire memory. (Other instruments require less; if you are concerned about this, consult the manuals for your instruments to see how large their dumps are.) In any case, if you plan to have this sequencer serve as the "central data storage facility for all the data that you use to set up your MIDI network" as claimed in the Q-80 owner's manual, plan on doing a fair amount of disk accessing. All sequence and system-exclusive memory may be stored to floppy disk, each disk holding up to 1,123 songs/150,000 notes.

The overall MIDI implementation is exceptional, including the ability to record on 16 tracks and 16 MIDI channels simultaneously. Rear panel jacks are provided for connecting the Q-80 to a tape recorder so that sequences may be synchronized to tape. MIDI clock is generated by the Q-80 when tape sync is used as a clock source allowing multiple devices (i.e., drum machines, computers) to be locked together with little effort. MIDI song position pointer is both sent and received.

Operation. On power-up, the Q-80 defaults to song play mode. Songs are selected using the alpha dial and begin playing when the dual-purpose "play/enter" button is pressed. Cursor controls allow the user to select tempo (40-250 bpm), which may be adjusted in real time. When the machine is in idle, tape-transport-style, buttons are used to maneuver through songs; specific sections may be accessed using fast-forward and rewind buttons to facilitate starting from particular bars or beats. Unfortunately, this locate function cannot be performed while the sequencer is running. During playback, tracks may be muted and unmuted, a handy utility. When a song has finished playing, a reset button must be pressed to start playback again from the beginning, or to select another song. Although a number of parameters are continuously displayed on the LCD, access is limited to those that directly relate to the currently selected operational mode (e.g., play, record). We have to wonder why the engineers designed so many mutually exclusive modes when numerous operations, such as changing tempo, could be executed from a single screen.

A number of steps are involved in starting recording. First select an empty song, then a record track. No, wait. First select a song, then the MIDI channel for the record track, then push the record track's function button, then the "record button, then play." Oops! That's not right either. First select the song, then the MIDI channel, then press "reset" and cursor to the track number, turn the alpha dial until your current record track is displayed, then press the "select" button to access one of the four banks of eight tracks, then press record, then press the record track function switch *twice*, then press play, and if you still have any energy left to play your parts... Maybe its time to consider live performance again! Doubtless you'll be able to commit the procedure to memory rapidly, as it must of course be repeated for each additional track. It is also necessary to press "stop" immediately after recording and/or use the "bar delete" command to make your sequence the proper length, as there is no provision for setting track length. Recording a motif is accomplished (unfortunately) in the same manner, except that the MIDI channel is selected in the "system" mode instead of by the track.

The primary difference between a track and a motif is that a motif may be overdubbed (i.e., recorded "sound on sound" style with new information added to the previously recorded material), whereas recording new data on a track erases whatever information existed prior to re-recording. Punch in/out is available only for track recording. Only the identifying number of a motif is stored on a track, not the information it contains, thereby saving memory. This also makes it easy to copy

---

Pros & Cons:

Pros: 32 tracks with independent looping and time signatures, advanced editing capabilities, system-exclusive storage, built-in disk drive.

Cons: Cryptic LCD displays, poor user interface, uninformative manual, limited auto-punch parameters.

sections of music without being concerned with bar numbers. Portions of tracks may be turned into motifs using the "make motif" command, and motifs may be "opened" for editing as a track. Having both modes allows you to compose in either short repetitive segments or long passages, or both, as dictated by the music.

Step mode recording provides a great deal of musical flexibility, despite its inherently rigid nature. All of the standard utilities for generating chords, ties, slurs, and rests are present, but the extra goodies are really impressive. Gate times, velocity settings, and note values as esoteric as sixteenth-note septuplets are all available, enough to satisfy even the most discriminating composer. What's the catch, you ask? Once again, somebody on the design team loves to push buttons—great if each button push provides results, but frustrating if multiple buttons must be pressed simply to access basic functions.

Punch-in recording is available in real- and step-time recording modes. When accessed from the Q-80's front panel, auto-punch in/out points must fall on bar lines, but when a footswitch is used, punches can be done in real time. It would have been more realistic, and considerably more useful, to allow auto-punches to be programmed with clock pulse resolution, especially since the Q-80 sports a respectable 96 ppq, but unless you are mighty fast with a footswitch, you'll have to settle for much coarser punching. (Kawai told us that clock-by-clock punching was originally implemented but was dropped due to memory constraints in the operating system.) One other annoying quirk in the punch operation involves punching in on multiple tracks. If you have tracks with different time signatures and consequently the start times of the tracks' measures are not always aligned, the punch will immediately affect only the track displayed by the LCD, but will punch in and out of the other tracks at their bar lines. This is a sure way to end up with unpredictable results, lost data, and frustrated users. But then again, how often are you going to have tracks with different time signatures?

Editing. The engineers at Kawai obviously did some homework when they designed the editing section of the Q-80. Almost everything one could expect (and hope for) even on the most sophisticated of sequencers has been included. Standard features like quantization have been given parameters to minimize the "machine" feel that generally results from auto-correction. (This is fortunate, as no quantizing is available on input.) One set of controls allows the user to draw a "tolerance window" so that notes falling within the window are left unquantized—perfect for keeping just the right amount of "slop" in an otherwise tight rhythm section. The option to selectively quantize specific notes, such as all *F3*'s in bars 15 through 24 is ideal for making subtle adjustments in drum and bass feels. It took us a while to get the hang of manipulating the parameters due primarily to the cryptic LCD messages, but the results were musically satisfying.

Edits are accomplished using Macintosh-style cut/copy/paste syntax, although the names have been changed. Most edit functions allow the user to define a range in which to perform the edit, although once again this is limited by bars. On the bar level, data may be erased, copied, deleted, mixed, and transposed, but the features that we liked were not only much more interesting, but real time-savers as well. "Note shift" allows all notes played at a specific pitch to be assigned to a different MIDI note number, ideal for auditioning different drums or drum tunings without reprogramming the whole sequence. "Note split" copies the notes in a specified range to a new track (and deletes them from the original), where they may be given a new MIDI channel, transposed, gated, or otherwise manipulated. "Move" shifts all of a track's data forward or backward by a specified number of clock pulses, useful for delay compensation as well as for adjusting a track's feel. "Event extract" copies selected controller information to other tracks, a perfect way of ensuring that all pitch-bends or volume modulation will be identical at specific parts of the sequence. Other options include velocity and gate time scaling.

Microscopic editing is available for those who dare, including the ability to reassign real-time controller information to another controller number. For example, pressure data may be edited to transmit as mod wheel information. The creative possibilities are endless. One edit feature that promised to be downright incredible was the "tempo track" function. Any one of the 32 tracks can be designated as a tempo map for the entire sequence. Although this feature allows for pulse-by-pulse tempo changes, we were really disappointed when it turned out that the map could not be programmed in real time. (Ever try to program a gradual tempo change over four bars in step mode?) Additionally, all attempts to copy the map so that it would appear several times during the seqence met with failure.

Conclusions. What ya got here, folks, is one mighty powerful piece o' gear. With its built-in disk drive, 32 record tracks, microscopic editing, and intelligent quantization features all packed into one very attractive housing, how could you go wrong? Sadly, Kawai found a way. This sequencer is about as difficult to use as any we've ever seen. The LCD display, one of the brightest and most easily read on any electronic device is virtually defeated by the impossibly cryptic information on its screen. The syntax is astonishingly convoluted (at least *we* were astonished), the inconsistency of commands is maddening, and if you think you're going to find the answers in the owner's manual, think again. (Kawai tells us a new manual is being written. Check with your local music store for details on its availability.) Data entry via the alpha wheel is manageable, but less than desirable: It takes 13 complete revolutions just to cover the entire range of gate time scaling. A numeric keypad certainly would be in order here, although it probably was not implemented due to price considerations. Other curiosities were the omission of an "erase song" function (erasing could only be accomplished using the bar delete command on a song-by-song basis), and the necessity to go to "save song" under disk utilities in order to name a song. (This was the only place where any sort of naming was available. Get out your pencil and paper if you plan on managing 32 tracks.) It really is unfortunate that the Q-80 is so confusing to operate, because in most other respects the machine offers such great potential. Considering its price point, however, its primary market comprises the

---

Kawai Q-80

Description: MIDI sequencer with built-in 3.5″ floppy disk drive.
Memory: 10 songs, 15,000 notes per song, 26,000 note total. 64K sys-ex storage.
Features: 32 tracks, independent track looping and time signatures, cut/copy/paste editing, microscopic event editing, tape-transport style controls, auto and manual punch-in/out recording, selectable data filtering, velocity scaling, programmable gate times, system-exclusive storage and transmission, non-volatile memory with battery backup.
Interfacing: MIDI in/out/thru, tape sync in and out, metronome out, footswitch in, 10V DC in.
Dimensions: 5.5″ x 9.2″ x 2.6″, 4.9 lbs.
Suggested Retail Price: $795.00.
Contact: Kawai America, 2055 E. University Dr. (Box 4095), Compton, CA 90224-9045. (213) 631-1771.

people who will find it the most frustrating. There seems to be no question that this sequencer was designed entirely by engineers, and we have a hard time believing that there was a musician/user among 'em.

If you think that lots of power at a reasonable price is worth any amount of aggravation, then we highly recommend the Q-80. If, on the other hand, you believe that the industry has come far enough to know that musicality is still the bottom line, we hope you'll join us in giving Kawai a rousing "we know you'll do better next time."

Keyboard, January 1989.

Yamaha QX5: MIDI Sequence Recorder

By Dominic Milano

Yamaha just brought out the best sequencer they've ever made—it's called the QX5. "Ho-hum," you say. "Here comes another review of a device only Michael Jackson can afford." Guess again. The QX5 is a dedicated hardware sequencer whose features put it in the same league as the best software-based sequencers, which require general puspose computers to run on, yet the QX5 lists for only $595. We find that stunning, especially since it's one-sixth the cost of Yamaha's flagship sequencer, the QX1. And it lists for just a hundred bucks more than the QX1's baby brother, the QX21. Yet the 5 blows the 21 completely away, and it is a better composition tool than the QX1, despite the fact that the 1 has more bells and whistles (like a built-in disk drive and eight individual MIDI outs). No wonder some keyboard players suffer from "I don't want to buy one now because something better for half the price will be introduced next month" phobia.

Panel Controls. The QX5 has a deceptively simple front panel consisting of 14 switches and a 16-character backlit LCD (no, they didn't put a contrast control on this one either). From the look of it, you'd never guess how many functions might be hidden behind those few controls, and it's surprisingly easy to get around from function to function. It doesn't hurt that the unit's architecture is printed on the top panel. If you forget what order to press the switches in, a quick glance will tell you.

The switches are organized such that the top row accesses different functions depending on whether you hit the switch once or twice or press it and the shift key together. The bottom row of switches (four altogether) select nested parameters (called jobs), move the cursor around, and increment/decrement the parameters. For example, pressing the measure switch along with the shift key puts you into measure edit mode. From there you can use the job switch to step through ten different job functions, including copy, delete, remove shift, quantize, transpose, velocity, gate time, crescendo, and create.

Recording. There are eight tracks, which can each hold information on all 16 MIDI channels. All recording takes place on track 1. When you want to do a second track, you need to move the data on track 1 over to another track. This can be accomplished by exchanging data between tracks (flip-flopping tracks), copying

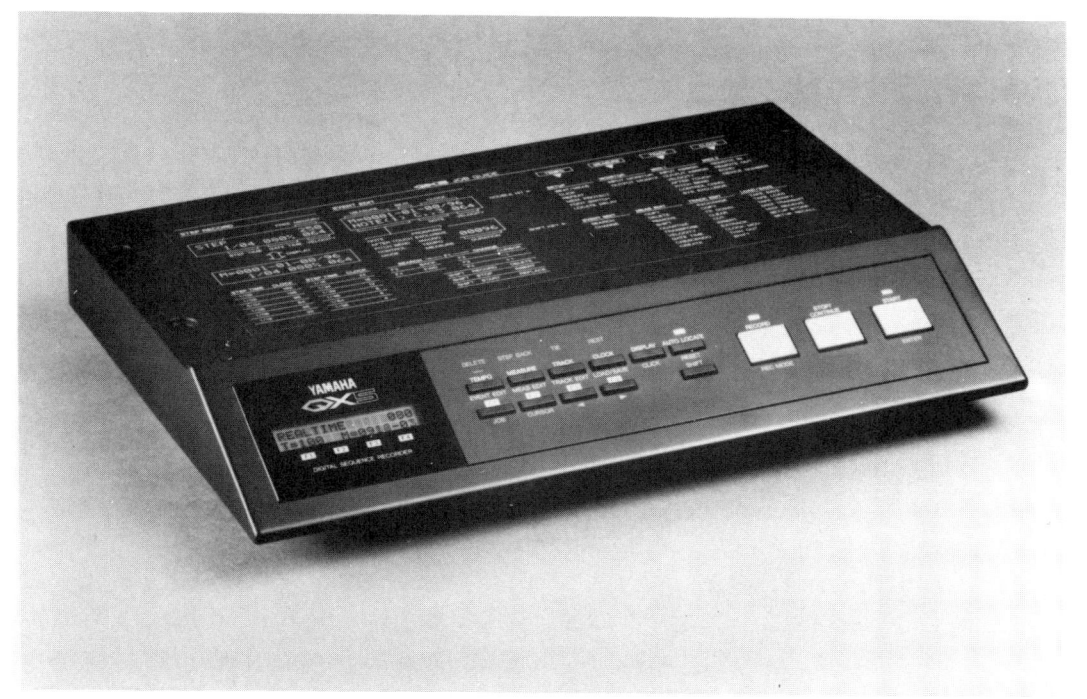

Figure 5.

track 1 to another track, mixing the data on track 1 with data on another track (more on that below), or inserting track 1 in front of some specified measure on another track. This should give you some idea of the kind of flexibility the unit offers.

Whatever data may be in track 1 when you start recording will be completely overwritten, so if you want to overdub into a part, you'll have to transfer the first part to some track other than 1, overdub the new material onto track 1, and then merge the old and new material into the same track using the track down function. One feature we felt was missing was some kind of individual track protection. As it is, you have to be very careful not to copy track 1 onto a track that already has data on it, although there is visual indication as to how much memory is being used on each track during exchange or copy functions. Tracks can be muted and unmuted during playback. One glitch we found was that a track has to be on when you start playback in order for you to be able to turn it on and off during the course of playback.

In addition to the eight tracks, there are 32 macros. A macro is a kind of floating track that can be called by another track, another macro, or itself (for looping) at any time. Macros can be any length within the limits of memory. For the record, that's 128k—roughly 20,000 notes without velocity data (15,000 with velocity data). You can have up to four macros playing at the same time.

Data that the QX5 will record includes all the standards and a couple of not-so-standards: MIDI note data, velocity, after-touch, pitch-bend data, program changes, channel data, mode data, continuous controller data (from modulation wheels, breath controllers, foot pedals, and so on), and system-exclusive data. System-exclusive data recording is nothing special in and of itself; there are hundreds of librarian and voice editing packages that do this, so why get excited about a hardware sequencer that has this ability? Simple—this sequencer will let you record sys-ex data along with the sequences! That's major exciting. For example, if you've got a DX7 set to system-info available, you can nest sys-ex patch data in each track of the sequencer. Instead of sending a program change message, the sequencer will send the entire sys-ex patch data to the DX. This way you don't have to use the internal memory of the synth at all. Likewise, if you've got an instrument that will send out sys-ex parameter-change data (like a Yamaha KX88, which has reprogrammable continuous controllers, you could cause a filter to open up, an operator's frequency to change, and so on by recording the proper sys-ex data along with the sequence. You can also use such a reprogrammable slider to send the QX5 tempo changes instead of using the increment/decrement buttons on the panel.

There are three recording modes: real-time, step, and punch-in. In real-time, notes and timing info, controller changes, and so on are recorded just as you play them (all quantizing operations are performed after the fact). The LCD gives you visual indication of how much memory is free, the current tempo setting (40-300 bpm), and the current measure and beat. The metronome click is a pitched beep (will we ever convince manufacturers that we want real non-pitched clicks?), and it can be set to beep whenever you toggle it on, during record only, or during record and playback.

Time signature can be set to anything between 1/4 and 32/16. To build up a track with constantly shifting meters, you'll have to record the desired number of measures in 1 signature, copy them to some other track or macro, then record another set of measures at the next meter and append those measures to the end of the other track, repeating as necessary until you've built up the desired measure structure. You can then copy that structure to track 1 for recording of note data—leaving the original track with the measure structure untouched so you can continue to copy it to track 1 for recording. Another way to do the same thing would be to extract the measure structure from 1 track and copy it to track 1. Again, this gives you some idea of the kind of flexibility you have with the unit—there are always a couple of ways to accomplish the same thing.

You can selectively filter velocity, after-touch, pitch-bend, control change, and sys-ex data on input. It's also possible to rechannelize data on input or on output, which can come in very handy. However, it's especially nice that tracks will retain channel data as it's recorded. This way you don't have to worry about channel data again unless you want to rechannelize something.

Punch-in recording lets you set punch-in and punch-out points. We consider this an essential feature to any sequencer. However, we have three complaints about the way it's implemented on the QX5. The first is that unlike the real-time recording feature, punch-in recording doesn't give you any visual feedback (like a measure countdown) of where you're at in the piece. That's all fine and dandy if you're working on a piece that you know inside and out, but if you're using the sequencer as a sketch pad and are caught up in the moment, the last thing you may want to do is try to keep track of where you are without some kind of visual indication to help you out. The second complaint has to do with the fact that you can only punch in at the beginning of a measure. What if you're trying to fix one phrase in a solo and it starts in the middle of a measure? Sure, you could edit it in step time, but it won't be the same as if you played in real time.

Our third complaint has to do with punching in and extending the length of a track beyond what it was originally. You can't do it without adding the desired number of measures onto the end of the track first. In other words, you can't just punch in and let the machine run until you feel like stopping. Some punch-out point has to be specified, and it can't be specified beyond the last previously recorded measure. This is the kind of thing you can get around by appending measures onto the end of a track, but it would be more convenient for sketch-pad improvisational composition if the unit let you punch in and play to your heart's content.

Step-time recording is fairly straight-forward, even if it is a little time-consuming. Fortunately, the QX5 has a way of making things go a bit more quickly. In step-time mode, note time value (half, quarter, quarter-note triplet, eighth, eighth-note triplet, sixteenth, sixteenth triplet, and so on), gate time, velocity, ties, rests, and so on can be specified. This can take hours if all you're using is the QX5's front panel. However, it's possible to route various MIDI controllers (a mod wheel, for instance) to adjust some of these parameters.

Editing. You can edit data on three levels—by individual events, by measure, or by entire track. At the event level, you can delete, insert, or replace events such as notes, pitch-bends, velocity, continuous controller data, sys-ex data, and so on.

At the measure level, you can copy, delete, remove, shift, quantize, transpose, change gate time, create measures, and set up crescendos/decrescendos. The difference between deleting and removing is that deleting takes the entire measure out of the measure structure, whereas removing allows you to remove a selected data type from a specified measure. Data types include channel, note, velocity, after-touch, program changes, sys-ex, macro numbers, tempo, and so on.

When copying, if you have a track devoted to drums, for example, and you want to copy a single pattern some number of times, you have to press the start button (to execute the function) as many times as you want to repeat the pattern. You can't just tell the unit to copy bars X to Y n-number of times.

Track editing functions include exchange (flip-flops tracks), copy, track down (merging), clear (erasing), cut (lops off the tail of a track at a specified point and pastes it to the end of another track), extract (takes specified data out of a track and puts it in another track), clock move (for moving tracks back and forth in time by single MIDI clocks), thin out (deletes about half of the selected continuous controller data from the specified track), and shift (bumps MIDI channels, notes, control data, or macro numbers over by some amount).

Miscellaneous. The QX5 will sync to FSK sync-to-tape tones and MIDI clocks both on record and on playback (unlike the QX1, which only syncs on playback). It also recognizes song position pointer, and recognizes and adjusts for minute time delays in external devices that are able to recognize song position pointer. You can also store up to four system setups, which are essentially user-programmable defaults for input filtering, beats/measure settings, metronome settings, and so on. Its output can echo the input, which is handy for listening to what you play while you're recording if you're using a master keyboard. And finally, data can be stored on cassettes or off-loaded to a MIDI sys-ex device. One nice aspect of the data dump feature (both cassette and sys-ex) is that you can store and load single tracks, groups of tracks, macros, or everything as desired. A sys-ex dump of full memory takes about 50 seconds, but a couple of tracks' worth is much, much quicker. The QX5 would be best used in conjunction with some kind of MIDI system-exclusive storage device. We thought that's what Yamaha had in mind when they introduced the DX7IIFD with a floppy disk built in, but we're told that the disk can only store 20k files, and sequence files will often be 128k or more. The Yamaha's MDF-1 MIDI sys-ex quick disk isn't much more help either, since it only holds 59k per side. JL Cooper's MIDI Disk, a computer with the appropriate software, or cassette tape are about your only alternatives at this point.

Conclusions. The QX5 is your basic workhorse sequencer. Its price tag puts it well within affordability for most home studio users, yet we wouldn't be surprised to see it showing up in pro studios too. The fact that it is a dedicated hardware device makes it extremely appealing for live performance use, since there's no monitor screen to get smashed if some roadie drops it off the back of a truck. Of course, since there is no monitor screen, you won't see frills like the ability to give tracks clever names, you won't see the ability to name entire sequences, you won't find any algorithmic composition capabilities, nor will you see dozens of bewildering quanitzation choices. And that's as it should be. Workhorses don't need to do everything, they just need to be able to get the job done. The QX5 does everything you should need to do and does it at a price just about everyone will be able to afford. What more could you ask for?

Yamaha QX5
Description: Dedicated hardware MIDI sequencer.
Memory: 128k—about 20,000 notes without velocity data, 15,000 notes with velocity data.
Interfacing: MIDI in, out, thru. FSK in and out. MIDI out can echo input. Cassette interface.
Features: 8 tracks, 32 macros, real-time and step-time recording, auto-locate punch-in, punch-out, song position pointer recognized, MIDI rechannelization, data editing on event, measure, and track levels, sys-ex data can be nested in sequences, real-time track muting and unmuting, and so on.
Dimensions: 13.75" wide, 9.5" deep, 2" high, 6.5 lbs.
List Price: $595.00.
Contact: Yamaha, Box 6600, Buena Park, CA 90622.

Keyboard, **March 1987.**

Q-Sheet: Event Sequencer And MIDI Automation Mac Software

By Dominic Milano

First, the good news: Q-Sheet is one of the slickest pieces of music software we've ever seen. Now, the bad news: Q-Sheet is not a program everyone will be able to take advantage of, because it's *not* the world's ultimate Macintosh sequencer for recording *music.* It's designed for recording MIDI *events* in sync with SMPTE time code. Which means it's a godsend for people who make their living putting sound effects into video and motion pictures. For those of us who are mainly concerned with musical applications, Q-Sheet turns out to be a fantastic tool for doing completely automated MIDI mixing, but in order to take advantage of this capability, you'll need to own a MIDI-controlled mixer and/or some MIDI-controlled effects.

System Requirements. We ran our tests on two different Mac Pluses: one with an external 800K disk drive and one with an external DataFrame 20Meg hard disk. Digidesign claims compatibility with all types of Macs except the extinct 128K model (Q-Sheet was developed on a Mac II). Q-Sheet takes up about 250K of memory. In order to make operations like selecting different windows nearly instantaneous, most of the program is loaded into RAM on booting up. If you're using a 512K Mac, this leaves little room for loading MIDI file sequences into the program. Our recommendation is to use a hard disk.

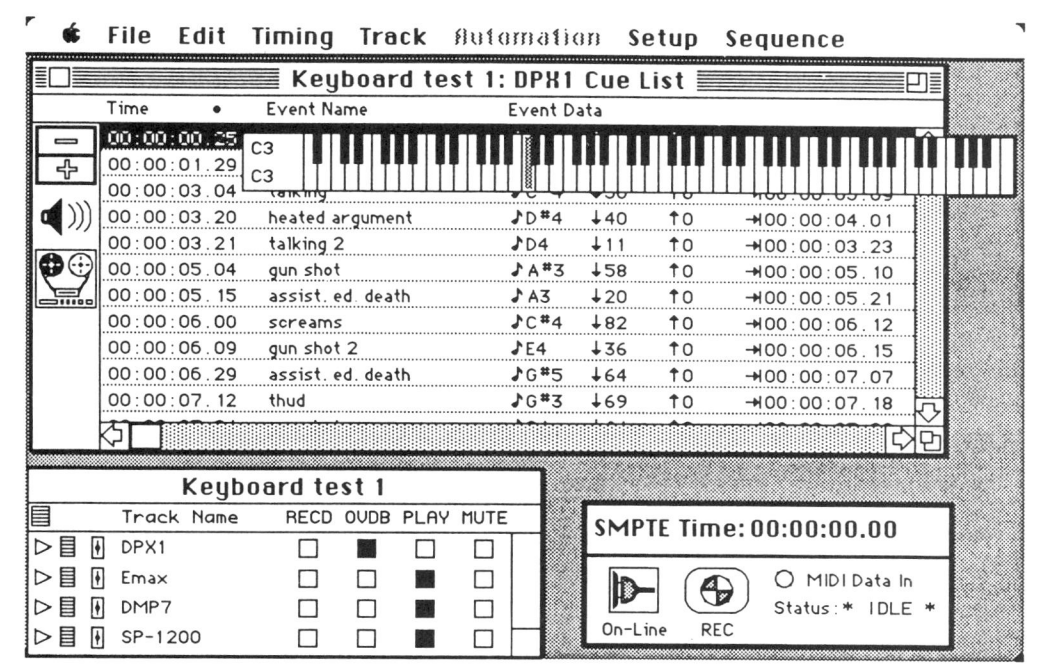

Figure 6. Editing a note event in the cue list involves using a pop-up menu keyboard, which plays the instrument remotely with the mouse.

If you're doing automated mixes, you can use Q-Sheet's internal clock, but if you're syncing to video or film, you'll need a SMPTE-to-MIDI Time Code converter like the Opcode Timecode Machine or JL Cooper's PPS-1. Our tests were conducted using an Opcode Timecode Machine. Our automation tests were performed with a Yamaha DMP7, an E-mu SP-1200 and Emax, an Oberheim DPX-1, and a Casio FZ-1, connected to a JL Cooper MSB Plus, whose panic button turned out to be invaluable, because the samplers tended to get stuck notes when we edited note events (more on this below). All of our sync tests were run with longitudinal time code on a Sony Beta VCR and an Otari MTR-90 24-track recorder; we had no opportunity to test Q-Sheet with a VITC (vertical interval time code) system.

Organization. Don't be confused when you see no reference to measures and beats, tempo and meter, and things like that. Q-Sheet is an event sequencer; as such, the aims of the program are wildly different from those of a music sequencer. Q-Sheet organizes incoming data into tracks, much like a music sequencer. However, a Q-Sheet track is more like a movie script that consists of a list of events and the exact SMPTE time they occur at—just the thing for syncing sound effects (fired from samplers) to video.

Screen displays include a track window, transport controls, cue lists, and animated automation windows. Overall, we found the program to be extremely intuitive, even though there's a lot of on-screen activity. Helping keep things simple during playback and editing are lots of dialog boxes and some useful pop-up menus for editing notes, attack and release velocities, and MIDI channels.

Interaction among windows is handled very well. If you insist on initiating every procedure with the mouse, instead of using keyboard equivalents, you'll find that selecting windows is virtually an instantaneous procedure. But if you really want to save time, we recommend using the keyboard command equivalents for the record, reset, start, and stop functions in the transport window.

Recording. Q-Sheet recording techniques vary depending on the kind of application you're working with. If you're syncing sound effects to film or video, the simplest way to work with Q-Sheet is to record in real time. But remember, Q-Sheet isn't a music sequencer, so there's no slowing the tempo down until you get it right. If you get it wrong, and chances are you will, you'll have to go in and edit the SMPTE

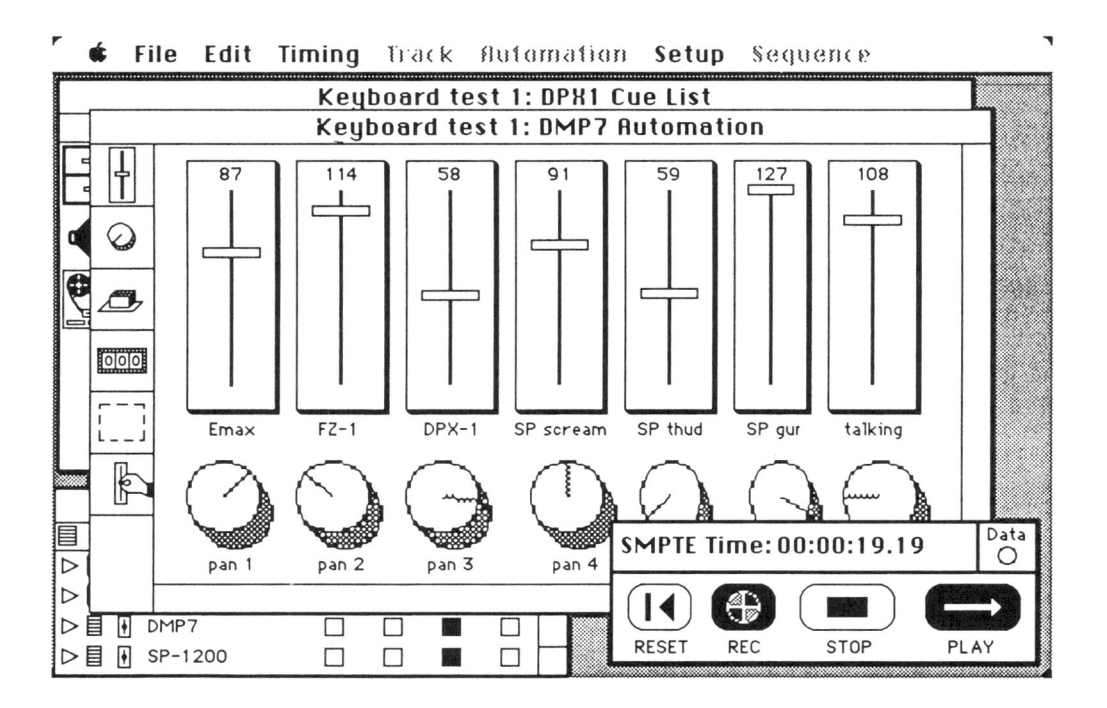

Figure 7. A Q-Sheet controller window showing animated faders and pan pots for DMP7 panel.

times, which is simple to do.

Another way to record is to input events one at a time—a process not unlike step-time recording. The difference is that rather than input a note and its duration, you input a SMPTE time and the corresponding MIDI event. If you're working with LTC (longitudinal time code, the kind that's striped on the audio track of a video or audio tape), as we were in our tests, you will have to input SMPTE times manually, since LTC's weakness is that LTC readers lose sync when the transport isn't moving fast enough (say when you're crawling through the picture looking for specific visual events to cue sound effects to). But if you're using VITC (vertical interval time code, which is nested in between video frames), you're in luck. Q-Sheet grabs VITC right off tape, no matter if it's crawling or stopped, so all you have to do is input your MIDI event, move to the next cue point, input that event, etc.

If you're inputting MIDI automation data—controlling a MIDI mixer or some

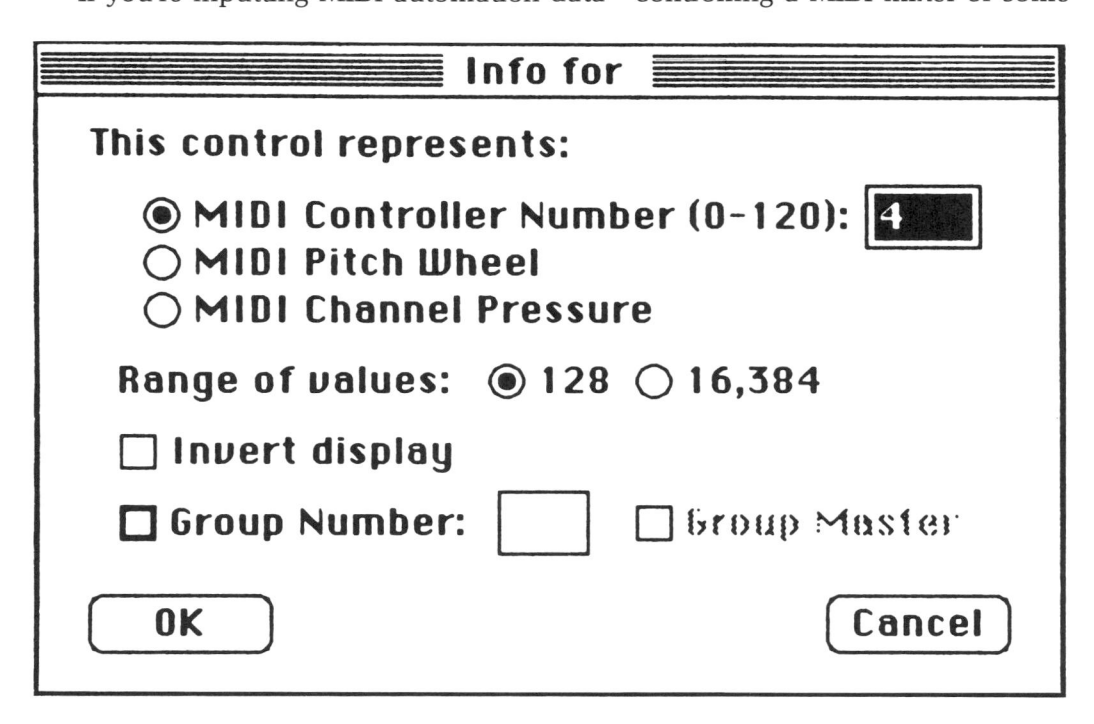

Figure 8. Dialog box for routing on-screen controllers.

110   Product Reviews

audio processor—the recording options are much different. In addition to recording controller changes the way you would when syncing to video, you can also open a controller window. Here, there is a tool box for building screen displays of any device—plans are to ship Q-Sheet with templates for a few of the most common MIDI-automatable boxes out there, including the Yamaha DMP7 and the Lexicon PCM-70. The version we looked at was a little more primordial, so we had to roll our own, which is a process that's time-consuming. But the fact that you can do it at all is a minor miracle.

At the left of each controller window are six icons: a slider, a rotary pot, a switch, an odometer, a Mac-style marquee, and a hand grabbing a slider. Clicking on any of the first four lets you reproduce that icon in the window as many times as you'd like, at any size you choose. The odometer indicates exact parameter values, while the marquee is used to select controls for performing cut, paste, and clear edits. When the hand-on slider icon is selected, you can update and record controller moves. Double-clicking on controls produces a dialog box in which you can map the controller number, group controllers, and determine the controller range (either 128 or 16,384).

Once you've assembled a "panel" of sliders, rotary pots, switches, and odometers, you can assign each to a MIDI controller number (corresponding, of course, to a control on some external MIDI box). Since you can open multiple Q-Sheet files simultaneously, we recommend taking the time to build a template file for any MIDI automation devices you have and transferring the appropriate templates to the file you're working on in order to save time.

Your panel of controllers can be used to record data (you grab sliders and rotary pots with the mouse—all controller movements are recorded in real time). If you prefer, you can record controller changes from the front panel of whatever device the controller changes are intended for. In either case, when you play data back, the screen display animates, showing all controller movements in real time. And if that isn't cool enough, you can have as many controller windows open on screen as you can fit (we found that three was the maximum reasonable amount to try to cram in). When you play back the cue list, all the controller windows will be animated. However, if you decide to get fancy and want to overdub controller moves on

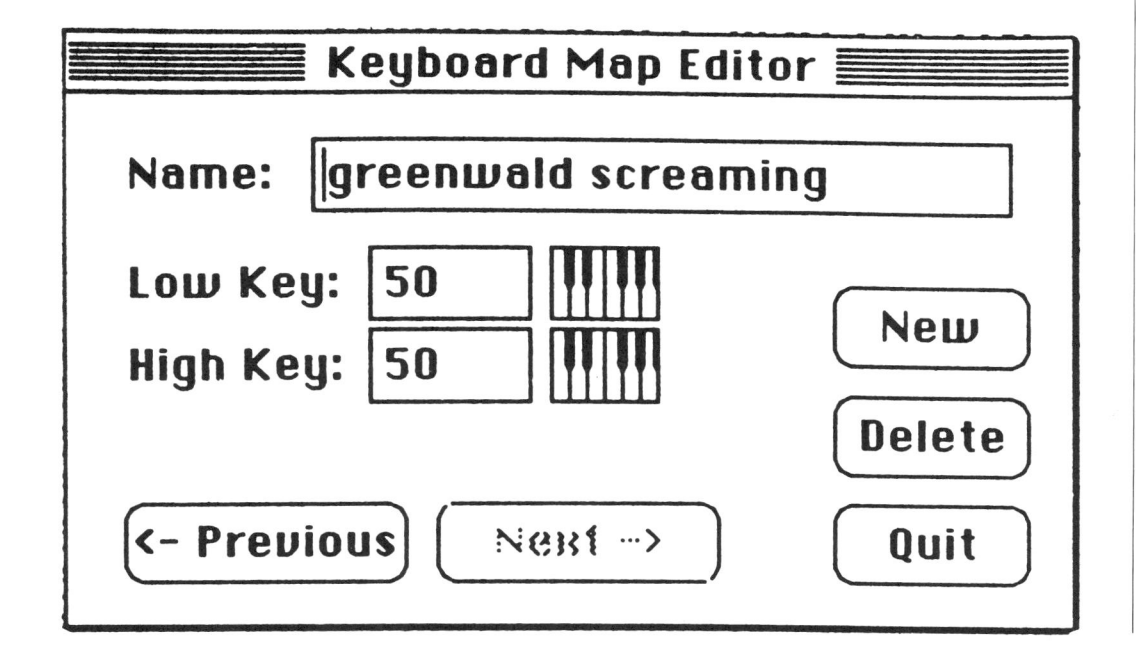

Figure 9. Keyboard icons in the map editing dialog box select pop-up keyboards.

multiple windows simultaneously, forget it. Even though all the controller windows animate simultaneously, you can only record in the window that's currently selected when recording from the Mac. If you're recording from external devices (playing keyboards, moving sliders, and so on), you can update any or all tracks, regardless if they're selected on the Mac screen.

Q-Sheet keeps controller messages grouped visually, so the cue list won't get overly cluttered with hundreds of controller changes. Each track has an independent stroke time parameter, which adjusts how far apart consecutive MIDI messages need to be before they will get logged as separate events in the cue list.

Other recording features include an input filter and an auto record mode in which up to 16 punch-in and -out points can be set. A keyboard map function lets you assign text names to any range of MIDI note numbers. For example: Middle C (MIDI note 60) could be a gunshot sample, 61 could be a thump, and so on. When those notes are recorded, the appropriate name appears in the event name portion of the cue list display. This function will definitely make life easier when you're trying to keep track of hundreds of sound effects events.

Editing. There are all kinds of useful editing functions in Q-Sheet, including the standard cut, paste, and clear Mac-style editing commands (keyboard equivalent commands are supported). SMPTE times for specific events can be incremented and decremented using icons in the cue list displays, or they can be changed by double-clicking directly on the time display, which calls up a dialog box in which you can type the desired SMPTE time.

Note events in the cue list can be changed by clicking and holding an eighth-note icon, which causes a pop-up menu keyboard to appear. Dragging the mouse across the keyboard will play the appropriate instrument remotely—very useful for doing sound effects on samplers, since it eliminates the need to remember what keys

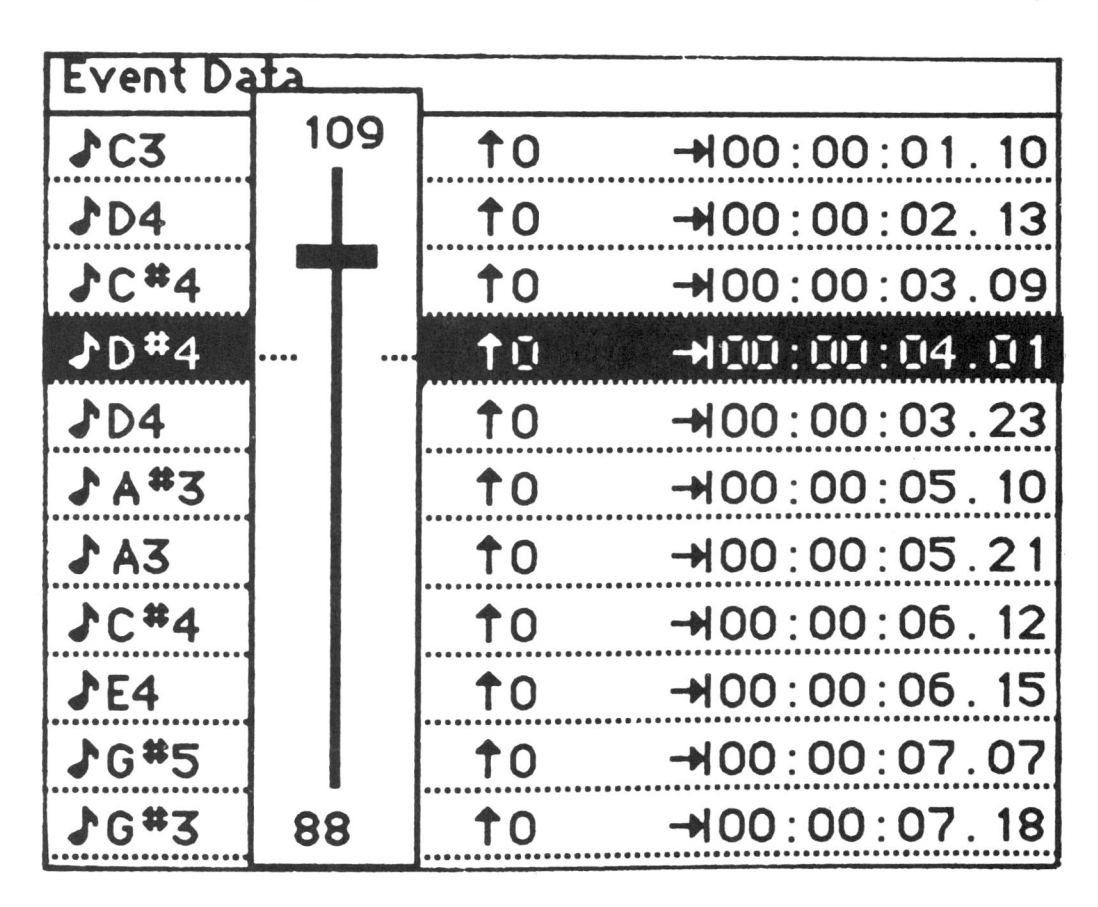

Figure 10. A pop-up slider for editing note-on velocity. The dotted line indicates fader position as originally recorded.

sounds are mapped on. On virtually all the keyboards/samplers we used Q-Sheet with, we experienced locked notes when using this function. At first we were using the MSB Plus' panic button to kill the endless note syndrome. Then we discovered the speaker icon in the cue list windows not only lets you sound the selected event, it sends out an all-notes-off. Every instrument we used recognized this command.

Editing note-on and -off velocities is handled with pop-up menus as well. The only difference is that a slider icon is used in place of the keyboard.

SMPTE times can also be messed with quite a bit. There are functions for offsetting time by any amount (all selected events are adjusted accordingly), aligning any number of events to a specific time, and repeating events any number of times at any specified number of frames (including the ability to randomize velocities and spacing by any percentage). Note lengths can be adjusted by quarter-frames (trying to adjust the length of a controller event by a quarter-frame happily produces no effect), and there is a special feature called event back-timing that sound effects people will love, it allows you to align the start of a sound effect for an action that begins off screen, with no visual cue to tell you when it should start other than a cue that tells you where it should end up (say a car zooming past the camera screen). This feature alone makes Q-Sheet worth its weight in gold.

Playback. When you're syncing sound effects to film, you frequently want to rewind to an earlier point, push play, and listen to what you've done so far. If you were working the old way—i.e., recording sound effects onto magnetic tape—all you'd worry about is whether you remembered to put the recorder in playback mode. When you're firing a bunch of samplers, automating effects, and driving MIDI mixers, there are a lot of other considerations. For example: Have you rewound to a place that requires the samplers to see six new program changes? Should your reverb parameters be different at the new locations? What about the audio levels and pan locations of the MIDI mixer you're driving? And worst of all—when you stop tape, will some of your instruments need to be reset in order to sync properly?

Happily (and somewhat amazingly) when you rewind Q-Sheet, it chases down program changes, controller positions, and so on. So when you start playback in mid-sequence, you needn't worry about the instruments being on the wrong programs. The one problem Q-Sheet can't deal with is that of an instrument needing to be reset to sync properly. We encountered this in our tests using an E-mu SP-1200 with SMPTE—you have to manually push the start/stop button twice for it to resync after it stops seeing SMPTE, which is a major pain. There's nothing Q-Sheet could possibly do about this, because it's a limitation of the SP-1200's design.

Some MIDI devices are more cooperative than others when receiving program changes. To accommodate the needs of different instruments, Q-Sheet features a chase delay for manually setting the number of milliseconds you need the program to wait before starting playback after chasing program changes, assuring that every instrument will have enough time to react to the program changes.

In a similar vein, instruments respond to MIDI data at different rates, which can be musically useful or musically horrible depending on your outlook. For syncing to film and doing automation, it turns out to be a nightmare. Which is why we were very glad to see that each individual track can be offset in quarter-frames during playback. The offset for each track is displayed on screen as part of the track window. Offsets can be positive or negative, so you can slide tracks forward and backward.

One fantastic feature lets Q-Sheet read and play back sequences created on any sequencer that supports MIDI files (we tested the function with a sequence created on

Opcode's Sequencer 2.5—it worked just fine). Start time, initial tempo, and a chase delay can be set from within a dialog box. You can also select which serial port the data will be sent out of.

Other playback functions include the ability to mute tracks, channelize their outputs, set which serial port they use, and sync to either external SMPTE or an internal timer. One very nice touch is the MIDI data indicator located in the transport control display. it blinks whenever MIDI data is received, which will come in handy in those rare situations when you're trying to figure out why the system isn't recording. We found ourselves forgetting (all too frequently) to put a track into record mode before starting recording using the transport controls.

If you're using a Mac II with a color monitor, you can color-coordinate animated controller displays, grouping sets of controls in the designer colors of your choice.

Conclusions. Q-Sheet is one of those programs that brings out the dreaded equipment-addict in us—once you've played with MIDI automation, you'll be loathe to go back to life without it. The only thing on our wish list is a feature that would slow the internal timer down to facilitate slower-than-real-time recording of controller data for doing automated mixes. It might also come in handy if you've already got a written-out cue list for sound effects. Suffice to say that if you've got the bucks to sink into a bunch of MIDIable mixing and processing gear, or if you do sound effects work with film and video, you'd be crazy not to add Q-Sheet to your list of must-haves.

Q-Sheet

Description: MIDI/SMPTE automation software, MIDI event sequencer.

System Requirements: 512K Mac minimum, Mac Plus, Mac SE, Mac II. Hard disk recommended. MIDI interface and SMPTE-to-MTC converter also required.

Features: Syncs to 24, 25, 30, and drop-frame SMPTE formats, input and output filtering, creates on-screen cue list of MIDI events and corresponding SMPTE times, text descriptions of keyboard mapping, track muting and overdubbing, extensive editing functions, event recording facilitates MIDI automation, MIDI files compatible.

List Price: $495.00.

Contact: Digidesign, 1360 Willow Rd., Suite 101, Menlo Park, CA 94025. (415) 327-8811.

Keyboard, **November 1987.**

Coda Finale: Music Notation And Transcription Software For The Mac

By Dominic Milano

Promises, promises. Would that every promise made was a promise kept. Take, for example, the pledge of salvation from the drudgery of notation nightmares offered in so many software advertisements. Throw away your notation pads, smash the points on your Rapidographs—notation software will do the dirty work for you. No more wrestling with beams and stems, no more blobby noteheads. Just click and drag, cut and paste to produce fit-to-print scores in no time at all.

Some notation packages make additional claims: Don't have time to transcribe your own music? Why not record your tune into a sequencer, save it as a MIDI file, export it to the appropriate notation/transcription software, and *voila!* Out comes a flawlessly transcribed publication-quality score.

Question is, is there any software on the planet that lives up to those lofty promises? According to the manufacturer's amazingly well-orchestrated marketing campaign, "Finale is the first music software that efficiently eliminates the pencil from the composing and publishing process." Naturally, we couldn't let such a bold claim go unchallenged, so we rolled up our sleeves, put our noses to the grindstone, and set about conducting our tests. Here's what we uncovered about Finale 1.0.0.

The Packaging. We all know that glitzy marketing campaigns and fancy covers do not a good book or software make, but Finale deserves some special praise here. Without a doubt, its packaging is the most stunning we've seen. Spot-varnished cover, gorgeous deco graphics, bound-in videotape, solid three-ring binder for not one but *three* spiral-bound manuals (tutorials, advanced applications guide, reference manual)—just the thing to convince buyers that Finale's $1,000 price tag is well worth it.

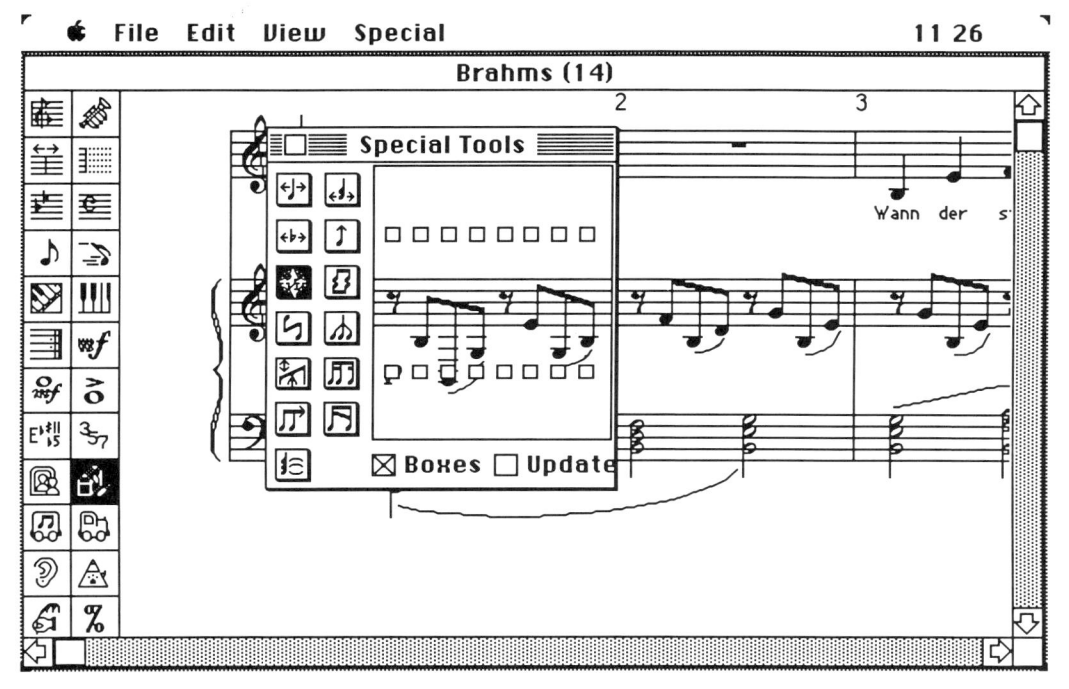

Figure 11. Finale's Special Tools dialog box is used to tweak the positioning of stems, beams, notes, ties, and accidentals.

The Package. Hidden away in one of the pages of the binders is the important stuff—four *uncopy-protected* disks: one master Finale system disk, one working copy of Finale, one copy of the Finale PowerPlus (more on this below), and one Hypercard Helpstack. Not copy-protecting Finale is a pretty gutsy move considering that the Hypercard Helpstack contains most or all of the information contained in the 301-page Reference Manual. Still, without the tutorial-oriented User's Guide or the Power User's Guide, even the most skilled pirate would have trouble figuring out how to run Finale.

The Approach. Organizationally, Finale is the most ambitious of any of the notation packages we've seen in that it attempts to be all things to all customers. For the music copyist Finale offers a number of note entry methods (MIDI included), extensive page layout facilities, custom shape-making tools for all sorts of non-standard notation symbols, tablature capability, score and part printing, templates for familiar staff combinations (grand, small orchestra, lead sheets), comprehensive stemming and beaming options, user-definable macros, and on and on. For the composer, Finale's disk set includes a completely independent program, Finale PowerPlus, designed to transcribe multi-channel sequences stored as MIDI files. The Finale program itself includes the ability to transcribe MIDI data directly, which is just the thing for transcribing long stream-of-consciousness improvisations. You can also overdub parts onto already existing scores and play the entire piece back as a MIDI sequence.

What this means is that two diverse sets of needs are being addressed simultaneously. And herein lies what we see as one of Finale's biggest problems: Despite claims made throughout the manual that Finale does not second-guess what it is you want to do, it does exactly that all too often. Copyists do not give a rat's posterior about hearing their work played back. They simply want to deal with graphic objects on a page/screen. Yet Finale forces you to play by rules that only make sense in a MIDI playback context. (The brochures tout this as one of Finale's main strengths: "... it assumes that any symbol—text or graphic—should be more than just a graphic element. It should do what it says.") As a result, getting exactly what you want to appear on the screen/printed page involves serious mental gymnastics of the "fool the program into thinking it's doing something that it's not" variety. Some of these tricks are well-documented in the manuals. Many of them, sadly, are not.

From the composer's point of view, listening back to your written notation without having to go through a sequencing program is wonderful. We think it's the best part of Finale. However, its transcriptions of MIDI files leaves a lot to be desired. We had to spend inordinate amounts of time massaging tracks and/or the transcriptions to even come close to what was originally played. The live transcription tool was much more useful—in fact, we found it delightful once we'd figured it out. The question is, will composers find Finale a more efficient substitute for pencil and paper combined with a good dedicated MIDI sequencer? We remain unconvinced.

To be fair, Finale is easily the most complex program we've ever seen. That there are *three* manuals, a Hypercard Helpstack, and more tutorial manuals on the way speaks tomes about its complexity. Anyone who buys the program shouldn't expect to be making publication-quality scores overnight. The time required to learn Finale is enormous. Certain aspects of it seem straightforward and easy to grasp. Yet other things strike us as completely unintuitive, needlessly convoluted, and impossible to deal with unless you have the patience of a saint and the mind of Sherlock Holmes. We've spent two months with it, and still don't feel we've come close to testing every feature to its limits. In other words, if you're looking for the instant gratification promised in the Finale brochures, you're not going to find it. On the other hand, we feel that if you're willing to devote serious study to learning Finale the way a concert violinist learns his instrument (and you're willing to put up with first-generation glitches and outright bugs), you may gain a great deal of satisfaction.

During our tests we regularly went through several distinct emotional states: (1) Joy. ("Wow. It'll do *that*?") (2) Curiosity. ("Now how do we get it to do it *right*?") (3) Aggravation. ("That took *how many* hours?") And finally (4a) triumphant relief (*That's* where that dialog box is!") or (4b) blood lust. ("Whoever designed this program should be shot.")

The Details. Finale, like many Mac music programs, prefers to see systems 4.2 or higher. If you boot with a system that doesn't have Finale's Petrucci font installed, you'll see a single measure with Greek letters in place of a treble clef, whole-note rest, and time signature when you boot the program. Needless to say, make sure you install Petrucci or use the system supplied with Finale. The 6.0 system gives Finale's Lyric tool problems, and the Speedy Note Entry tool isn't compatible with Multifinder versions 1.0 or 6.0, though Coda is fixing this problem in a soon-to-come update. We recommend using Finale with a hard drive, as the program is 789k—too big to fit any files on the program disk, so you'll be in for plenty of disk swapping.

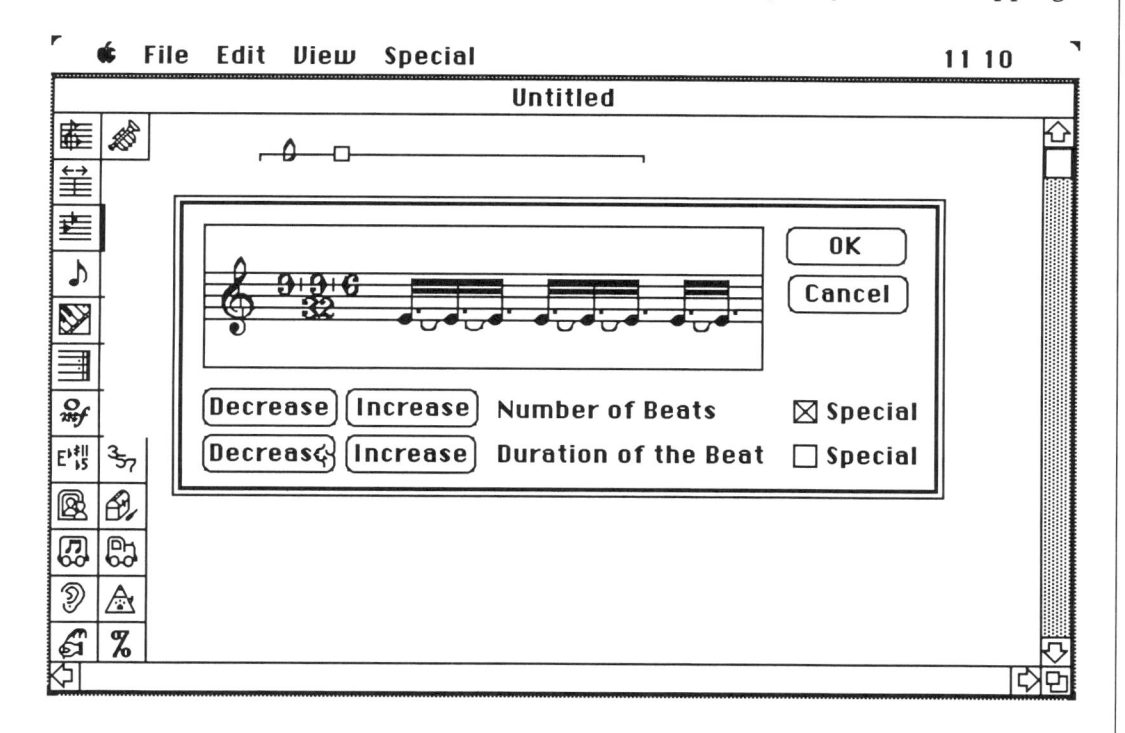

Figure 12. Dialog box for setting time signatures in Finale. An unusual meter is shown.

Once you've booted up, you are greeted with a display of a single staff/single measure in the working area of the screen (called the Score Window). Stacked vertically along the left of the screen are 32 tool icons. (Actually, only 24 of them are visible on a standard Mac screen; all 32 are visible on a standard Mac II monitor. If you want to use a full-page-display monitor.) On an SE, which 24 tools are visible at any time is completely up to you, since you can store four tool palette configurations—very handy once you've learned the program, though we found the default arrangement as good as any.

Working with the tools is a simple matter of point and click and click again on the target for that tool's operation. Or we should say, it becomes that once you've gotten familiar enough with the program to remember which tool to select for the task at hand. It can't be all that hard to remember each tool's function, right? Oh yes it can, considering that tools perform multiple functions. The function you get may depend on whether you're option/clicking, shift/clicking, or command/clicking, or it may depend on your selecting different functions in any one of the dialog boxes.

In fact, we've heard Finale nicknamed "OK," because there are so damn many dialog boxes. For example, want to transpose a measure? Select the Mass Mover tool (one click), select target measure/staff by double-clicking on it (two more clicks), select the desired operation in the first dialog box (edit, erase, delete measures, insert measures, or add measure—click), answer the next dialog box question (items to edit—clicks), answer the third dialog box questions (entry modifications: a couple of transpose options, stemming choices, rebeaming selections—another click and some typing if you are transposing), and finally answer the fourth dialog box if you chose to rebeam or transpose (click). That's seven clicks.

Coda Finale   117

Figure 13. The page layout functions allow you to view multiple pages of a score simultaneously. You can also adjust layout of measures, input headers and footers, determine percentage of reduction, and so on.

Got it? Most of the tools are like that. But there's a way to avoid endless dialog boxes—the Meta tools. These are both user-definable and preprogrammed macros. The programmable Meta tools can be used to streamline the operation of eight tools: Chord, Key Sig., Note Expression, Repeat Score Expression, Staff Expression, Time Sig., and Tuplet tools. Preset Meta tools exist for the Mass Mover and Playback tools. So, for example, the transpose operation described above becomes a mere five-step operation (click Mass Mover, double-click the target measure(s) while holding down the number 6, type the transpose value, click "OK"). Take our word for it, it's a lot faster. Our advice is to learn to use the Meta tools right away. They'll save you from hours of clicking on "OK."

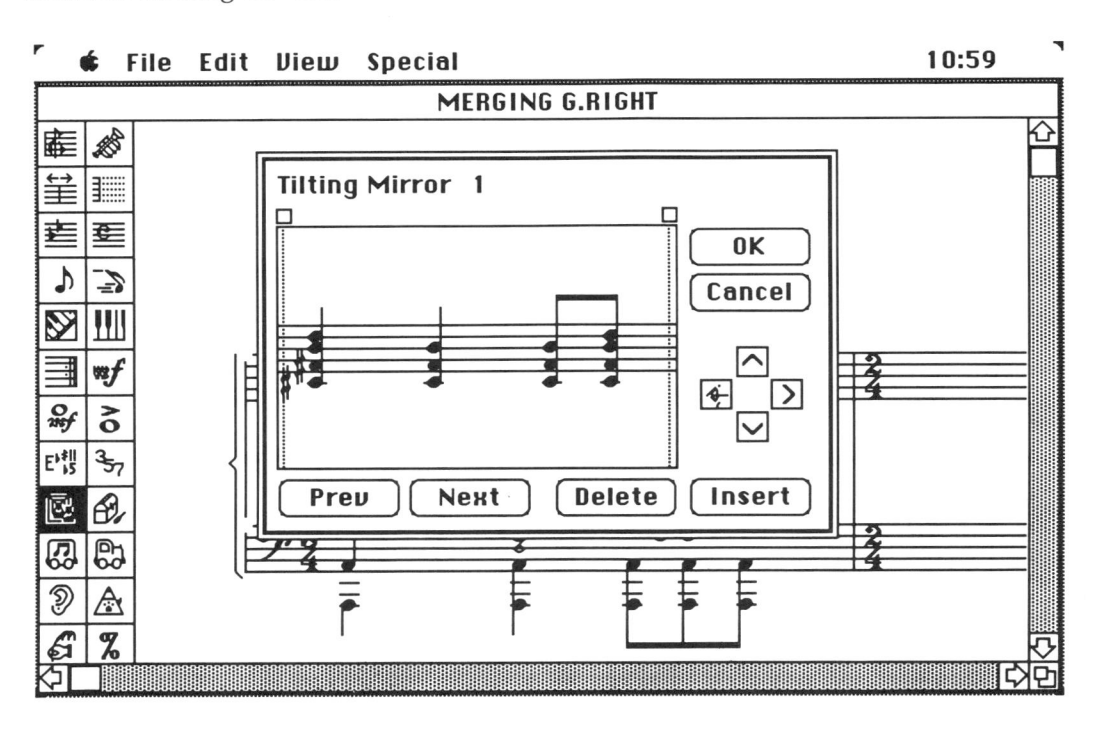

Figure 14. The Tilting Mirror tool is one of many "intelligent" ways of manipulating portions of a score.

Unless you've opened a template file (a blank collection of staves with preset instrument/staff definitions), the first thing you'll be doing is setting up how many

118   Product Reviews

staves will appear in your score, grouping them together in various ways, and specifying their starting clefs, time signatures, and key signatures. We recommend that you spend some time building template files if you plan on doing a lot of scores that involve particular instrumentations (string quartets, guitar trios, synth quintets, etc.), as it will save you much time in the future.

You'll be using ^ix tools to build your instrument/staff definitions: the New Instrument tool, the Instrument Attributes tool, the measure Attributes tool, the Key Signature tool, the Time Signature tool, and possibly the Measure Add tool, though its function (adding new measures onto existing staves) happens automatically in most of the note-entry methods.

Speaking of note-entry methods, Finale offers no less than seven of them. These include HyperScribe (instant on-screen transcription), transcription (play in notes via a MIDI instrument and superimpose or tag the measure breaks), simple note entry (click and drag notes onto the staff via note tools), simple note entry with MIDI (enter the notes via MIDI and add the rhythms using the mouse), speedy note entry (select pitches with the arrow keys and time values with the numeric keypad), speedy note entry with MIDI (note values from MIDI, time values from the numeric keyboard), and the seventh method, which allows the alpha keys to dictate pitch and the numeric keys to dictate rhythm. An eighth method is provided by the PowerPlus program. As mentioned above, it offers the ability to transcribe pre-recorded MIDI sequence files, though we found that it took so much to massage these files into shape that we would have a hard time recommending this as a serious way to transcribe even old sequences.

By far our favorite note entry method for composing was to use the Transcription

Figure 15. The ideal way to get around Finale's quirky multiple voice implementation is to input each independent voice on a separate staff and then merge them as shown here.

Coda Finale 119

tool combined with the Speedy Note Entry tool, the latter to clean up the default accidentals Finale insists on (argh), as well as to massage time values and the like. There were times, however, when the Speedy Note Entry tool simply froze up, or user error ended up trashing a measure accidentally. A couple of tips for using the Transcription tool: Keep your parts as simple as possible. The more you throw Finale at once, the more cleaning up you're likely to have to do later. And don't make the same dumb mistake we often did: Remember to set the keyboard function to play while doing your time tags. (A time tag is a manually played metronome reference that tells Finale where to put the beats in a transcription.) Otherwise the program will transcribe the note you play as a time tag as part of the piece. Also before playing a note, use the Measure Attributes tool to set the measure width to a value greater than the default of 600 (we preferred a setting of 1200). This ensures that the notes won't be jammed together.

Putting ourselves in the shoes of a music copyist, we found the Speedy Note Entry tools quickest for raw inputting of notes from an already existing score. Depending on your sight-reading chops, you may prefer some other method.

Dynamic markings are more easily dealt with, although occasionally we found them appearing double-vision fashion in our scores, with the only way to eliminate the extra symbol being to erase both of them. Fingerings are another story. Rather than simply type them in as you would lyrics, you use a combination of the Note Expression tool and the Meta tools, the former to enter the numbers, the latter to

Figure 16. Finale printout. Top to bottom: Linotronic, Laserwriter, and ImageWriter.

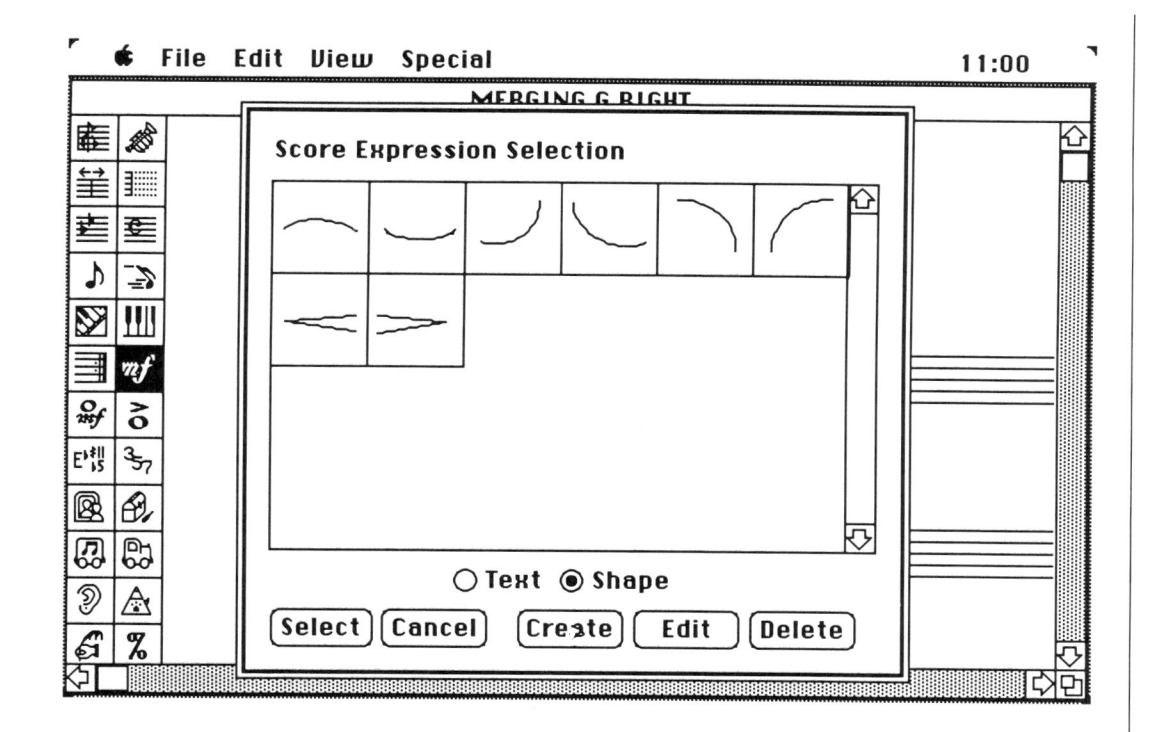

Figure 17. The Score Expression library. Shapes created with the Shape Designer tool are stored in this library for selection and placement. This is our least favorite aspect of Finale; we're told it's being completely redesigned.

automate the process of assigning them to notes. Point size and font of the finger markings can be adjusted, but we still haven't figured out how to get chord fingerings.

Other editing functions you'll no doubt need (especially if you're a copyist) are your basic cut, copy, paste, insert, and merge commands. Finale has these covered

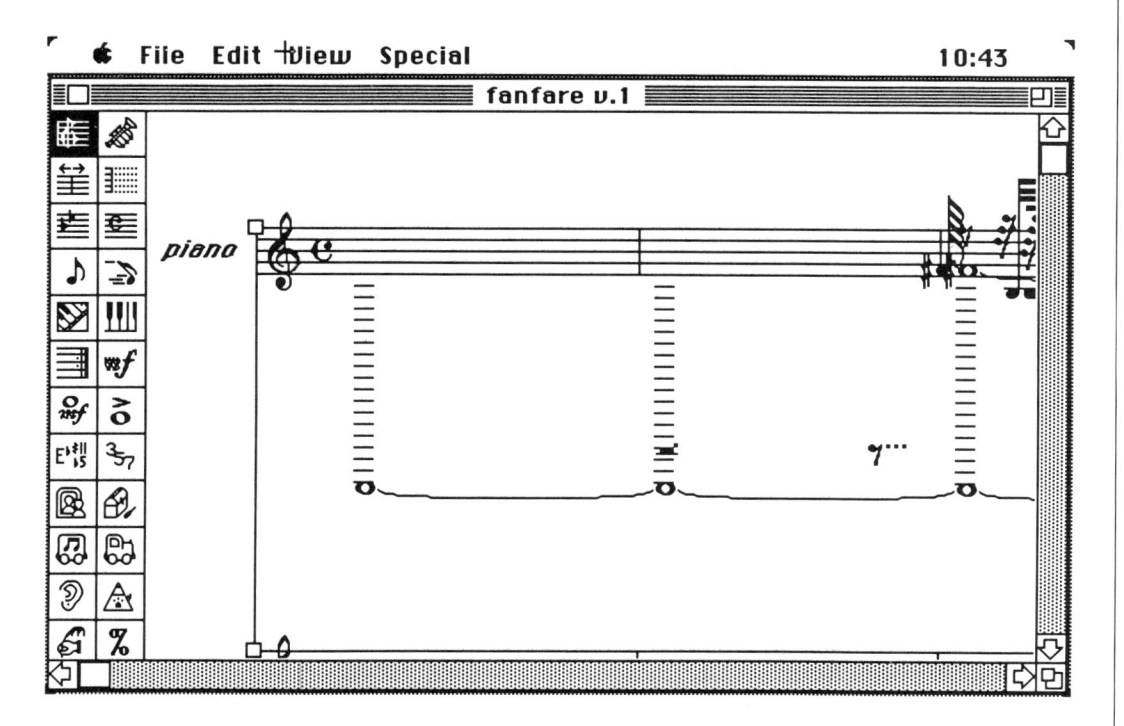

Figure 18. Unless you massage your sequence and set Finale's parameters properly (a time-consuming process of trial and error), the program can produce peculiar transcriptions like the one above.

very well. The Note Mover's dialog box lets you choose from a plethora of options for destructive and non-destructive merging and copying. And for performing operations on large portions of your score, the Mass Mover tool generally does a great job, though learning all its uses will take some time and it's not quite bug-free. (It tends to lock up in the middle of massive computations.) It would also be nice if the insert, delete, and add measures commands in the Mass Mover didn't have to affect every staff in a system. As it is, you can't add a measure to a vocal part's staff without

Coda Finale 121

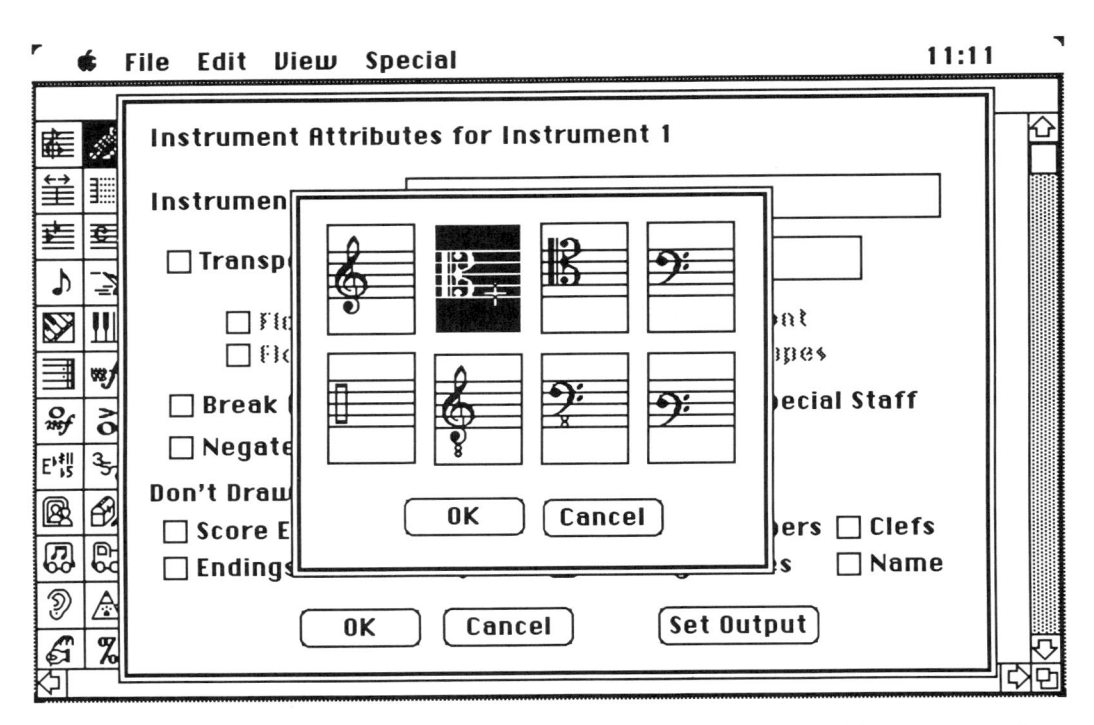

Figure 19. The Instrument Attributes tool allows you to select the default clef for a staff.

also adding a measure to the rest of the instruments in the score. These operations should be available both globally and locally, and they should be undoable.

Playback. Despite the inconveniences to the raw entry of notes due to restraints imposed by playback considerations, actually being able to click an icon (and an "OK" or two in a dialog box) and listen to your score is quite a cool thing. What's even cooler is that there are all kinds of facilities for assigning different staves to MIDI channels, nesting program changes, record/playback of continuous controller data, and so on. On top of that, the dynamic markings in the score will be translated into MIDI data (one of the tools determines which notes the expression markings will affect). These playback facilities make Finale one of the first serious stabs at doing a "sequencer" that does not follow the tape recorder metaphor. And that deserves major kudos in and of itself.

Think of it this way: Instead of tracks, you have staves, each of which holds data (notation-based MIDI note information). These are assignable to different MIDI channels. If you want to overdub a part, you can either play it using one of the transcription tools, or manually input it using Note Entry or Speedy Note Entry tools. Editing the tracks is a matter of massaging the score with the editing tools.

Finale supports display of multiple simultaneous time signatures, so you can score, for example, 3/4 against 4/4. But playback does not, unfortunately, produce anything resembling three-against-four polyrhythms. Rats. This capability is high on our wish list, though if you're doing pop tunes, we doubt you'll care. The same complaints we made about massaging the score apply to Finale as a sequencer. At the very least, cutting and copying functions should be available as global and local commands, and dealing with multiple voices should be simpler than it is. The score can be set to scroll during playback, though we found that our Mac SE and Plus couldn't keep up with even a simple four-voice, two-staff piece. By the time the third and fourth measures were redrawn, bars 8 and 9 were already playing. You'll need a Mac II to make the best of this capability.

Page Layout And Print Quality. For copyists and composers both, printing and page layout facilities are very important. After all, getting a score laid out for publication or for session players is not a trivial consideration. Finale allows you to shift measure widths, view multiple pages, print music at nearly infinite reduction percentages, design headers and footers, print out individual parts from a master score, and so on.

Finale's insistence that you distinguish between voices on any given staff was by far its most infuriating shortcoming. It has a two-voice limit per staff! (The voices are polyphonic, of course. The distinction between them is for purposes of stem and rhythmic independence.) We could go on for days listing the glitches in this implementation and the trouble it causes. For example, when a simple four-voice chorale on two staves (like most anything by Bach) is being input, the program insists on counting each note as a beat in that measure. Go past the allotted number of beats in the time signature, and up pops the most annoying dialog box of all to ask you if you want to chop off the offending notes or simply dump them into the next measure. Fortunately, there's a simple way around this problem that isn't in any of the manuals. You can enter each voice on a separate staff, use the Special Tools tool to adjust the relative positions of the voices as needed to prevent notes from colliding, and then drag the staves together (merge them) using the New Instrument tool.

Massaging Your Work. After you've got all your notes input, there are a number of stages you'll go through before you have a visually polished score. There will no doubt be aspects of its initial appearance that you don't like—measures too narrow, beams not grouped or angled in the proper direction, stems pointing in the wrong direction, etc. To massage note-oriented objects, you'll use a combination of the Special Tools tool, the Tuplet tool, and the Mass Mover and Note Mover tools. The Special Tools will be particularly important in that they are the main way you go about moving notes around (be sure you've selected one of the non-default positioning modes via the New Instrument tool), changing stem lengths, beam angles, and things like that.

Pros & Cons
Pros: Combined graphic and MIDI playback orientation. Transcription capabilities. Beautiful printed output. Extensive documentation.
Cons: Complex and difficult to learn. Playback orientation gets in the way of graphic capabilities. Extensive documentation.

There are a couple of frustrating glitches within this tool, however. The most serious is that the tool itself is a sort of window that appears over the target measure. This window can't be shifted up or down, though you can shift what's under it to the left or right. This is a problem because notes you may need to move may fall above or below the boundaries of the window, making those notes, beams, or stems unreachable.

Another problem for copyists worried about publication-quality scores: The Special Tools will only work on notes, stems, and beams. They will let you push and pull rests in a left-right axis, but forget moving them up and down. This problem is particularly evident when you change the stem direction of a group of eighth or sixteenths that have nested rests in them. The stems will flip up or down just fine, but those rests stay where the stems used to be. Oops. You can sometimes get around the problem by pulling voices out of the staff, which if you're lucky may cause the stems and rests in your sixteenth-note (or whatever) grouping to flip direction. This technique is a little iffy for our taste.

The other kind of tweaking you'll want to do involves putting in dynamic markings, slurs, ties, and crescendos/decrescendos, not to mention fingerings and lyrics. The latter is a snap. We found that automated lyric entry worked wonderfully, though we're told it sometimes goes to Mars if you're running on the wrong system. Slurs and crescendos/decrescendos are another story altogether. The good news here is that this part of the program is being completely reworked—very fortunate since the current implementation flat-out sucks.

To make a very long story short, in the current implementation, slurs have to be designed, saved to a library, and then entered into the target measure(s). Yes, you can tweak them after they're in that measure, and yes, you can automate some of the process by using Meta tools. Inputting a slur should be as simple as clicking on the first note, last note, and some secondary plane to define the angle. Instead, you get to attempt deciphering the Shape Designer—a process that's not unlike trying to learn Adobe's Illustrator without a manual. Coda is planning to release an update that will include the ability to draw slurs and hairpin crescendos by specifying a start- and end-point. We're told the shapes will expand or contract as the measure widths are changed and will wrap around the end of staff systems on the page as necessary.

The way stems fit noteheads, the distance between accidentals and notes, the beam widths, and so on, can all be adjusted from one of Finale's many menus. The defaults looked quite good to us, but if you intend to tweeze them, be prepared for some serious trial and error. These parameters are not for the weak at heart.

As far as the print quality of the music font, Finale uses its own custom font called Petrucci. It is by far the best we've seen, though the differences between it and the Sonata font used by most other programs is fairly subtle.

Documentation. During our first week or so, we were going around telling people that Finale's documentation was the best we'd seen in a long time. The first of the three manuals, the User's Guide, is packed with tutorials that do a great job of getting you into the first layers of the program. We got a lot out of them. The frustrating thing is that the tutorials stop there. What you're left with are essentially two Reference Guides that explain the functions, but don't necessarily walk you through their application. Instead, you're left to your own experiments—which is where our needing the mind of Sherlock Holmes statement comes from. We were constantly discovering new ways to do things, which was both exciting and maddening. Finale is full of redundancy—it is possible to accomplish certain tasks in a variety of ways. Discovering which way is best for you takes time and practice.

The Hypercard Helpstack is excellent (it contains virtually all the information in the third manual, the complete Finale Reference Guide), yet it cross-references all of the functions related to performing a given task. Too bad the Speedy Note Entry tool has trouble running under Multifinder, because ideally, you'd want to be able to access the Helpstack without quitting Finale.

We're told that Coda is planning to release a new set of tutorials filled with tidbits to help you get into the less obvious aspects of the program. These should be a help to users who don't have the hours it takes to track down solutions to problems.

Conclusions. Finale is an incredibly powerful program. And like all too many first releases it's not without its glitches and bugs (many of which we're told are being fixed in the next software revision). Getting familiar enough with Finale to even feel comfortable writing a review took us a full two months. During that time, we constantly flip-flopped between loving Finale and hating it. So how do we feel now? Finale's printed output is gorgeous, no doubt about it. Getting to that output is not as straightforward as we wish it was. Anyone who is willing to spend the time to master the program will no doubt go through the same love/hate thing we did. While anyone who's looking for the instant gratification promised in the Finale ads and brochures is going to hate it, pure and simple.

Rating Finale's Notation Power

There are certain notation conventions and non-conventions that have given earlier so-called first generation notation programs fits. They are also the reason that so many composers and copyists have resisted computerizing their notation operations for so long.

Below is a small sampling of bench marks followed by their Finale version and our comments and tips. We encountered many glitches in various tools throughout the process of creating these and other examples. The most frustrating were those that totally destroyed 15 to 20 minutes worth of work in an instant. For example, we were experimenting with doing tuplet grace notes when we realized the target staff for some cross-stave beaming was in the wrong clef. We exited the Special Tools and selected the Instrument Attributes tool, but after we changed the clef, our stream of would-be grace notes turned into chords.

Of course, if you aren't concerned about whether your beams extend across staves or your triplets are bracketed or slurred, you needn't worry. Finale version 1.0.0's output looks fantastic.

There's a lot of raw power in Finale's Notation capabilities, but it takes time to learn the program, and it takes time to figure out how to overcome its shortcomings. We were constantly surprising ourselves by thinking up ways to do things we initially thought Finale would never be able to do. Just as often, we'd try to produce something

---

Coda Finale (Version 1.0.0)

Description: Music notation, transcription, and sequencing software for the Macintosh.

Requirements: Macintosh Plus, SE, or II with at least 1 meg RAM. Hard disk recommended. LaserWriter or other PostScript-compatible printer for PostScript printout. Imagewriter for bit-map printout. Optimal configuration for professional use: Mac II with full memory, hard drive, accelerator card, full-page display, Linotronic or other PostScript-compatible typesetter. IBM version being developed.

Features: Eight input modes including MIDI transcription. Support of non-standard time signatures and key signatures. Display of multiple meters and clefs. Automatic transpositon to any key. Support of nested tuplets. Comprehensive stemming and beaming options. Automated mass entry of lyrics. Custom shape design for non-standard notation symbols. User-programmable and preset macros. Extensive cut, copy, paste, merge, insert implementation. Display of chord symbols, etc.

Printing: PostScript output in Finale's Petrucci font. Parts may be extracted from scores for individual part copying. Extensive page layout capabilities.

Playback: Audition mode allows quick playback of score over MIDI. Individual staves can be assigned to different MIDI channels. Nested program changes. Dynamic markings interpreted as MIDI velocity values. Captured MIDI performance data may also be played back as part of a score/sequence. Up to 32 MIDI channel playback if interface allows.

Documentation: Three-volume manual (Finale User's Guide, Unlocking the Power of Finale, Finale Reference Manual), Hypercard Helpstack, 25-minute video cassette. Inside Finale booklets available soon. Customer support phone line available from 6 A.M. to 8 P.M. Central Standard Time.

List Price: $1,000.00.

Contact: Coda, 1401 E. 79th St., Bloomington, MN 55425-1126. (800) 843-1337.

in the way you'd expect to do it, found it didn't work or glitched too much, but later came back to it and figured out a completely new approach that *would* work.

Is it faster than doing notation the old-fashioned way? If the "old-fashioned way" means pen and paper, Finale's output will look a lot better, no question about it. But if forced to choose between Finale and a manual music typewriter, we'd be inclined to stick with the typewriter. We still feel that version 1.0.0 puts too many roadblocks in the way of getting what you want on the printed page. Aside from some obvious bugs, the rules you have to play by to get the benefit of listening to your scores are just too cumbersome. The metaphor that comes to mind is that of having a word processor that insists on checking your grammar on a sentence-by-sentence level. So it won't let you write a sentence that ends with a verb. Or won't let you write sentence fragments or haiku poetry without first fooling it into thinking you're writing something else.

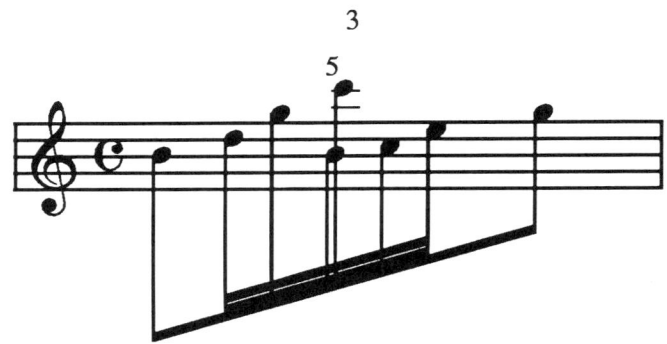

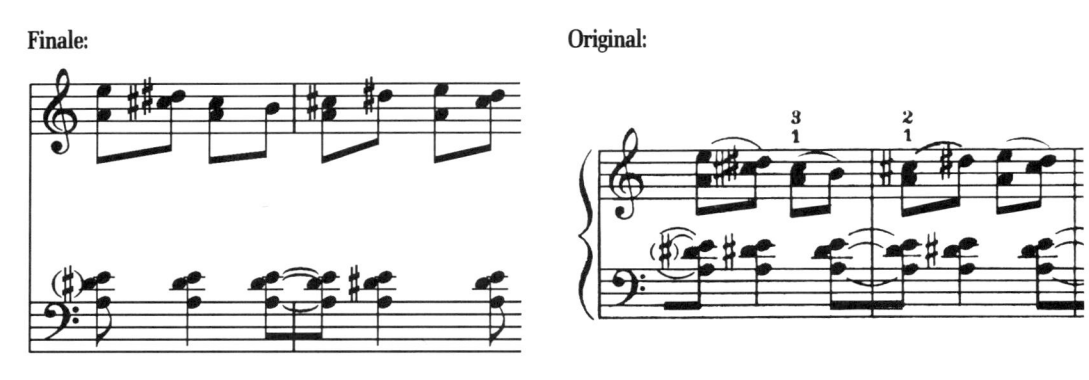

Figure 20. There are two ways to do nested tuplets in Finale. Here, we've superimposed a quintuplet with a triplet by merging two different staves.

Figure 21. Cross-bar beams, as in this passage from Bartók's Mikrokosmos, are tough with Finale. Though there is a tool in the Special Tools for extending beams, just for this purpose, it will not convert a flag into a beam, which meant that the eighth-quarter-eighth pattern in this example required a more creative solution. The way we accomplished it was to enter this example as a bar of 4/4, then use the Shape Designer tool to fake the bar line. We can't tell you how many times we had to fight the program wanting to un-beam the center eights, even though the barline is artificial.

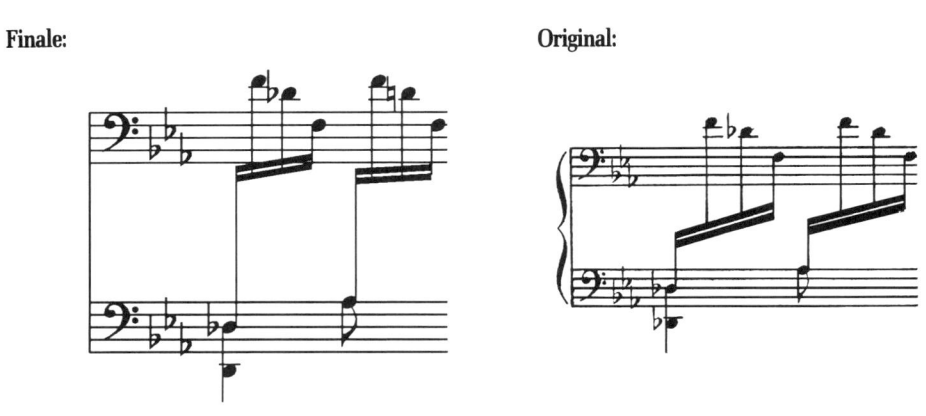

Figure 22. We found cross-stave beaming with Finale, with stems pointing in opposite directions, a real bear to get just right. For this example from Debussy's Jardins sous la pluie, we used three staves and merged the bottom two to get the multiple voice effect.

If, on the other hand, "old-fashioned" means choosing Finale over copying endless parts by hand, our decision is less clear cut. Finale's ability to print out individual parts from a larger score, its ability to transpose an entire score to any new key you tell it to, its ability to produce templates and copy sections *en masse* makes it a very powerful tool for the composer/copyist who is willing to learn their way around the program and all its idiosyncrasies.

***Keyboard*, February 1989.**

Ludwig: Algorithmic Composition For The Atari ST

By Jim Aikin

Musical ideas I've got plenty of. What's in short supply is the time needed to shape those ideas into finished pieces. So when somebody comes along with yet another program that will generate raw ideas, I'm skeptical. I want to know how hard the program will be to learn and to use, and how well it will function in a sequencing environment with the gear I've already got.

Ludwig, the new algorithmic composition package from Hybrid Arts, looks and sounds quite exciting in its own terms. It will perform a host of unusual operations on raw musical data and play back the results as a MIDI performance. In terms of ease of use and integration within an environment, it's merely adequate, not spectacular. If Ludwig were a prototype for a program that was going to have some new features added before its release, we'd be ecstatic, It stimulated us to think of lots of musical textures that we might never have considered if we hadn't taken it out for a spin. But it isn't a prototype, it's a finished product, and we're told that Hybrid Arts probably won't put version 2.0 onto the agenda unless sales of the first version warrant it. Given the amount of competition these days in algorithmic music generators, they may be looking at an uphill fight.

Overview. More than anything else, Ludwig resembles a drum machine that went to Mars. Not that it's limited to drum sounds, you understand. It will play up to eight channels of MIDI notes at once. But like a drum machine, it makes music by stringing together short patterns. The Mars part comes in because Ludwig doesn't simply play back the patterns; it allows the user to transform them in very complex ways, using commands called "operators." An entire piece could conceivably be built up by putting a single simple pattern through dozens or hundreds of different transformations.

The program can contain up to 96 pitch patterns and 96 rhythm patterns. Each of these can be a maximum of 32 events long. (A pitch "event" can consist of a single MIDI note or a chord. The chords can contain up to 16 notes each, but these must be contained within a span of a minor tenth—an odd but workable limitation.) Thirty-two events may not seem like much, but if you happen to need longer patterns you can always string two shorter ones together. We found that even patterns of five or six pitches and seven or eight rhythms actually produced more possibilities than we had time to explore.

The patterns can be strung together in eight simultaneous parallel tracks, each with its own MIDI channel. Each track can be a maximum of 1,024 "cells" long, where a cell contains either a pattern or an operator that transforms the pattern in some way. Actually, it's a little more tangled than that: Each track has both a series of pitch cells and a series of rhythm cells. The two series within an individual track play back concurrently, and both are required in order to produce music. That should be obvious—the pitches must be played back with some rhythm. The neat, and powerful, thing about Ludwig compared to a drum machine is that the two series of cells within a track don't have to line up. You could have a single short series of pitch cells being played back in many different rhythms, or a long series of pitch cells (including complex operations) being played back in a simple repetitive rhythm.

If you'd prefer, you can force a linkage between the two cell series within each track. Or, if you want to get fancier, you can force either the pitches or the rhythms of any track to sync their starting points to those of any other track. These are handy shortcuts if what you want to do with Ludwig is make "normal" music. But Ludwig is frankly a poor environment in which to create normal music, so it's hard to see why anybody would bother.

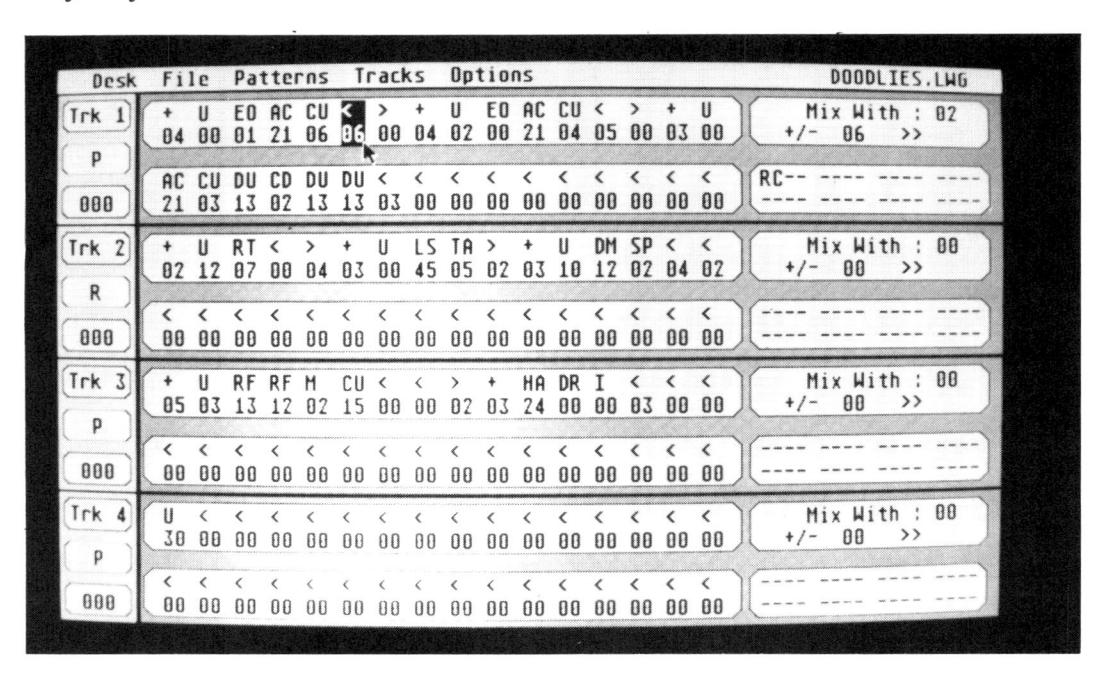

Figure 23. Ludwig's main screen. Pitch series are shown for tracks 1 and 3, and a rhythm series for track 2. (Track 4 is empty.) The "Mix With" windows are used to choose a second pattern for each track's random combining operations. For meanings of symbols, see pages 126 and 130.

Recording Patterns. Before you start assembling a Ludwig track, you'll need a few raw patterns to work with. (Actually, the program is shipped with a disk full of raw material to get you started. The disk is called "Bones," which is part of an obscure joke about a dog named Ludwig. We promised the guys at Hybrid Arts we would try to mention the dog somewhere in the review. Arf.)

There are two record/edit screens, one for pitch patterns and one for rhythms. If you'd like, you can link pitches with rhythms prior to recording, and record both at once. Quantizing occurs on input, and quantization values of quarter-, eighth-, sixteenth-, and thirty-second-note are supported. (The only way Ludwig can play triplets is through a rather roundabout rhythm transformation.)

On your first attempts to record a pattern, you're liable to think that Ludwig is mangling your input. This is because it doesn't record like a sequencer. Whenever two notes, or a longer group, overlap by even a millisecond, it assumes that you are playing them as a chord. They will all be quantized to the start time of the first note in the group.

This vertical-chunk orientation is one of Ludwig's more subtle but problematical limitations. If you should happen to envision a part that contains both sustained notes and moving notes, you'll have to use two or more tracks to play it, and will quite likely have to use a pencil and paper to figure out how many iterations of rhythm pattern 04 correspond to how many of rhythm pattern 05.

The pitch-editing screen sports a large grid containing rows and columns of note names. Clicking on a note selects it and highlights it in inverse video; clicking again deselects it. If no notes are selected, a column will be played as a rest. Each column contains 16 notes within a chromatic scale. You can move this scale around wherever you like in the full MIDI note range, but all of the notes in a given step of the pattern must fall within that 16-note span. We're not sure why the program was designed to allow chords only within such a narrow range, but it's a limitation that we found easy enough to work with, especially since many of the pitch operations that can be inserted into a track will expand the range of a pattern.

A random pitch generator is included. It can be used several times to layer random pitches on top of one another. Curiously, this is the only place in the program where patterns can be layered. There is no "merge patterns" utility, and no operation that will allow a single track to play two patterns at once.

Both pitch and rhythm patterns can be given 15-character names. These won't appear on the main track screen, but you can call up a pattern list that displays them, which is handy.

Rhythm patterns can be recorded by tapping from a MIDI controller, or manually edited. The pattern is displayed as a row of notes, and the lengths of individual notes can be adjusted by left- or right-clicking on them. A row of letters beneath the notes indicates whether each step is to be played (N) or a rest (R). Clicking on these letters toggles them back and forth. A "condense" command can be used to convert all note/rest combinations into notes of longer duration.

Pitch And Rhythm Operations. This is the heart of Ludwig—the trip to Mars. Both

---

Pros & Cons

Pros: Powerful system for generating complex sequences of notes from simple pitch and rhythm patterns. Eight tracks can all access the same pattern data and produce independent transformations.

Cons: Cramped, counter-intuitive user interface. Limited velocity and duration processes. MIDI file storage not yet implemented.

---

pitches and rhythms can be manipulated so thoroughly as to become virtually unrecognizable. In fact, we could envision doing an entire piece of music in Ludwig (if that were practical at all, which we have some doubts about) using only a single pitch pattern and a single rhythm pattern, and subjecting these to endless permutations.

Some of the pitch operations are simple: You can transpose a pattern up or down either chromatically or diatonically (with reference to one of eight user-defined scales). You can play it backwards, or truncate the start or end. You can tell the machine to play only the highest or lowest note in each step, eliminating the other tones in chords. You can break chords into arpeggios or combine adjoining notes into chords.

As already mentioned, you can perform a different operation every time the pattern is played. What's a whole lot more fun is that you can combine a number of operations, so that the machine will calculate the results of all of them together and then play whatever notes it arrives at. This "combine" operation is a gas, especially when the more esoteric operations are put together with the basic ones.

The esoteric pitch operations require a bit more explanation. "Expand/compress" will find the midpoint of a chord and then stretch or squash the intervals with reference to this point. This can lead to some pretty strange chords, so you might want to use it in combination with "force diatonic," which adjusts every note up or down a half-step to bring it into line with one of the user-defined scales. "Accompany" takes the top note in each pattern step (eliminating any chords) and then inserts a first-inversion triad from one of the scales below each note.

"Warp melody" doesn't actually warp anything; what it does is insert a pitch from one of the scales between some or all of the existing notes. By doing several warps in a combination, you can create an ostinato figure in which the notes of your original pattern only show up at a few points. "Substitute rest" causes a rest to appear at a specified step, while "no rests" shortens the pattern by eliminating any rest steps. Obviously, several "substitute rests" could be used in a combination with a "no rests" to change the content of a pattern.

Other operations, which we don't have room to explain, include "echo," "exchange adjacent," "play even," "play odd," and "harmonize above." And then there are the randomizing operations (see below).

Another important operation is looping. Loop start- and end-points can be inserted anywhere within a pitch or rhythm series. The number of repeats for the loop can be specified (00 means "loop forever"), and loops can be nested within other loops. This type of structured series is great to work with. We could imagine other possibilities (conditional branching, for example) that would let you do some really twisted structures, but the results would be hard to control, so we're not going to complain. Nested loops are enough to keep us happy for quite a while.

Most operations allow the user to specify an argument—in layman's terms, a two-digit number. The meaning of this number depends on the type of operation being performed. In the case of a chromatic transposition, it is a simple quanitty—a number of half-steps. But in many cases the number is not a quantity; it has a special meaning. For example, in a "harmonize above" operation, the left digit tells the machine which user-defined scale to get a note from, while the right digit tells it what interval within that scale to play. (We found a bug in this feature: When we specified an interval of 1—a unison—the machine gave us two-note unisons but only shut off one of the two notes when we hit the stop button.)

We had questions at a couple of points about why the arguments were defined in the way that they were. For example, the "accompany" operation lets you choose a scale (the left digit) and then specify whether to put a triad under every note (right digit 1), every other note (right digit 2), every third note (right digit 3), and so on. There is no way to accompany two notes out of every three, or three out of every five, or to control where the accompany operations starts counting notes.

Some of the rhythm operations, such as looping, combining, exchanging, and truncating, are identical to the pitch operations. As you'd expect, there are a number of new possibilities as well. "Divide/multiply" divides or multiplies a rhythm by some whole-number. If the number is 3, you get triplets, which is nice, but dividing or multiplying by numbers larger than 4 tends to result in either lugubrious adagios or chattering prestissimos. We think it would have been far better to use the available integers to offer the option of multiplying or dividing by some simple fractions, such as 1.5 or .66.

"Legato/staccato" is used to change the gate time of notes, from 1 percent to 99 percent of their rhythmic value. This setting is used to control a playback of a given rhythm pattern, so it will always be the same throughout the pattern. We think it's a shame that you can't set up independent legato/staccato loops, or set duration to more than 100 percent.

"Rotate" moves all of the rhythm values backward or forward in the pattern by up to nine places, wrapping the end around to the beginning. We found a cool application for this: We set up three tracks to use the same rhythm pattern, but gave each of them a different rotate value. The result contained some unexpected syncopations, while the total phrase lengths of all tracks remained identical. Other operations include "invert note/rest," "randomly drop some," "force the number of beats," "substitute rest," and so on.

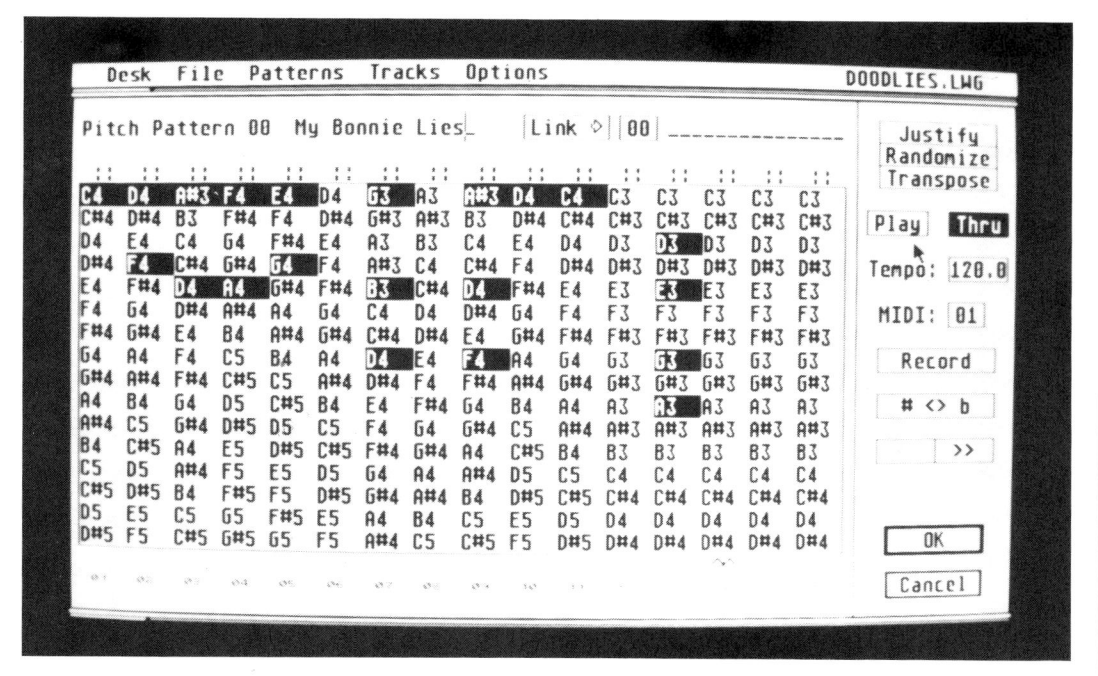

Figure 24. Ludwig's pitch pattern edit screen.

Random Functions. You say you can't bear to assemble a completely deterministic piece, that you insist on machine improvisation? We've already mentioned the function that fills a pattern with random pitches, and the operations that drop random chords or rhythm steps from a pattern. Many of the operations that use one of the user-defined scales let you select scale 0, which causes the machine to select a scale at random. These options are fairly simple. Ludwig is not the most sophisticated randomizer we've ever seen. But it does have a couple of other slick ideas.

You can let the machine randomly determine the length of a pattern (that is, the number of chords or rhythms within it that will be used during playback). The length can be constrained within a user-specified range. Ludwig can do this while playing the elements of the pattern forward, backward, or in a random order, which leads to some very pretty accompaniment patterns with unpredictable notes in the arpeggios.

On a higher level, you can mix two patterns together according to any of a number of different schemes. The way this works is perhaps a little more rigid than it might be, but we wouldn't want to be too critical until we had spent more time with the program. Basically, you choose one pattern as the mix material for each pitch or rhythm series (that is, one pitch pattern and one rhythm pattern per track). This will be used in conjunction with any and all patterns in that track that you select to be randomized. A little window at the side of the track has an empty slot for each of the 32 possible steps in the pattern. In each slot, you specify what mixing operation will be carried out at that step. For the pitch patterns, the operations include simple combining, selecting notes randomly from either or both chords, and generating entirely new diatonic or chromatic notes or chords at random. The correspondence between the two patterns will always be item-for-item, however. There is no way to tell the machine, for example, to replace the sixth chord in a pattern with some unspecified chord from the other pattern. In this case, it will always go to the sixth chord in the other pattern.

The mixing of rhythm patterns is necessarily somewhat more limited, and includes only a few simple randomizing options, none of them especially geared toward good-feeling grooves, as far as we could determine.

Track Operations. Any four or Ludwig's eight tracks can be displayed at a time. For each track, either the pitch, rhythm, or velocity series (see below) can be displayed. In the case of pitch and rhythm, 32 of the possible 1,024 cells can be displayed at a time. By incrementing a little counter with the mouse, you can put the 32-cell window anywhere in the series that you like.

Each cell appears as a mnemonic (usually two letters, but sometimes only one letter or a symbol) above a two-digit number. A typical Ludwig passage might look something like this:

```
+     U    WM  AC   EX   FD   <
05    12   32  21   15   02   04
```

If you're beginning to get the idea that this type of input structure is something only a computer programmer could love, we won't argue with you. Of course, there may not be any better way of designing an interface for the types of operations that Ludwig performs. If you want to dance, you've got to pay the piper.

Choosing operations for the cells is a two-step process. When you click on the upper symbol, a window pops up. This window, which fills half the screen, lists the available operations. When you click on one, it is automatically loaded into the cell that you had previously clicked on. You then increment or decrement the two-digit number using the mouse buttons, and finish by clicking anywhere outside the cell with the left button to confirm the new element, or with the right button to cancel.

This process is fairly tiresome, for a couple of reasons. As we said, the two-digit numbers mean different things with different operations, and there is no on-screen help to let you know what the values will do. So you'll have to leaf through the manual almost constantly, at least while learning the program. Fortunately, the manual is printed on nice thick stock, and should stand up to a good deal of leafing. Unfortunately, the list of operations in the manual is not alphabetized, so you'll have to leaf back and forth through ten or twenty pages every blessed time in order to find what you're looking for.

A more serious problem is the absence of block copy utilities for the tracks. Let's say you've set up a nice loop containing a couple of dozen cells—the type of data shown above. You'd like to copy this loop into another track. But that track already contains some cells, and you don't want to replace these. you want to tack the copied material on at the end of the series. No can do. Ludwig will let you copy an entire pitch or rhythm series from one track to another, but not a portion of one. The only way to make such a copy is by manually reentering the whole damn thing. Block copying is not an esoteric process; it's found on just about every sequencer still being manufactured. So its absence from Ludwig is mystifying, to say the least.

Ludwig does not record or play back pitch-bends, after-touch, or MIDI controller data. Each track can be given a patch number, which will be sent out each time playback is started, but there is no way to insert patch changes anywhere else in a track. Each track can be given a default legato percentage (which will be overridden wherever a legato/staccato operation appears in the rhythm series).

We were pleased to discover that Ludwig's tracks (though not the contents of the patterns themselves) can be edited without interrupting playback. It's neat to be able to insert new patterns and hear the results a few seconds later. We wish the edits could be heard instantly, but the program has to calculate a few seconds ahead of the current playback position, in order to ensure timing accuracy. Thus it's generally possible to enter new values that won't be heard, even though they're in front of the current playback point. This is confusing at first, but quite easy to get used to. It would be a mistake, however, to think of the real-time editing ability as suiting Ludwig for live performance. Clicking on little alphanumeric items in a list and selecting new ones from a pop-up window just isn't an organic, gestural process, no matter how you slice or dice it.

We wish Ludwig had a cuing function. Due to the way the tracks are structured, there is no way to start a cue in the middle of a piece. Every time you hit the play button, playback will start from the top. There ought to be some way to instruct the machine which cells you want playback to start at, but since most users will probably be generating only short phrases with Ludwig, this may not be much of a problem.

Velocity Processes. We have deliberately avoided talking about note velocity until now, because generating velocities is one of the least interesting aspects of the program. To begin with, each track has a set of exactly 32 velocity cells, each of which contains one of eight user-specified velocity levels. These levels can be specified differently for each track, which is certainly a nice extra. The track can cycle endlessly through all 32 of its velocities, or it can be forced to restart each time a pitch and/or rhythm cell starts. It will not, however, cycle through a smaller number of cells continuously (unless that number happens to be one of the factors of 32).

Two more types of velocity processes can be used—random accents and determined accents. The random accent feature allows you to instruct the track to choose random notes for shifts in velocity. The shift will be of whatever size you specify. The determined accents can be placed on all instances of a specified pitch, all instances of a specified note length, or both. Thus you could have all quarter-notes and C's accented and all sixteenth-notes and A♭ de-accented, but the accent/de-accent amount would be the same for all four types of notes, and the same from one end of the track to the other.

It may be true that velocity is less noticeable than pitch and rhythm, and therefore doesn't require the same degree of sophisticated programming. But we can't help feeling that this area of the program short-changes the musician. For starters, there is no way to do sweeping crescendi or decrescendi, no way to include accents in one section of a long track but not in another section, and no way to provide various pitches with various accent levels.

The Big Roadblock. Coming up with some provocative musical phrases with Ludwig is easy, but constructing an entire piece with it would be nearly impossible, unless (a) you're an unemployed masochist, or (b) you're fascinated by thick, repetitive, and relatively colorless jumbles of notes. So the question arises, how can you transfer phrases from Ludwig into your sequencer to use them as starting-points for compositions?

If you already own Hybrid Arts' SMPTE Track sequencer, you're in luck, because Ludwig stores its performances in a playback buffer, from where they can be saved as a SMPTE Track .SNG file. The HybriSwitch multiple program handler can hold both SMPTE Track and Ludwig in memory at the same time, allowing the contents of the performance buffer to be transferred directly, without saving to disk. If you own a sequencer that doesn't run on the Atari, you can record Ludwig's output into that,

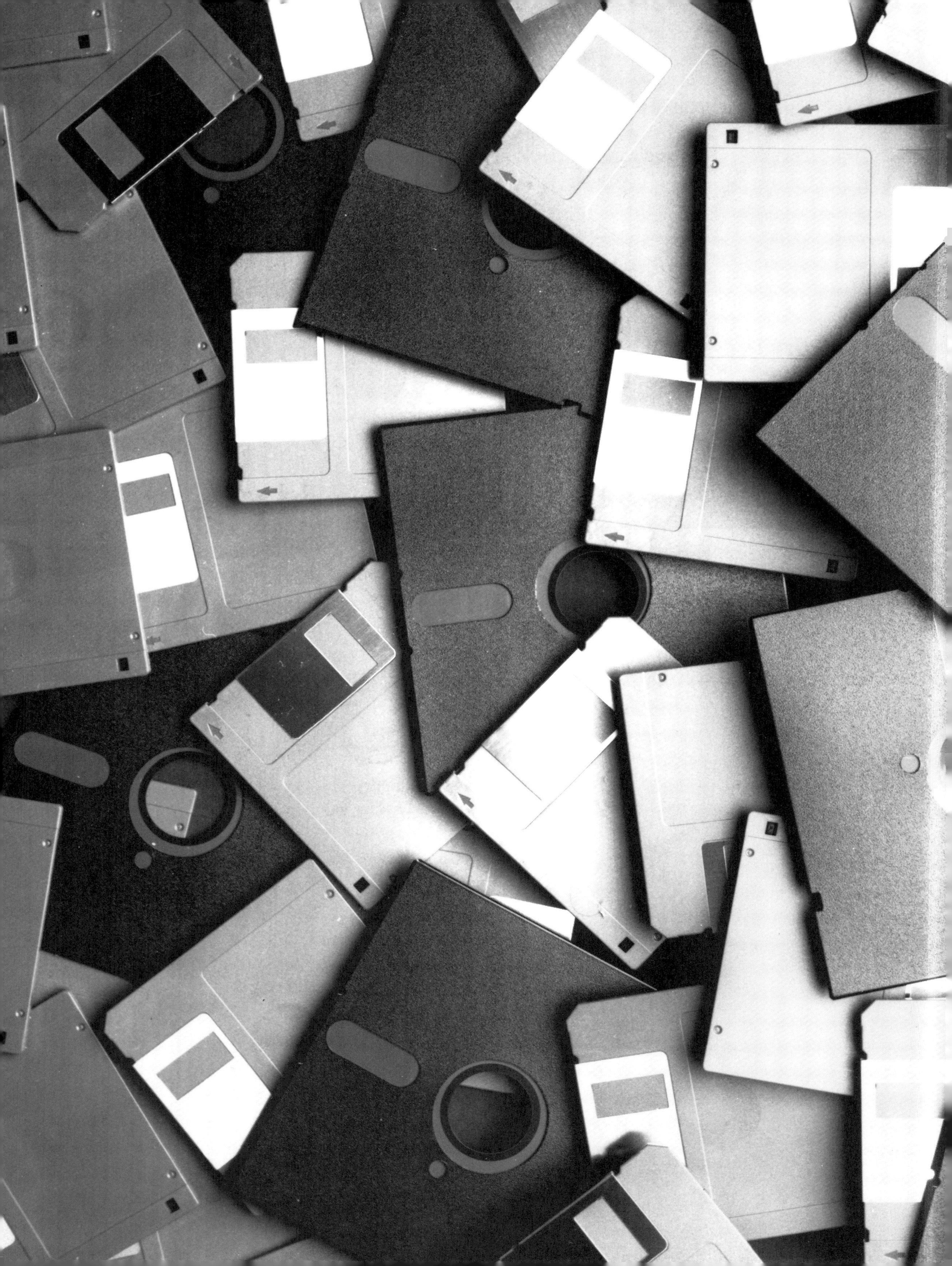

from where it can later be played back across into an Atari sequencer if desired. Ludwig can transmit MIDI clocks, and we had no trouble dumping its material into the sequencer in our Ensoniq SQ-80.

But unless you own a second sequencer, you're out of luck, because Ludwig doesn't store MIDI files. Incredible? We thought so. When we asked Hybrid Arts about the oversight, they indicated that they're planning to release the MIDI file conversion module from SMPTE Track as a free public domain utility. Some snags came up in the development of this utility, and they chose not to hold up the release of Ludwig until the utility was available. Unfortunately, the utility was not yet available when we wrote our review. Unless you're a SMPTE Track user, we would recommend that you wait to purchase Ludwig until the conversion program is actually in your hot little hands, because "a few days" can easily stretch into a few months in the music software business.

Conclusions. Evaluating a program like Ludwig is a lot tougher than evaluating a sequencer or editor/librarian. Those types of programs are designed to do familiar things. Ludwig is designed to do unfamiliar things, so it has to do them in unfamiliar ways. In other words, it takes time to learn. So are the musical results worth the effort? We'll answer that with a guarded "yes."

There's no question Ludwig will do lots and lots of stimulating musical tricks. As we leafed through the manual, we kept thinking, "Wow! This looks like fun." And as we delved deeper, we did come up with some astonishing syncopated chord patterns, quite unlike anything we had ever heard before. But using the program was less fun than we had expected. The control structures take some time to memorize, important dimensions of control (such as the ability to start playback or send patch changes in the middle of a piece) are missing entirely, and some method of block copying ought to have been provided.

There's a lot of power slouching around inside Ludwig. But we wonder how many people are going to have the patience to pry the power loose. Compared to other programs that serve the same purpose, Ludwig is rather counter-intuitive. And unless you have some method of getting its output into a form that your sequencer can use, we can't recommend that you buy it, because it simply isn't a full-function music production environment. When Hybrid Arts releases their MIDI file conversion utility, the program would definitely be worth considering for anybody who wants a way of generating some new kinds of ideas.

Ludwig

Description: Algorithmic composition software.
Hardware Requirements: Atari ST or Mega computer (black-and-white or color monitor), any MIDI sound module.
Features: Eight independent tracks with pitch and rhythm processing operations. 100 pitch and rhythm patterns. Interval and rhythm expansion, automatic accompaniment chords, transposition, nested loops, rhythm cell rotation and truncation, and many other automated operations. Random mixing of patterns, accenting of specific pitches, forced linkage between tracks. Performances can be saved in SMPTE Track sequencer format.
Suggested Retail Price: $149.00.
Contact: Hybrid Arts, 11920 W. Olympic Blvd., Los Angeles, CA 90064. (213) 826-3777.

Keyboard, **March 1989.**

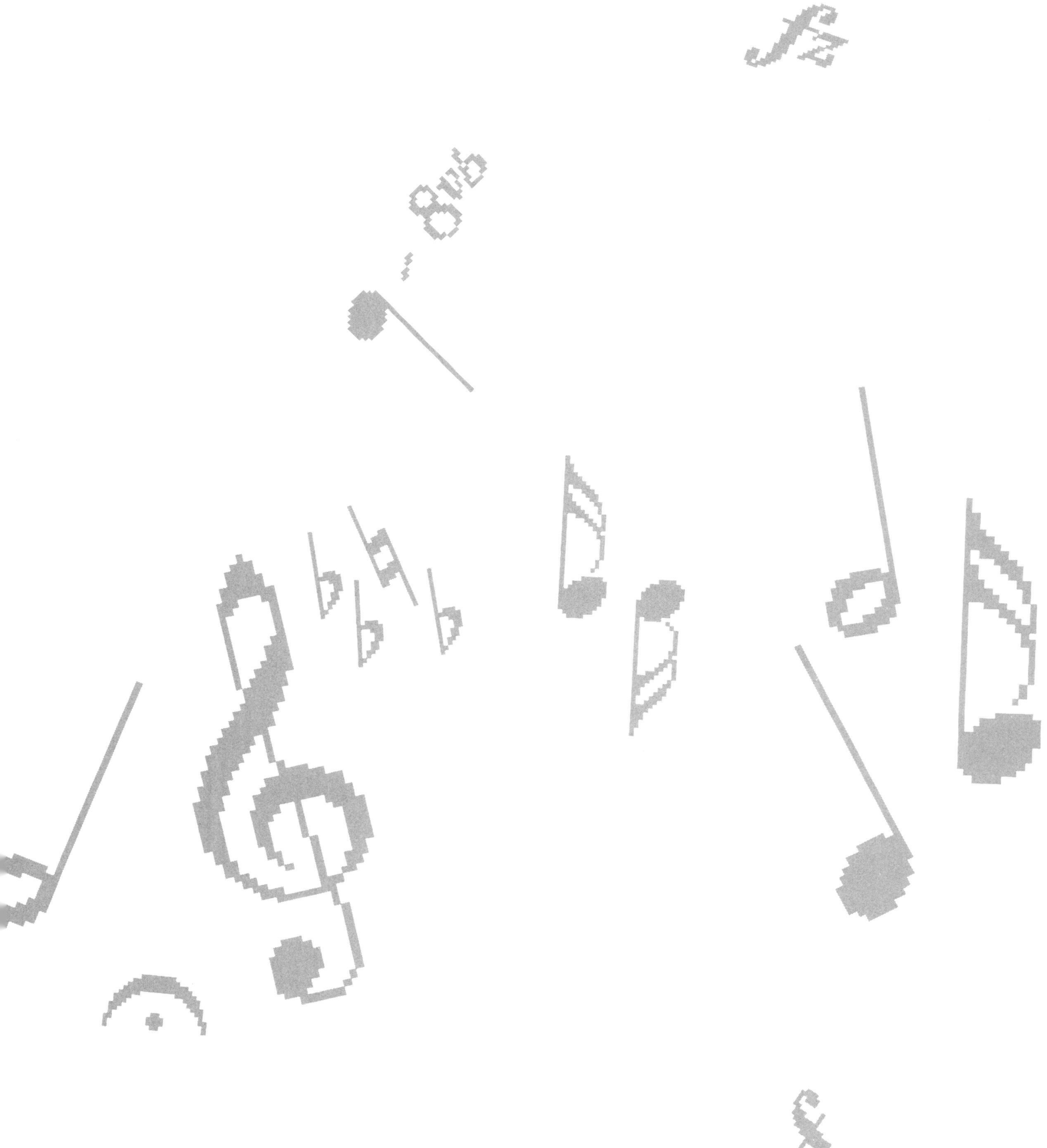

About The Authors

Jim Aikin is the senior associate editor of *Keyboard* magazine. Most weekends you'll find him recording in his home MIDI studio, where he uses Atari ST software for sequencing. He has also published some science fiction, and he plays a dangerous game of pool.

Dominic Milano is the editor of *Keyboard* magazine. He studied electronic music composition at the Chicago Musical College, and has written volumes on every aspect of the subject over the past 15 years. He is active as a performer, programmer, design consultant, and visual artist.

Michael Marans is an assistant editor at *Keyboard* magazine. An admitted techno-junkie, he spent several years in L.A. as a professional programmer, sound engineer, and system designer. Prior to joining the *Keyboard* staff, he was an engineering associate and product specialist at E-mu Systems.

From GPI Books

SYNTHESIZER BASICS (Revised)

A valuable collection of articles from the pages of *Keyboard* magazine covering all facets of electronic music. Includes chapters on: perspectives on synthesizers, understanding synthesis, MIDI, sound systems and components, and recording electronic music. Also included are hardware and software manufacturers' addresses, recommended books, and a complete glossary. Contributors include: Helen Casabona, Ted Greenwald, Bryan Lanser, Dominic Milano, Bob Moog, Bobby Nathan, Tom Rhea, and the staff of *Keyboard* magazine.
ISBN 0-88188-552-5 $14.95   From Hal Leonard Publishing.

SYNTHESIZERS AND COMPUTERS (Revised)

A comprehensive overview, useful for beginners or seasoned pros, or anyone interested in the future of music. Includes discussions of digital audio, synthesis, sampling, MIDI, choosing software and interface hardware, and choosing the right computer. Also included is a section on Programming Your Own Software—which leads the reader step-by-step into the world of writing music software, and covers many insider's programming tips. From the pages of *Keyboard* magazine, with articles by Steve De Furia, Dominic Milano, Jim Aikin, Ted Greenwald, Jim Cooper, Bob Moog, Craig Anderton, and other leading experts.
ISBN 0-88188-716-1 $14.95   From Hal Leonard Publishing.

SYNTHESIZER PROGRAMMING

Don't be satisfied with factory presets! Get the most out of your instrument, whether it's a battered Minimoog or the latest digital dream machine. You can create your own unique sound with the concrete and understandable information in this practical introduction to programming and synthesis. With contributions by Wendy Carlos, Bo Tomlyn, and the editors and staff of *Keyboard* magazine. Includes specific guidelines for the DX7, Oberheim Xpander, CZ-101, Roland JX8P, and JX10.
ISBN 0-88188-550-9 $14.95   From Hal Leonard Publishing.

SYNTHESIZER TECHNIQUE (Revised)

How to utilize all the technical and creative potential of today's synthesizers, with discussions of Recreating Timbres; Pitch-Bending, Modulation and Expression; Lead Synthesizer, Soloing and Orchestration. Hands-on practical advice and instruction by leading practitioners, including Bob Moog, Tom Coster, George Duke, Roger Powell, and others. Diagrams, illustrations, and musical examples throughout. Edited from the pages of *Keyboard* magazine.
ISBN 0-88188-290-9 $14.95   From Hal Leonard Publishing.

MULTI-TRACK RECORDING

Information on the latest home and studio recording techniques and equipment, edited from the pages of *Keyboard* magazine by Dominic Milano. Includes chapters on Getting Started, Outboard Gear, Synchronization, Keyboard Recording, and Advanced Techniques And Technical Change. With contributions by Bobby Nathan, Bryan Lanser, Dave Frederick and the staff of *Keyboard* magazine.
ISBN 0-88188-552-5 $14.95   From Hal Leonard Publishing.

MULTI-TRACK RECORDING FOR MUSICIANS

How to make professional quality recordings at home or in the studio—comprehensive, creative, practical information including basic theory and up-to-date guidance on the latest equipment.
ISBN 0-88284-355-9 $17.95   From Alfred Publishing.

BEGINNING SYNTHESIZER

A step-by-step guide to understanding and playing synthesizers with discussions of how to use and edit presets and performance controls. A comprehensive, easy-to-understand, musical approach, with hands-on lessons in a variety of styles, including rock, pop, classical, jazz, techno-pop, blues, and more.
ISBN 0-88284-353-2 $12.95   From Alfred Publishing. Item Number 2606.
BEGINNING SYNTHESIZER is also available in a two-volume set of shorter Special Focus Guides, including:
Playing Synthesizers: A Beginner's Guide To Effective Techinque
ISBN 0-88284-362-1 $8.95   Item Number 4110.
Programming Synthesizers: A Beginner's Guide To Editing Preset Sounds
ISBN 0-88284-363-X $8.95   Item Number 4121.
All from Alfred Publishing.

THE ART OF ELECTRONIC MUSIC

The creative and technical development of an authentic musical revolution, from the Theremin Electrical Symphony to today's most advanced synthesizers. Scientific origins, the evolution of hardware, the greatest artists—including Tangerine Dream, Vangelis, Keith Emerson, Wendy Carlos, Jan Hammer, Kraftwerk, Brian Eno, Thomas Dolby, and others—in stories, interviews, illustrations, analysis, and practical musical technique. From the pages of *Keyboard* magazine, and with a foreword by Bob Moog.
ISBN 0-688-03106-4 $15.95   From Wm. Morrow & Co.

MIND OVER MIDI

A comprehensive and practical introduction to this crucial new technology, including: What MIDI Does, Data Transmission Tutorial, Channels, Modes, Controllers, Computers, Interfaces, Software, Sequencers, Accessories, SMPTE & MIDI, MIDI systems, and more. Edited by Dominic Milano from the pages of *Keyboard* magazine.
ISBN 0-88188-551-7 $14.95   From Hal Leonard Publishing Corp.

USING MIDI

The first comprehensive, practical guide to the application of Musical Instrument Digital Interface in performance, composition, and recording, including: basic MIDI theory, using MIDI performance controls, channels and modes, sequencers, MIDI synchronization, using MIDI effects, MIDI and computers, alternate MIDI controllers, and more. A definitive and essential tutorial.
ISBN 0-88282-354-0 $12.95   From Alfred Publishing. Item Number 2607.
USING MIDI is also available in a three-volume set of shorter Special Focus Guides, including:
What Is MIDI?: Basic Theory And Concepts
ISBN 0-88284-364-8 $8.95   Item Number 4126
Basic MIDI Applications: Sequencers, Drum Machines, And Keyboards
ISBN 0-88284-365-6 $8.95   Item Number 4139
Advanced MIDI Applications: Computers, Time Codes, And Beyond
ISBN 0-88284-365-6 $8.95   Item Number 4143
All from Alfred Publishing.

BASIC GUITAR (Revised)

Chet Atkins, Arnie Berle, Paul Chasman, Dan Crary, Rik Emmett, Brad Gillis, Edward Van Halen, John Hammond, Bill Keith, Steve Morse, Arlen Roth, Mike Seeger, and other distinguished players and writers present a comprehensive, practical introduction to the technique and art of playing guitar. Edited from the pages of *Guitar Player* and *Frets* magazines by Helen Casabona, with a foreword by Les Paul.
ISBN 0-88188-906-7 $14.95   From Hal Leonard Publishing Corp.

ROCK GUITAR (Revised)

Carlos Santana, Eric Clapton, Lee Ritenour, Steve Morse, B.B. King, Rik Emmett, Steve Vai, Edward Van Halen, and others tell you how to get started, solo, and more. Music examples. From the pages of *Guitar Player* magazine.
ISBN 088188-908-3 $14.95

ELECTRIC BASS GUITAR (Revised)

All you need to know about getting started, reading music, practicing, techniques, soloing, progressions, patterns, bass lines, scales, chords, and ways to modify your instrument. Filled with productive lessons and musical examples, all from the pages of *Guitar Player* and *Bass Player* magazines.
ISBN 0-88188-907-5 $14.95

THE GUITAR PLAYER BOOK

The most comprehensive book on guitar ever produced, from the pages of America's foremost magazine for professional and amateur guitarists. Any style, any level, whether player or fan—this is the book. Includes definitive articles on all the important artists who have given the guitar its life and expression, plus design, instructions, equipment, accessories, and technique. Edited from the pages of *Guitar Player* magazine.
ISBN 0-394-62490-4 $11.95